Manchester Sounds

Volume 4 ~ 2003–2004

Editor: Martin Thacker

Manchester Sounds

Editorial address: Martin Thacker, 24 Eagle Brow, Lymm, Cheshire WA13 0LY.
Telephone: 01925 757 114
E-mail: mthacker@manchestersounds.org.uk
Reviews material and enquiries about advertisements should be addressed as above.

For current subscription rates please enquire to John Turner, 40, Parsonage Road, Heaton Moor, Stockport, SK4 4JR or at e-mail recorderist@zoom.co.uk

Manchester Sounds is published by The Manchester Musical Heritage Trust (Registered Charity no. 1076473) in association with Forsyth Brothers Ltd.

ISSN 1471-3659
ISBN (Vol. 4, 2003-2004) 0 9539010-3-3

The publication of volume 4 of Manchester Sounds is made possible through the generous support of the Ida Carroll Trust.

Manchester Sounds is printed by the Arc & Throstle Press Ltd, Nanholme Mill, Shaw Wood Road, Todmorden, Lancs., OL14 6DA.

Single volumes are available from Forsyth Brothers Ltd., 126, Deansgate, Manchester, M3 2GR, price £10.00.

Please visit our website at http://www.manchestersounds.org.uk

Cover: caricature of a conductor by Thomas Pitfield, from his *Limusics: 40 Limerics*

The logo of The Manchester Musical Heritage Trust is designed by Melanie Young.

Editorial

Welcome to the delayed fourth issue of *Manchester Sounds*. We are dating it 2003-4 to give it a longer currency, but, although it is the biggest number so far, it is in no sense a double issue: we hope to produce volume five somewhere around the end of 2004.

We hope, too, that you will find in this volume, as in its predecessors, a blend of solid research with more immediately digestible items. Several of our articles are prompted by anniversaries: the centenaries of Eric Fogg and Thomas Pitfield, and the thirtieth anniversary of the Manchester Camerata; and other momentous events of 2003, although not directly referred to outside this editorial, link in various ways to current or previous articles. When we ran, in volume three, an article about one characteristic haunt of the Manchester musician, Wright Greaves' music shop, we little thought that a further year would see the closing of the doors of another – Gibb's book and record shop. However, it is comforting to know that the shop still exists in cyberspace, where it can be entered via your computer terminal.

Another important event of 2003, the opening of the new School of Music and Drama building at the University of Manchester, is linked to this issue by our coverage of the achievement of the late Professor Humphrey Procter-Gregg, who pioneered the music department in its modern form, and to whom belongs much of the credit for the success of the just-vacated Denmark Road premises, the acoustics of whose concert hall have been surpassed in the new building only with the aid of design techniques unavailable in P-G's day. At the opening, on 21 October, the University conferred honorary doctorates upon the soprano Amanda Roocroft, upon our President, Michael Kennedy, and upon the writer and performer Ben Elton. Between Dr Roocroft's singing of Strauss' *Zueignung*, and the eloquence and wit of the speeches of Drs Kennedy and Elton (diverse, as may readily be imagined, in their starting points) a good time was had by all those lucky enough to be at the ceremony.

In presenting Michael Kennedy for his degree, Professor David Fallows began by referring to his role in rallying support for the Henry Watson Music Library, some four years ago when it was feared that it might share the fate of the once great public music library at Liverpool. Coincidentally both libraries, as Professor Fallows pointed out, were the subject of a letter by Michael Bryant in the issue of *Private Eye* which was currently on the news stands:

Cllr. Mike Storey… has failed to justify the sale of music and irreplaceable reference works from Liverpool Public Library to the second hand market… another
home could and should have been found for the music. Manchester's Henry
Watson Library now remains the only collection of its kind in the north of England.[1]

So how safe *is* the Henry Watson Music Library? In the first place, let
it be said that Manchester City Council is greatly to be congratulated
for bearing the whole expense of the preservation, staffing and development of the collection since Dr Watson's death ninety-three years
ago in January 1911. However, councils are sometimes subject to forces
beyond their control. The agenda currently set by the government places
social inclusion, lifelong learning, and the provision of computer facilities way ahead of the maintenance of what some people see as an
elitist library of printed music and books on music. Indeed, in the report of the 2002 inspection of Manchester Libraries by the Audit Commission, not only was no credit given to the council for the discharge of
this essentially regional function, but there was no sign that the inspec-
tors were even aware of the existence of the Watson collection.[2] It is
not surprising, therefore, that in order to address the new agenda, the
Manchester Libraries are now implementing a staffing structure which
combines supervision of the Henry Watson Music Library with other
city-wide responsibilities.

Perhaps the Henry Watson is better placed to weather the storm than
its former sister at Liverpool. It has a higher public profile, and a coherent
group of influential supporters, including the readers of this journal.
Moreover, its supporters have been promised the willing cooperation
of the library management. In 2000, the Director of Libraries and
Theatres wrote to a number of eminent musicians and writers, including
our President, to ask them to become patrons of a trust which would
support the Watson Music Library and help to obtain all-important
regional funding so that it could go forward on a new footing. Almost
all replied in the affirmative. As Sir Peter Maxwell Davies recorded in
a letter to the editor of *The Daily Telegraph*,

The council has given assurances that the materials will remain intact, that there
will be a librarian with musical knowledge, and that the collections will be

maintained and renewed. Further, a 'Friends of the Henry Watson Music Library Trust' is proposed, to support and extend the library's work, and the council has stated its wish to work closely with the newly-established Manchester Musical Heritage Trust in raising the profile of Manchester's musical history and heritage.[3]

For the Henry Watson, the days of adequate funding from a single source may be over, but it is reasonable to hope that a viable future may be found in a framework of partnership and co-operation. Suitable models are few, but there are two which should be mentioned. First, the Central Music Library Ltd has shown itself effective in collaboration with Westminster City Council in the maintenance of the largest of the public music libraries in London. Its Chairman, Lewis Foreman, is a contributor to this issue of *Manchester Sounds*. And second, the Surrey Performing Arts Library at Dorking, having been threatened with closure some years ago, is now a remarkable example of public-private partnership, having its staff provided by Surrey County Council and its premises by local business. That these premises happen to be on a real live vineyard encourages the hope that a rosy and mellow future may yet be in store for the Henry Watson Music Library.

Martin Thacker
Manchester, February 2004

[1] *Private Eye,* 17 October - 30 October 2003, 14.
[2] www.audit-commission.gov.uk/reports
[3] *Daily Telegraph*, 14 February 2000.

MANCHESTER CAMERATA
2003-2004 CONCERT SERIES MANCHESTER CONNECTIONS

Manchester Camerata – at the centre of musical life in Manchester for over three decades.

SATURDAY 24 JANUARY 2004 7:30pm RNCM
TELEMANN Suite in D
MOZART Piano Concerto No 12 in A
HANDEL Concerto Grosso in F Op 3 No 4
HAYDN Symphony No 45 in F Sharp Minor, *Farewell*

NICHOLAS KRAEMER Conductor
STEVEN OSBORNE Piano

SATURDAY 14 FEBRUARY 2004 7:30pm BRIDGEWATER HALL
MENDELSSOHN A Midsummer Night's Dream Overture
BRUCH Violin Concerto No 1 in G Minor
BEETHOVEN Symphony No 2 in D

DOUGLAS BOYD Conductor
JENNFER PIKE Violin

SATURDAY 6 MARCH 2004 7:30pm RNCM
MOZART String Quintet in G Minor K516
BEAMISH Sextet, *The Wedding at Cana*
BRAHMS Sextet in B Flat Op 18

MANCHESTER CAMERATA ENSEMBLE

SATURDAY 3 APRIL 2004 7:30pm BRIDGEWATER HALL
BEETHOVEN Leonore Overture No 1
SCHUMANN Piano Concerto in A Minor
BRAHMS Symphony No 1 in C Minor

DOUGLAS BOYD Conductor
MARTIN ROSCOE Piano

RNCM 0161 907 5555   BRIDGEWATER HALL 0161 907 9000

W.J. Robertson and National Identity

HAZEL BUCKLEY

The Parson in his pulpit,
The Critic in his chair,
Assumes, in his vocation,
A self-important air:
No matter what he preaches,
His flock has no reply;
And so, the lying scribbler
His victims may defy.
Oh! Could one mount that rostrum,
Upon that seat sit down,
Some points might be disputed,
Some arguments o'erthrown;
For 'tis vain to argue
With this pragmatic pair,
Unless in that same pulpit,
Unless in that same chair.
George Linley[1]

THIS SECTION of George Linley's poem written in 1862 seems an apt denunciation of music criticism in general. It is perhaps especially pertinent to the journalism of the Victorian period, full as it is of rhetoric and purple prose. Despite the inherent accuracy of such comment, music journalism of this period should not be overlooked as a fundamental tool in music research of this period. Once the overblown language has been sifted through, vital information can be gleaned about performers, concert life and how public taste was constructed. Although Linley's description of the relationship between critic and reader is accurate, 'No matter what he preaches, His flock has no reply', the critics are of course not safe from criticism once they themselves become the subject of study. The critic under scrutiny here is W.J. Robertson of the *Manchester Guardian*. His writings can be found in the Robertson *Scrapbook*, which is an interesting and important document for several reasons. Barry Cooper discovered this remarkable text in the Henry Watson Music Library, Manchester, in December 2001. It consists of music journalism contributions, mainly to the *Manchester Guardian*,

---

[1] *Musical Cynics of London* (London, 1862), pp. 10–11.

by the previously unknown author W.J. Robertson. The newspaper reviews, articles and criticisms on music cover the period 8 August 1882
– 1 November 1887, in 201 pages.[2]

Although there is an increasing interest in provincial Victorian Britain, there is much work still to be done before an overall impression of
musical life can be accurately gauged. Provincial music criticism has
been almost entirely overlooked for the period in question. The
Robertson Scrapbook can be seen as a summary of music criticism in
1880s Manchester and therefore provides unique opportunity for research. It contains over 100,000 words, including seventy-four music
reviews and fifty-seven articles on musical subjects. To some extent
provincial music journalism has been ignored because research is con-
centrated on London. Another reason is that journalism at the time was
anonymous. This is why the Scrapbook is so interesting. The majority
of music journalism in its earlier days being unsigned also prompted
interest at the time, as can be seen in one of Robertson's articles about
a new *Quarterly Musical Review* (1884) to be edited by Henry Hiles,
in which he makes a point of stating 'The articles are to be signed.'[3]
Although some critics' work has been identified through stylistic analysis or in biographical or autobiographical writings, much remains
unascribed. It is not certain whether all the main music critics have
even yet been catalogued. Some have been named in various sources,
including such books as David Ayrest's *The Guardian: A Biography of
a Newspaper* (London, 1973) and Charles Kent's articles, but biographical information on many of them is still difficult if not impossible to
locate.[4] Robertson is not mentioned in any of the usual biographical

[2] Unless stated otherwise, articles quoted are from Robertson's writings in the
Manchester Guardian, rather than his few contributions to the *Manchester Courier*.
[3] Saturday 20 December 1884; Robertson Scrapbook (*RS*), 78. Dr Henry Hiles (1826–
1904) was an organist and conductor in several Manchester musical societies. He also
taught at Owens College and Victoria University, and in 1893 became professor of
music at Manchester College. As a composer he wrote an oratorio, cantatas, anthems,
glees, organ music, operetta, an orchestral overture, songs and piano pieces. He also
wrote several books on music, including *Harmony of Sounds* (London, 1872, R/1878),
Grammar of Music (London, 1879) and *Part-Writing or Modern Counterpoint* (London,
1884). See James D. Brown and Stephen S. Stratton, *British Musical Biography*
(Birmingham, 1897), pp. 197–8.
[4] Charles Kent, 'Periodical Critics of Drama, Music & Art, 1830–1914: A Preliminary
List', *Victorian Periodicals Review*, 13 (1980), pp. 31–55, and 'More Critics of Drama,
Music and Art', ibid., 19 (1986), pp. 99–105.

NEWSPAPER CUTTINGS.

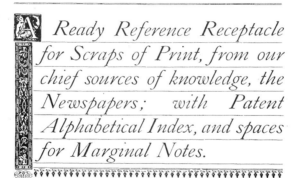

Ready Reference Receptacle for Scraps of Print, from our chief sources of knowledge, the Newspapers; with Patent Alphabetical Index, and spaces for Marginal Notes.

"*When found, make a note of.*"—CAPTAIN CUTTLE.

London:
MARCUS WARD & CO., LIMITED,
AND ROYAL ULSTER WORKS, BELFAST.

1. Initial page of a newspaper cuttings scrapbook, taken from one of the Darbyshire Scrapbooks

sources.

This Scrapbook appears to be one of the pre-printed versions available at the time, as can be seen in illustration 1.[5] The Henry Watson Library holds several such scrapbooks, with identically ruled margins and pagination, but in varying sizes. A comparative study highlights their original form. A similar set is that of the Alfred Darbyshire Scrapbooks, 1868–1906.[6] Alfred Darbyshire (1839–1908) was an architect and amateur actor and also a journalist, and the inscription on one of the preliminary pages reads: 'This Book contains my Contributions to the Manchester "Press"'. An additional feature of the Darbyshire Scrapbooks is that they contain many pages for indexing items within the Scrapbook, with thumbnail cut-outs for each letter of the alphabet (see illustration 2). Plainly such personal collections of a journalist's published contributions were not an isolated occurrence. Unfortunately this front portion of the Robertson Scrapbook is entirely missing.

As W.J. Robertson is not mentioned in any of the usual reference texts or those of the period, it is necessary to use other means to discover even basic biographical details about him. The 1881 census has records of over 32 million people who were living in Britain on 3 April 1881. The records list the full name of everyone in the household, their age, sex, occupation, marital status, relationship, birthplace and the census place. Certain assumptions had to be made in order to limit the search of the census. There are two reasons to assume that Robertson was living in Manchester or the surrounding area. First, he had his first visible contact with the *Manchester Guardian* in the form of a letter written on Thursday 3 August 1882 (appearing on page 7) in response to a review of the newly published English translation of the book *Life and Letters of Berlioz* that had appeared in the previous day's edition. And second, he would have needed a local base in order to write regularly for the *Manchester Guardian*, as travel was more difficult than it is today, and there are many reviews in the Scrapbook of concerts in Manchester. With this in mind, the census catalogue for the north-west of England was searched. It is a happy coincidence that a census was taken in 1881. The start date of the writings being 1882, it can be rea-

---

[5] All illustrations are reproduced by permission of Manchester Public Libraries.
[6] Manchester Central Library: Alfred Darbyshire Scrapbooks 1868–1906 (12 vols.), BRff720.92Da.

Art Treasures Exhibitions   4 5 6 7 8 9 10 11 12 13 14 15

Manchester

Academy of Art   17 18

Arts Club   21

Acton Mr Henry M   46

Ashland Mr Alfred Death   112 of

Antiquarian Society of Lanca-   104 shire & Cheshire

Athenaeum Graphic, Manchester   121

Ackworth School   143

Architectural Association Man   179, 199, 200 chester

Ashton John Mr Funeral of   196

Antony & Cleopatra at the   197 Prince's Theatre

Alston Hall, Preston   200

2. Indexing feature of the Darbyshire Scrapbook

sonably assumed that the author may well have been in the same place of residence at the time of the census.

Other valuable research tools of the period were of no help in this investigation, as the Trade Directory is useful only if a person's trade or address is known.[7] The Local Studies archive catalogues at Manchester Central Library were also searched without a positive result. There are several categories of catalogue and there is no mention of a W.J. Robertson, or any variation thereof, in the name index, which indicates that there are no documents specifically relating to him, such as wills, letters, deeds or other written material. Nor is there any entry in the Autograph letters index.

The identity of our W.J. Robertson is still uncertain. However, the most likely candidate found in the 1881 census is William Robertson (b. 1835, Flae, Mauritius) of Mereside House, Castleton, Lancashire. His occupation is listed as 'Reporter & Author' and he would have been 47 at the time he first wrote to the *Manchester Guardian*. His household consisted of his wife Elizabeth (40), schoolmistress, children Albert William (11), Bertha (9) and Maud (5), all born in Rochdale, unspecified relative Elizabeth Thomas (50, from Tynault, Wales) who was a household assistant, and relative Alfred Thomas (18, born in Chester), reporter's apprentice (presumably Robertson's).

Earlier research has however removed the possibility of a conclusive answer to Robertson's identity. There was a William Robertson living and writing in the nearby town of Rochdale at the time in question. He was the author of *The Life and Times of the Right Honourable John Bright* (Rochdale, 1887) and several other local histories published at various dates. The preface of the single-volume edition of the work offers a clue to support a possible identification with the Scrapbook Robertson: 'The author of this work has been a reporter for the last twenty-four years in different parts of England. During the last seventeen years he has resided in Rochdale.'[8]

---

[7] Manchester Central Library, Manchester Archives and Local Studies, has very helpfully compiled indexes of the Trade Directory by surname for the census years only, to provide a starting point for research.

[8] There is also a six-volume version of the same title (London, 1887). The author's other works consist of *Rochdale Past and Present: A History and Guide* (Rochdale, 1875; 2nd edition with additions and illustrations 1876), its companion volume *Old and New: Rochdale and its People* (Rochdale, 1881), *The Social and Political History of Rochdale* (Rochdale, 1889) and *Rochdale and the Vale of Whitworth* (Rochdale, 1897).

The fact that the Rochdale Robertson was a journalist makes him a strong candidate. Another interesting detail can be found in an advertisement for *Rochdale: Past and Present*.[9] Under the title details is the legend 'By Wm. Robertson, (Reporter, and Correspondent of the London and Provincial Daily Press)'. In addition to writing his books, then, Robertson was also active in several locations as a journalist. It is highly probable that he wrote for his local paper, the *Rochdale Observer*, and there is some evidence to suggest this. Several of his books were published at the Observer General Steam Printing Works.

3. Robertson's name as it appears on the form of the Bibliotheca Lancastriensis

4. Robertson's signature from the letter

5. Robertson's name from the handwritten title of the Scrapbook

---

[9] The newspaper advertisement is in a compilation at Manchester Central Library, Manchester Archives and Local Studies, RIM–ROB in BIOG CUTS 153, under 'Robertson, William'.

This identification, however, is not beyond dispute. A further adver-tisement by William Robertson entitled 'Opinions of the Press on Rochdale Past and Present', has attached behind it a form and hand-written letter, both with Robertson's signature.[10] The form is signed 'William Robertson' (illustration 3), and the letter 'W. Robertson' (il-lustration 4). Neither of these matches the signature in the front of the Scrapbook, 'W.J. Robertson' (illustration 5). A comparison of these two samples of handwriting with that contained in the Scrapbook adds further confusion.

As can be seen, the signature in illustration 3 taken from the form is not in the same hand as that in illustration 4, from the letter. It is how-ever entirely possible that the signature on the form is that of an offi-cial, and not that of William Robertson. The form, on which there is no date, is from the Bibliotheca Lancastriensis. The signature in illustra-tion 4, taken from the letter, is again substantially different from that in the Scrapbook shown in illustration 5. The letter itself does mention a forthcoming visit to Manchester, but the reason for the visit, or indeed to whom the letter was addressed, remains a mystery. The trend in the handwriting of William Robertson of Rochdale in the letter as a whole is often to join the last letter of one word with the first of the next, as with the signature. This trend is not shown in the handwriting in illus-tration 5.

There are two possible explanations for the differences in handwrit-ing. One is that it was not Robertson himself who compiled the Scrap-book. His wife Elizabeth was an educated woman, a schoolmistress, and may have compiled the Scrapbook of her husband's writings. Al-ternatively Alfred Thomas, as apprentice, may have been given the task of compiling it. The second possibility is that when the front por-tion of the Scrapbook became detached, a librarian at the time may have copied the details onto the first page in order to preserve its prov-enance. A further piece of evidence is a stamp with the initials W R at the top of the letter. This is obviously something that William Robertson felt necessary to include as a letterhead, and its exclusion from a scrap-book of journalistic contributions, of which he was proud enough to make a compilation, would therefore seem implausible. However, again the answer to this may lie in the missing front section of the Scrap-

---

[10] Manchester Central Library, Manchester Archives and Local Studies, RIM–ROB in BIOG CUTS 153, under 'Robertson, William'.

book.[11]
The journalism collected in the Scrapbook covers various subjects. Some columns consist purely of music news from the continent, often with forthcoming opera programmes, with very little continuous prose for study. However, even such items of seemingly little scholarly interest in the area of social construction can be useful as easily accessible archival material. There are several neat and careful alterations and corrections in blue ink added to the writings. These are most likely to be Robertson's own, as they are either factual or vocabulary changes.

6. The stamp from the top of Robertson's letter

The Scrapbook has now been surveyed and all the contents of significant length have been indexed by genre: musical reviews, articles on musical subjects, obituaries, theatre reviews, reviews of books on music and articles on non-musical subjects. The range of topics covered under the banner heading 'articles on musical subjects' is enormous. Some of the articles are on specific subjects of contemporary interest.[12] Robertson's articles sometimes reflect the sentiments of music

[11] The lines of investigation suggested by the evidence of Robertson's identity will be followed up and concluded in my ongoing doctoral research.
[12] The subjects of the articles can be summarized as follows: Balfe, Wallace and English opera, Paris opera houses, opinions on Wagner, poetry adapted as libretti, the new dictionary from the French Academy, Shakespeare as libretto, a tribute to Auber, registration of works in France and Germany, English music festivals, Rubinstein as virtuoso, James Leach, the state of English music, blind orchestra 'experiment' in Germany and France, French opera composers, Jules Pasdeloup, French Concerts Populaires, the Paris Opéra finances, the state of London opera, successes of English composers, music education in South Australia and France, municipal libraries and fine arts, French musical competitions, eisteddfodau, Johann Strauss's popularity and reputation, the place of the pianoforte in musical life, the secularization of the Panthéon in Paris, the Inventions exhibition of 1885 and the heritage of music, the Handel Festival, the Carl Rosa Opera Company and the arguments over foreign operas being produced in English, English composers on the continent, copyright legislation in Belgium, Francis Hueffer as a writer, Wagner in France, the Saint-Saëns 'incident', foreign attitudes to English philistinism, the art and state of singing, the reputation of the Marseillaise, the

journalism as a whole. He speaks for the majority of critics at the time when he says:

Arthur Sullivan with a fine vein of melody and some sense of dramatic and instrumental effect, seems to have finally forsaken the higher paths of his art for the ephemeral popularity of musical burlesque. Are we then, on the eve of that era of artistic sterility, which has been predicted by some of the most intelligent musical critics of the time?[13]

He is of course referring to the Savoy operas taking precedence over such works as oratorios, which were indeed perceived to be academically preferable, in Sullivan's composing schedule.

There are many reviews of performances in the Scrapbook.[14] These, like the articles, vary greatly and are centred on performances in the Manchester area. Many of the major musical events in Manchester are reported on, such as the Charles Hallé Grand Concerts,[15] the Athenaeum Musical Society[16] concerts and reviews of performances by visiting foreign musicians, such as an organ recital in Eccles by the French organist Alexandre Guilmant.[17] As well as large-scale orchestral concerts, the local concert series are well represented in Robertson's writings. The J.A. Cross Popular Concerts series, Mr. C.E. Rowley's Musical Union Concerts at Cheetham Town Hall, the Gentlemen's Concerts[18] and other chamber concert series, and such events as a piano recital in Broughton by Mr W.H. Shore[19] (with a guest appearance by

---

Bayreuth Festival, the Berlin Royal Academy of Fine Arts Centenary Exhibition, Rubinstein as musical philanthropist, an American opera company, Stanford on Sullivan, the New Guildhall School of Music, Verdi's *Otello*, Gounod, women's place at the piano, and musical destiny.

[13] Tuesday 12 September 1882; *RS*, p. 5.

[14] They include reports from London as well as of the local performances mentioned below.

[15] See Michael Kennedy, *The Hallé Tradition* (Manchester, 1960).

[16] The Manchester Athenaeum was opened in 1839 'as a centre for the development of intellectual and physical aspirations of the people'. See Louis M. Hayes, *Reminiscences of Manchester* (London, 1905), pp. 28–30.

[17] Alexandre Guilmant (1837–1911), French organist, teacher, composer and editor.

[18] See Wilfred Allis, 'The Gentlemen's Concert in Manchester 1770–1921', M.Phil. dissertation (University of Manchester, 1995).

[19] Not to be confused with William Shore (1791–1877) the founder and musical director of the Manchester Madrigal Society, and honorary secretary of the Gentleman's Glee Club.

Mr S. Speelman[20] for Alard's 'Valse for violin and piano-forte'[21]), and a concert by Miss Amina Goodwin,[22] are reviewed in varying degrees of depth.

Opera and operetta, from a variety of Manchester venues, are of course also covered: St James' Theatre, the Prince's Theatre, the Theatre Royal, the Free Trade Hall and the Comedy Theatre.[23] The reviews differ greatly in form. Some concentrate purely on the performances and set design of the work, while others provide the reader with a more balanced review, including a history of the work and opera company, and even on occasion critical comment about the music itself. Many of the operettas reviewed in the Scrapbook are now almost unknown, including Alfred Murray's *Dick*, Edward Terry's *Falka*, and Alfred Cellier's *Nell Gwynne*. Discussion of such works is invaluable for the information it provides on concert life and contemporary taste. The Robertson Scrapbook reveals much important detail about these and other long-forgotten works, which might otherwise have remained secreted in the mass of newspaper archives.

Robertson does not attempt to disguise his distaste for comic opera in an article that he seems to have written grudgingly.[24] His opening sentence, couched in the splendid Victorian prose that typifies his writings, sums up his revulsion:

---

[20] Possibly Samuel Speelman, principal second violinist in the Hallé and the second violinist in the Brodsky Quartet. With Simon Speelman, he also played regularly with the Liverpool Philharmonic, as the orchestra relied heavily on Hallé players at that time. See Kennedy, *The Hallé Tradition*. The Speelman referred to may be he of Speelman's Blackpool Orchestra: according to Neville Cardus, the Hallé members in 1901 used to keep themselves warm in winter by playing there. See Sidney H. Crowther, *Huddersfield Glee & Madrigal Society Centenary 1875–1975* (Kirklees, 1975).

[21] Delphin Alard (1815–88) was a French violinist and composer (best remembered today as the teacher of Pablo Sarasate from 1856 at the Paris Conservatoire and owner of the famed 'Messiah' Stradivari violin), to whom Gounod dedicated, among other things, his *Hymn to St Cecilia* in 1865.

[22] Amina Beatrice Goodwin (dates unknown) was born in Manchester and made her piano debut at the age of six. She studied initially with her father, John Lawrence Goodwin, then went on to study with Reinecke and Jadassohn at the Leipzig Conservatoire, Delaborde in Paris, Liszt in Weimar, and Clara Schumann. She had a very successful career and in 1895 founded a Pianoforte College for ladies. See Brown and Stratton, *British Musical Biography*, p. 167.

[23] See Alan J. Kidd, *Manchester: Illustrated from the Archives and with Contemporary Photographs* (Manchester, 1993); Terry Wyke and Nigel Rudyard, *Manchester Theatres* (Manchester, 1994).

[24] Tuesday 9 September 1884; *RS*, p. 67.

The musical historian of the latter half of this century will wonder at the immense development of comic and burlesque opera, and will hardly understand how the same conventional types of character, the same absurd stage situations, the same well-worn rhythms and imitated melodies, drew audience after audience, simply by a little variation on the familiar theme, and with the help of a little clever acting.

His comment was prescient. Robertson was of course correct in his evaluation. And yet formulaic entertainment is still being manufactured at an alarming rate. The gap between what is considered high art and low art, what is worthy and what is produced for popular consumption, will probably always exist. Robertson scathingly yet dutifully relays the convoluted plot of one such comic opera, *Dick* (1884) by Murray and Edward Jakobowski, that comes under scrutiny in this article. And then he begins on a barrage of faint praise and insults:

The new work is not much worse than most of its fellows – nor much better … It seems ungrateful to find a little too long an opera which is in two acts only, but the incidents of the drama are hardly enough to keep up the interest throughout … from this point the work is almost pantomime, sometimes running into broad farce … Here and there is a scrap of melody….

In his review of a performance of *The Rose Maiden* (1870) by Frederic Hymen Cowen[25] at a Manchester Athenaeum Musical Society concert, Robertson provides only a brief description of the performance before embarking on a relatively detailed account of the work itself.[26] While deprecating the fact that it shows 'little … lyrical originality and contrapuntal skill' he admits that it does possess 'graceful and pleasing

---

[25] Cowen (1852–1935) studied piano with Benedict and composition with Goss; in 1865 at Leipzig he was taught by Hauptmann, Moscheles, Reinecke and Plaidy, and in 1867 at the Stern Conservatory, Berlin, by Kiel. He became a well-respected composer and conductor. He conducted the Philharmonic Society in London (1888–92, 1900–7), Hallé Orchestra (1896–9), Liverpool Philharmonic Orchestra (1896–1913), Handel Triennial Festivals (1902–23), Bradford Festival Choral Society and subscription concerts (1897–1914), Bradford Permanent Orchestra (1899–1902) and Scottish Orchestra (1900–10). Elsewhere he appeared frequently as a guest conductor. See Christopher J. Parker's website <www.btinternet.com/~john.parker17/>

[26] There was a large audience and the choral pieces were 'admirably rendered by the well-balanced chorus which is so ably directed by Dr. [Henry] Hiles'. From the article of Tuesday 16 October 1883; *RS*, p. 39.

music'. This is typical of the way he strives for balance in assessing a work. He often cites the airs or choruses as evidence of their failings or praiseworthiness, for example:

Mr. Cowen's genius is essentially lyrical, and his style rarely swells with emotion or throbs with passion. Even where the writer of the words has given him an opportunity he has failed to avail himself of it, as where the Rose Queen suddenly exclaims to the personified Spring, "But Hear Me!" before which words Mr. Cowen's comparatively long instrumental *intermezzo* takes away all the force of the words.

Robertson's praise at times becomes poetic: such statements as 'Of melody pure and simple there is an abundance, and it runs in a clear and sunny stream, which sparkles as it flows' at first seem to sit somewhat strangely with his generally analytical approach. But it soon becomes evident that a marriage between fact and poetry is possible:

Mr. Cowen is so enamoured of rhythm and melody that he often repeats a few words without fresh meaning rather than lose the whole measure of a melodious phrase, and will miss a chance of dramatic effect rather than deny himself the charm of a smooth cadence.

Robertson also writes about some one-off events of interest, including a Welsh National Concert in aid of the Moss Side Welsh Chapel in Association Hall; the Royal Normal College and Academy of Music for the Blind concert in Brussels for the royal family;[27] a show given by Haverly's American Minstrels;[28] Mr Millar Craig's Glasgow Select

---

[27] Formed in 1872, the Royal Normal College and Academy of Music for the Blind is now known as the Royal National Institute for the Blind. It was based in Windermere House and Walmer House, Westow Park, Croydon. See W.H. Illingworth, *History of the Education of the Blind* (London, 1910).
[28] The first successful black songwriter in America was James Bland. His most famous songs were 'Oh dem Golden Slippers' and 'Carry me Back to Old Virginny'. Among his more than seven hundred songs are celebrations of the end of slavery: 'De Slavery Chains am Broke at Last', 'Keep dem Golden Gates Wide Open', 'In the Morning by the Bright Light'. In 1880 he came to England with the Haverly Coloured Minstrels and organized his own troupe there. The troupe performed for the royal family and also became very popular in Germany. See Donald Clarke, 'Minstrelsy, and the War between the States' (Chapter 2), *The Rise and Fall of Popular Music* (New York, 1995).

Choir concert,[29] and Mr. J.H. Greenwood's Annual Performance at the Comedy Theatre. He also reports on pantomimes, theatre productions and London concert life. In addition Robertson reviews a number of newly published books on music[30] and writes three obituaries, of Liszt, Smetana and Pasdeloup.[31] The few articles on non-musical subjects cover a wide range of topics, including the regulation of cremation; crime and punishment in France and England; and Russian-Jewish agriculture.

Two of the most interesting subjects, addressed repeatedly throughout the Scrapbook, are the condition of English music, and concepts of what constitutes national identity. Recognition for British composers was an important issue for Robertson. The term he uses is English, meaning English-speaking or British, a typical Victorian locution.[32] In an article on Michael William Balfe (1808–70) Robertson commends the unveiling of a medallion in Westminster Abbey as an apt remembrance and recognition of one of the few popular opera composers of England.[33] He later mentions Balfe's native city of Dublin and recognizes that both Balfe and William Vincent Wallace (1812–65) are 'na-

---

[29] John Millar Craig (1839–?) succeeded James Allen as conductor in 1886 and was still involved with the choir in 1895 when he took part in a competition judged by, among others, Ebenezer Prout. He went on to conduct the Edinburgh Bach Choir in 1910, resigning the following year. As a baritone he had studied with A.W. Smith and Signor Bucher in Edinburgh (where he was born), Leoni in Milan and Romani in Florence. See Brown and Stratton, *British Musical Biography*, p. 105.

[30] W.S. Rockstro, *George Frederick Handel*, H.R. Haweis, *My Musical Life*, Ernest David, *A Life of Handel*, Hector Berlioz, *Autobiography*, trans. Rachel and Eleanor Holmes, Amy Fay, *Music Study in Germany: From the Home Correspondence of Amy Fay*, August Reissmann, *The Life and Works of Robert Schumann*, John Frederic Rowbotham, *A History of Music*, vols. 1 and 2, Sarah C. Bull, *Ole Bull: A Memoir*, Hubert H. Parry, *Studies of Great Composers,* Emil Naumann, *The History of Music* trans. F. Praeger, and Arthur Pougin, *Verdi: An Anecdotic History of his Life and Works* trans. James E. Matthew. All were published between 1883 and 1887.

[31] Jules Pasdeloup (1819–87) was the founder and director of the popular concert series in Paris in 1861. See E. Bernard, 'Jules Pasdeloup et les Concerts Populaires', *Revue de musicologie*, 57 (1971), pp. 150–78.

[32] Occasionally it is also used to mean resident and working in England.

[33] Saturday 21 October 1882; *RS*, p. 9. Other tributes paid to Balfe are testimony to his popularity at the time. In April 1879 a stained-glass window was erected in his honour in St Patrick's Cathedral, Dublin, and a large marble statue of him stands on a pedestal in the centre of the entrance foyer to the Theatre Royal, Drury Lane, London. Balfe was from Dublin, but moved to London after the death of his father in 1823. Then in 1828 he moved to Italy, returning to London in 1835.

tives of the sister island'.[34] Robertson felt that the future of English opera lay in the Irish. He cites Balfe and Wallace as examples, although presumably they are meant to be paradigms for the new generation of Irish composers, as by this time both were dead. In the same article he credits them with a 'spontaneous spring of pure melody, coloured with the peculiar character of the native song of Ireland'. The generalizations about race so characteristic of the Victorian era are typified by Robertson's sweeping and patronizing tribute to the Irish:

The northern Celtic peoples are peculiarly adapted by their emotional nature for the utterance of musical speech, and in fact the popular songs of the Irish are the richest in melody and the deepest in expression which we possess as national property.

But Robertson is not isolated in his praise for Irish musical talent. Hubert Parry expressed the same sentiment (though on spurious grounds) in 1893:[35]

Irish folk-music – probably the most human, most varied, most poetical, and most imaginative in the world – is particularly rich in tunes which imply considerable sympathetic sensitiveness … as a simple emotional type the following Irish tune is one of the most perfect in existence.[36]

While seeming to disapprove of operetta in general, Robertson does not flinch from a fair appraisal of one of Balfe's best-loved works. He both condemns and extols the virtues of *The Bohemian Girl* (1843) in

---

[34] Wallace was from Waterford, Ireland. In 1835 he emigrated to Tasmania, and founded a music academy in Sydney, Australia. He moved to New York in 1844, where he left his wife Isabella Kelly to marry the pianist Helen Stoepel. In 1845 they settled in London, where Wallace stayed for twenty years before going to the Pyrenees (where he eventually died) for the benefit of his health. His extensive travels included visits to India and South America.

[35] C.H.H. Parry, *The Evolution of the Art of Music* (London, 1896), p. 79 (2nd edition of *The Art of Music*, London, 1893). Sir Charles Hubert Hastings Parry (1848–1918) was appointed Director of the Royal College of Music in 1893, where he taught Ralph Vaughan Williams, Gustav Holst, George Butterworth and Herbert Howells. In 1898 he became Professor of Music at Oxford.

[36] Parry here is mistakenly referring to the Londonderry Air as an example of the 'emotional nature' of the Irish, and depth of expression in melody that Robertson had earlier observed. See Brian Audley, 'The Provenance of the *Londonderry Air*', *Journal of the Royal Musical Association*, 125 (2000), pp. 205–47.

his writings: '[though] full of faults from the dramatic point of view [it] is rich in melody, and the pathos … has turned a commonplace libretto into pure poetry, which will certainly last as long as there is an English musical language. He criticizes Balfe's style, however, arguing that it suffers from following Italian models and citing the 'artificial cadenzas with which he weakens the simple effect of his finest airs' as evidence. Unfortunately the article is quite short and Robertson does not go into more detail.

The propensity of Robertson to claim 'foreign' composers for the greater glory of 'English' music is again evident in an article from Wednesday 16 May 1883.[37] Arthur Goring Thomas's *Esmeralda* (1883) and Alexander Campbell Mackenzie's *Colomba* (1883)[38] are cited as successes abroad following Carl Rosa productions in Hamburg.[39] Robertson goes to the trouble of explaining their foreignness, stating that Thomas was 'by education and choice a disciple of the contemporary lyrical school of France' and that Mackenzie 'by birth belongs to the northern Celtic race'.[40] He then proclaims that they 'are none the less to be fairly claimed as English composers, and as such their work is welcome'. This fixation whereby national identity was first defined and delineated, and 'foreigners' were then claimed as 'our own', may be symptomatic of an era when hierarchic demarcation and segregation were sociologically important.

An important leap in the logic of Robertson's stance on national

---

[37] *RS*, p. 29.
[38] Mackenzie (1847–1935) was Scottish, from Edinburgh. He studied at Sondershausen in Germany between 1857–62 and later at the Royal Academy of Music, London. Between 1879 and 1888 he lived partly in Italy. From 1888 to 1924 he was Principal of the Royal Academy of Music, and from 1892 conducted the Philharmonic Society of London. He was knighted in 1895 and created KCVO 1922. His compositions displayed some stylized Scottish folk music elements.
[39] Carl August Nicholas Rosa (1842–89) moved to England in 1866 from Hamburg and formed an opera company that became the pride of the British operatic scene. Internationally famous singers flocked to take part in his productions and the company often toured abroad, also to great acclaim. His surname was actually spelt Rose, but because of common mispronunciation by the British he changed the spelling to Rosa on the formation of his opera company in 1873. The Carl Rosa tradition lived on after financial crisis by merging with Sadler's Wells Opera in 1958. See Eric Walter White, *The Rise of English Opera* (London, 1951, R) and *A History of English Opera* (London, 1983), pp. 368–72.
[40] Thomas (1850–92) displays a clearly foreign influence in his music, having studied with Durand in Paris and later orchestration with Max Bruch. Cecil Forsyth calls Thomas, among others, a 'denationalized Englishman' in his book *Music and Nationalism* (London, 1911).

identity occurs in an article he wrote about regional musical festivals.[41] He thought that it would 'not be amiss to reckon also as a tribute to English musical art, the oratorio of *St Ludmilla*, which has been commissioned from Mr. Antonin Dvořák' for the Birmingham and Leeds festivals. But the reasoning behind this remark – 'since this highly endowed Bohemian musician owes to the enlightened love and liberal patronage of music which prevail in this country his rapid rise from comparative obscurity' – is obscurely compelling. Robertson was correct in his evaluation: the rise of Dvořák's fame was largely due to his reception in England. In 1884 the composer travelled to England for the first time, at the invitation of the Philharmonic Society, London, to conduct performances of his own works. All were favourably reviewed. The London musical world hailed his works and his presence in England, and the Philharmonic Society made him an honorary member. Although Dvořák never lived in England, his great success prompted eight more visits over the next few years, bringing new works each time. In Germany and Austria, political feeling hindered the reception of his work, whereas England was unaffected by the political issues and free to appreciate his music without bias. Unfortunately Robertson did not write any reviews or articles concerning Dvořák or his music, other than in passing in brief articles of music news. Dvořák wrote *The Spectre's Bride* (1884) and the Requiem Mass (1890) for the Birmingham music festival, the Seventh Symphony for the Philharmonic Society (1885) and *St Ludmilla* for the Leeds and Birmingham music festivals (1886). He also received an honorary doctorate from Cambridge in 1891, so Robertson was not entirely alone in his affectionate adoption of Dvořák. His comment was probably more a flippant statement of possessiveness of a well-loved composer than a declaration meant to be taken seriously.

Another English success abroad is listed as *Fenice* (1853) by Henry Hugo Pierson (originally Pearson; 1815–73).[42] Pierson moved to Germany in 1839 to study under C.H. Rinck, Tomaschek and Reissiger. He was appointed Professor of Music at Edinburgh in 1844, but because of a disagreement with the establishment resigned the following year. He then embraced Germany as his home and at the same time Germanized his name. Regrettably, Robertson writes nothing in this

[41] Saturday 21 August 1886; *RS*, p. 154.
[42] *RS*, p. 29.

article or elsewhere in the Scrapbook about either his music or its reception. Indeed, he seems almost to resent the success of English composers who, like Pierson, moved abroad. At the same time he expounds
the virtues (and implied loyalty) of those who stayed at home, such as
the Irishman Stanford.[43] Robertson seems to be arguing that the success of these composers should be seen as greater than those who have
deserted England, thereby absolving themselves of responsibility for
the country's place in musical heritage:

> It would, of course, be easy to attribute too much importance to such patronage
> of English music on the Continent, since the recognition of such of our compos-
> ers as have settled abroad from time to time has not been grudging, though it has
> never done much for the development of musical life in England. But the present
> run upon the works of English composers who have not left their native land is
> noteworthy in many ways, and may even be enough to warrant the hope that this
> country is at last prepared to take her place in that movement which has pro-
> duced such large and rich results elsewhere.

Robertson was by no means unique in his anti-nationalist sentiment. At
a dinner during a visit to Ireland in 1837, Balfe mentioned the fact that
on his return to London he was considered a foreigner, an Irish Italian.[44]

Nationality appears as a topic of the day once more in 1885,[45] in an
article alluding to a recent contribution to the German magazine *Die
Grenzboten*, about English music from Purcell to the present. Robertson
appears to be quite sensitive about criticism of native talent from foreign sources, although admitting himself the overall lack of an English
musical voice:

> Whether in ignorance or to lend colour to his contrast between the productive-
> ness of the good old days and the poverty of later times, our critic then leaps with

---

[43] Charles Villiers Stanford (1852–1924) was born in Dublin. After his graduation at
Cambridge, he left for Germany, studying at Leipzig and later in Berlin. He travelled
throughout Germany and France listening to the contemporary music. After his studies
he returned to England and became simultaneously Professor of Music at Cambridge
and Professor of Composition at the Royal College of Music, remaining in those posts
for nearly forty years.
[44] See Basil Walsh, 'Balfe the Irish Italian', *History Ireland*, 11/1 (spring 2003).
[45] Monday 21 September 1885; *RS*, pp. 107–8.

one bound to Sterndale Bennett [1816–75] (from the 'Arnes, Arnolds, and Bishops of a later time').

The German critic acknowledges no composers of worth in English musical heritage between Arne and Bennett, other than Arnold and Bishop, and 'not unfairly characterises them as meritorious writers scarcely original enough to entitle them to a place apart'. Obviously affronted by those views, Robertson begins to set the record straight on behalf of the grievously omitted English composers:

> He does not seem to know that Balfe, Wallace, Loder, and others of their period composed some respectable operas, and, perhaps for the same reason, he omits entirely the English composers of church music, who, for dignity and devotional feeling no less than for sound artistic workmanship, have no reason to look for rivals anywhere.

Although agreeing with some of the German journalist's points, he cannot resist arguing that he reached his decisions on 'imperfect evidence'. His chief disappointment, Sullivan, is compared with 'some injustice' to Franz Wilhelm Abt (1819–85), which Robertson surmises must be because Sullivan is known in Germany only for his comic operas, rather than for his serious music. Apart from his fame as director of numerous choirs, Abt was celebrated for his vocal music, especially male choral music: 'His style was popular, his melodies simple and fresh, with a pleasing and varied accompaniment … [so that they] are easily mistaken for genuine folksong.'[46] Unfortunately Robertson did not review any of Abt's works in the Scrapbook.

Robertson goes on to comment that 'our foreign critic metes full justice out to us when he says that, paradoxical as it may sound, "the love of music in England is greater than with us in Germany"'. Robertson continues: 'This assertion does not seem to be promoted by what Mr. Herbert Spencer calls the anti-national bias, or even by a light spirit of

---

[46] Edward Kravitt, 'Abt, Franz Wilhelm', *The New Grove Dictionary of Music and Musicians*, ed. Stanley Sadie (2nd edition, London, 2001), i, pp. 39–40.

epigram, of which German writers, as a rule, are all too guileless.'[47] After having commented that England suffers periodically from a lack of notable composers, the German critic says that nonetheless the English love music more than the Germans. But Robertson states that this assertion is not supported by the 'anti-national bias', a dislike of the product of one's own country, as exemplified in Act I of *The Mikado* (1885): 'The idiot who praises, with enthusiastic tone, / All centuries but this, and ev'ry country but his own'. Nor can it be accounted for by a German sense of humour, which he suggests is, as a rule, non-existent.

In Robertson's opinion the love of music in England is a result of other factors:

It is founded rather on an intelligent discernment of some strong forces in English character and history. Chief among these is the musical training of our churches and cathedrals, in which so many learn not only to recognise good music but to take part in it themselves. No doubt the excellence of our choral singing and the fact that we are better able to enjoy the harmonious elements of the oratorio than any other people is due to the culture thus received; and the practice of singing now adopted as part of our national school system can hardly fail to increase this culture to a high degree. Our composers also will do well to keep a firm hold on the national characteristics if they wish to ensure a lasting success. Any attempts at the mere imitation of German solidity or French delicacy can only end in failure, unless the lines of national development are followed. The fact that so many English composers are now working for our great festivals is the most encouraging sign of musical revival we have seen in this country for many years, and if they will only free themselves from the imitation of some models to which they have shown a too conventional attachment in the past we may be privileged to welcome the time, foretold by our own German critic, 'when England shall again take an important place in the development of music'.[48]

---

[47] The philosopher and sociologist Herbert Spencer (1820–1903) was a major figure in the intellectual life of the Victorian era. A prolific author, he was one of the principal proponents of evolutionary theory in the mid nineteenth century, and his reputation at the time rivalled that of Charles Darwin. Spencer was initially best known for developing and applying evolutionary theory to philosophy, psychology and the study of society, in what he called his 'synthetic philosophy'. See his *A System of Synthetic Philosophy* (1862–93). See also S. Andreski, *Herbert Spencer: Structure, Function and Evolution* (London, 1972); T.S. Gray, *The Political Philosophy of Herbert Spencer* (Aldershot, 1996).

Robertson has finished his sermon on a positive note. Although covering many diverse topics both musical and non-musical, the Robertson Scrapbook provides, among other things, an interesting addition to the discourse on issues of national identity in English Victorian music. The campaign to recognize national talent, though perhaps less ardent than at the time of the Society of British Musicians (1834–65), still existed alongside sentiments of self-loathing and xenophilia in the dialogue of music journalism.[49] W.J. Robertson displays a great enthusiasm for a national school of composition and is vigorous and wholehearted in his remarks on the state of English music. Another possible legacy of his writings, among others, is to illuminate the prose that would have helped to inform the tastes and positions of Manchester's intelligentsia in the national debate on musical composition.

[48] There were and still are many regional music festivals in England. At the time under discussion the Three Choirs Festival, as well as those of Wolverhampton, Leeds and Birmingham, commissioned and put on many new works, from both home and abroad. See Watkins Shaw, *The Three Choirs Festival 1713–1953* (Worcester and London, 1954); A. Boden, *Three Choirs: A History of the Festival* (Stroud, 1992); D. Lyons and others, *Origin and Progress of the Meeting of the Three Choirs of Gloucester, Hereford and Worcester* (Gloucester, 1932); F.R. Spark and J. Bennett, *A History of the Leeds Musical Festivals 1858–1889* (Leeds, 1892); W.C. Stockley, *Fifty Years of Music in Birmingham from 1850–1900* (Birmingham, 1913).

[49] See Leanne Langley, 'Sainsbury's *Dictionary*, the Royal Academy of Music, and the Rhetoric of Patriotism', *Music and British Culture 1785–1914: Essays in honour of Cyril Ehrlich*, ed. C. Bashford and L. Langley (Oxford, 2000); Simon McVeigh, 'The Society of British Musicians (1834–1865) and the Campaign for Native Talent', ibid.; Gerald Newman, *The Rise of English Nationalism: A Cultural History, 1740–1830* (New York, 1997); Hans Lenneberg, 'Collective Biography and National Pride', *Witnesses and Scholars: Studies in Musical Biography* (New York and London, 1988).

Some Notes on the Music of Anthony Gilbert

DOUGLAS JARMAN

FIRST, THE ESSENTIAL biographical information.

Born in London on 26 July 1934, Anthony Gilbert was a relative latecomer to composition. Not until he was 19 did he start to study part-time at Trinity College of Music, London, and not until he was 23 (by which time he was working as a translator and interpreter at the London offices of the Société des Fonderies de Pont-à-Mousson of Nancy) did he begin to study composition, largely as a private pupil, with Anthony Milner, Mátyás Seiber and Alexander Goehr. It is a mark of Gilbert's determination that for the next ten years, while working in a variety of both non-musical (warehouseman and accounts clerk) and musical jobs (freelance copyist, proofreader and arranger) for Schott, and full-time Music and Record Library Assistant at the City of Westminster Public Library, he not only devoted his summer holidays to studying at Dartington and Wardour Castle (with, among other teachers, Nono and Berio) but also found time to produce a whole series of works, including an unpublished *Elegy* for piano, a Duo for violin and viola, the Piano Sonata no. 1, *Serenade*, the *Missa Brevis* and the *Sinfonia*.

In 1965 he left his job as Library Assistant to take up the position of Music Editor and Head of Production of Contemporary Music at Schott's, a post he held for five years, during the course of which he also studied at Tanglewood with Carter, Schuller and Sessions, received his first commissions and composed many of the works – *Brighton Piece*, *Nine or Ten Osannas*, *The Incredible Flute Music* and *Spell Respell* – that first brought him to public attention.

In 1970, the year which saw the première of his one-act opera *The Scene Machine* in Kassel, Gilbert became Granada Arts Fellow and Composer in Residence at the University of Lancaster. The next year he was appointed Visiting Lecturer at Lancaster, a post that he continued to hold until 1973, while working at Morley College and as acting Director of Music at the Department of Adult Studies at Goldsmiths College. He took up a post in 1973 at the newly instituted Northern College of Music (made 'Royal' the following year) where he was responsible for setting up the composition department and where, as tutor and eventually Head of the School of Composition and Contemporary Music, he stayed until his retirement in 1999.

As the only full-time tutor in composition Gilbert taught some hundred would-be composers in his twenty-eight years at the RNCM, and it would not be an exaggeration to say that he was single-handedly responsible during this time for what might justly be called a Second Manchester School, among whom can be numbered Simon Holt, Martin Butler, Robin Grant, Kate Romano, Paul Newland, Ian Vine, Cheryl Camm, Anwen Lewis, Paul Clay and many others.

Nor has Gilbert's influence as a teacher and moving force been confined to his work in Manchester. In addition to the many periods he has spent teaching in his beloved Australia, Anthony Gilbert, with his abiding interest in the work of young composers and his unstinting work on behalf of his colleagues (he was one of the founders of the SPNM Composers' Weekends in 1967, has acted as panel member and adjudi-

cator for numerous national awards and has been a long-standing member of the score-reading panel of the SPNM and New Music Panel of
the BBC), has for over thirty years been somewhere near the centre of
British musical life.

If such a brief biographical summary seems unsatisfactory what follows will be even more so, for it is hardly possible, in an article of this
length, to deal adequately with Gilbert's own creative output. It is an
output that now runs to some ninety compositions, covering over forty
years' work and ranging from the tough serialism of the early Piano
Sonata of 1962 (Gilbert's first published work) to the wit and sometimes broad humour of the *Bestiary* pieces, from the incisiveness of
Nine or Ten Osannas to the meditative *Moonfaring* and the lyricism of
the recent Violin Concerto *On Beholding a Rainbow.*

Rather than give a general, and inevitably somewhat vague, 'over-
view' of Gilbert's output, which would do less than justice to one of the
most vital, interesting and original composers at work in the UK, this
article will concentrate on a few works from different periods of Gilbert's life in the hope that a discussion of these pieces (and occasional
references to other works) will not only show the development of Gilbert's musical language but also provide a starting point, and a stimulus, for a more complete and thorough study of his music.

Since what follows will be primarily concerned with the development of various technical procedures, and since, in choosing works
most of which involve keyboard, I am ignoring one of the most striking
aspects of Gilbert's music – his acute ear for, and often virtuoso handling of, orchestral colour (witness the crystal-hard clarity of the orchestration in the chamber concerto *Towards Asâvari* or the sumptuous
textures of *Vasanta with Dancing*) – it will perhaps be as well to begin
by trying to summarize the constant and individual characteristics of
his music.

Gilbert began to study composition at time when, in what was still a
relatively conservative and traditional musical atmosphere, many young
British composers were eager to get to grips with the new musical
developments that had taken place in Europe in the years after the Second World War. As a pupil of two composers whose natural orientation
was European – the Hungarian Mátyás Seiber and Alexander Goehr
(who was not only linked to the Schoenberg school through his father

Walter Goehr, but had also recently studied in Paris with Messiaen) – Gilbert inherited not only a tradition of fastidious technical craftsmanship but was, through both his own inclinations and those of his teachers, plunged into a musical world that was a ferment of new ideas. Anthony Gilbert's music may have become more accessible over the years, as has that of many other composers of his generation, but the technical bases of his music and his essential 'voice' have never changed.

The bases of Gilbert's music spring from a wide diversity of sources: from the music of India and Indonesia, from his study of birdsong, from early music, from change-ringing and, of course, from the twelve-note techniques of the Second Viennese School and the rhythmic techniques of Stravinsky and Messiaen, procedures which, from Gilbert's earliest compositions, were taken as given, as they were by any serious composer of his generation. Filtered through Gilbert's own individual compositional concerns, such techniques have remained a permanent part of his vocabulary.

Some of the permutational methods and the intricate formal structures in Gilbert's music – the view of the work as a single whole rather than a collection of movements, the intricate cross-references and maze-like constructions of some pieces – may remind one of the music of Berg but, from the earliest pieces, Gilbert's emotional world is closer to that of Stravinsky and Varèse than to that of the Schoenberg School. Indeed the importance of the influence of Varèse and Stravinsky has been explicitly acknowledged in many of Gilbert's works: *Regions* for two orchestras is dedicated to the memory of Varèse while *Igórochki*, which draws on the *Symphonies of Wind Instruments*, is dedicated to the memory of Stravinsky. There is no hint in Gilbert of the neo-classicism of the twelve-note Schoenberg that one sometimes finds in the music of his teacher Alexander Goehr. Nor, despite the fact that the *Missa Brevis* makes reference to *Pierrot Lunaire,* is there any hint of that fascination with the 'Angst' of Viennese expressionism that one finds in the music of Maxwell Davies. Similarly when, as in the Third String Quartet which is based on Machaut's *Hoquetus David*, Gilbert turns to earlier music, it is not, as so often in Maxwell Davies's forays into the past, to use the original as a basis for expressionist distortion but to transform the string quartet medium into an energetic, raucous hurdy-gurdy – a descendant of the organistrum used by medieval monks to teach plainchant.

The rhythmic energy of the Third Quartet is as characteristic of Gilbert's music as the sheer oddity of the idea. Indeed, along with its meticulous craftsmanship and its eclecticism – which somehow manages to combine a wide variety of both musical and non-musical sources and inspirations into a totally individual language – Gilbert's music is characterized by its energy, its sheer wit and quirkiness.

If the analyses that follow seem remote from the highly individual musical experience of the works themselves, the reader should remember that the techniques described are a means to an end and not an end in themselves; the technical procedures employed are determined by the nature of the initial musical idea rather than the music being determined by the technique. As a corrective balance to the description of what, to non-composers, may seem abstract or mathematical technical procedures (a 'criticism' to which I shall return in the final paragraph of this article) it will be as well to bear in mind that we are here dealing with a composer who was inspired to create a whole series of pieces by the bizarre nature of a categorization of animals discovered in the writing of Borges and who, in the *Quartet of Beasts*, chooses to compound the flight of fantasy by extending it to include the visual aspects of the score, so that in the movement entitled 'Those which are Mythological or Fabulous', for example, musical beasts (including two strange flying creatures, a brontosaurus and a beautiful unicorn) stare out at us from the printed score while in manuscript (the last page of which is reproduced in facsimile in the published score) even the piano pedal marks start to develop into sheep.

How many composers would choose to set the lines 'On yonder hill there stands a coo, if it's no there, it's awa noo'? Perhaps the Stravinsky who set the nonsense poems of *Pribaoutki* and whose last work was a setting of *The Owl and the Pussycat*. Not, one feels fairly certain, Schoenberg or any of the members of the Second Viennese School.

The Piano Sonata no. 1 of 1962, the first of Gilbert's works to be published, immediately reveals the influences of both Schoenberg and Messiaen. The Schoenbergian influence is evident in the fact that, unusually for Gilbert, the piece is a twelve-note work. From the outset, however, Gilbert handles the system with considerable freedom, repeating and omitting notes at will, using only half rows, and deriving major triads from it in a way that is distinctly un-Schoenbergian (and, despite the ingenious construction of the original note row, distinctly un-Webernian also).[1] Equally un-Schoenbergian, but indicative of the kind of techniques developed in Gilbert's later work, is the fact that the row itself is subjected to various permutations – permutations of groups of notes within set segments in the first movement, more radical permutations in the second and third movements, which use derivative rows that spring from new horizontalizations of material presented as harmonies in the first. Thus, for example, the second of the two Trios in Movement III derives its material from the final chords of Movement I, which it then employs as harmonic units within which the notes are constantly permuted.

While the rhythmic structure of most of the Sonata seems to be instinctive and unsystematic, the influence of Messiaen is clearly evident in Trio I of the third movement *Scherzo* (and, indeed, the influence is acknowledged since the rhythmic pattern involved is a quotation from *Oiseaux exotiques*) in which a twelve-note row is treated as a repeating pitch cycle and linked to a repeating durational cycle of fifteen, or sometimes fourteen, notes. Equally Messiaenic is the structuring of the five bars of the same Trio, the lengths of which define the following mathematical sequence:

$$\frac{7+7+10}{16} \qquad \frac{9+9+9}{16} \qquad \frac{11+11+8}{16} \qquad \frac{13+13+7}{16}$$

before the return of the original 7+7+10 bar presents the twelve-note set in retrograde.

By the time of the op. 20a String Quartet, ten years later, the relatively unstructured handling of the relationship between pitch and rhythm in Piano Sonata no. 1 has given way to a more systematic and individual technique in which the pitch collection (in the case of the Quartet the pitch collection is a twelve-note set) remains untransposed and, instead of (or, in some works, as well as) being subjected to the traditional Schoenbergian transformations of inversion, retrograde and

---

[1] The original row of the Sonata is constructed in such a way that the first tetrachord is its own inversion, while the second and third tetrachords are inversions of one another:

Db C A G# : E G F# B : F D Eb Bb

As a consequence, at the inversion a fifth above, the first tetrachord reverses itself and the other two simply exchange positions:

G# A C Db : F D Eb Bb : E G F# B

retrograde inversion, is subjected to a series of systematic permutations, the effect of which is to generate a sequence of fluid, ever changing but interrelated pitch groupings.

Given Gilbert's interest in, and knowledge of, the music of Messiaen it is tempting to trace the origins of these procedures to the kind of permutational techniques found in works such as the *Ile de feu II*, *Livre d'orgue* or *Chronochromie*. They are however, equally reminiscent of, and owe as much to, the change-ringing patterns of bell ringing.

Thus, in the radio opera *The Chakravaka-Bird* (1977), the music associated with the main character, the young poetess Mahadevi, is based on the following seven-note set: C F sharp G B C sharp D A flat. These notes are permuted according to the scheme in Ex. 1.

$$
\begin{array}{ccccccc}
1 & 2 & 3 & 4 & 5 & 6 & 7 \\
6 & 3 & 4 & 7 & 2 & 5 & 1 \\
5 & 4 & 7 & 1 & 3 & 2 & 6 \\
2 & 7 & 1 & 6 & 4 & 3 & 5 \\
3 & 1 & 6 & 5 & 7 & 4 & 2 \\
4 & 6 & 5 & 2 & 1 & 7 & 3 \\
7 & 5 & 2 & 3 & 6 & 1 & 4 \\
\end{array}
$$

Ex. 1

The complementary seven-note set associated with the Prince Kausika (the inversion of the prime set above at a level which provides the five notes missing from Mahadevi's set) is subject to the same permutational method.[2]

Although Gilbert's scheme breaks one of the first rules of change-ringing – that each bell or pitch moves, at the most, only one position forward or backward – it is the kind of permutational method familiar to any bell ringer: each of the seven notes follows the same pattern (that plotted for note 4, B natural, in Ex. 2) but starts at a different point. Here, in *The Chakravaka-Bird*, then, the two heptachords associated with Mahadevi and Prince Kausika respectively are defined not by ordered succession, as in a Schoenbergian note row, but by their different harmonic identities.

---

[2] Priti Paintal, 'A Comparative Study of the Integration of Eastern and Western Music in Two Compositions', unpublished M.Mus. (Composition) thesis (RNCM, 1985).

	1	2	3	4	5	6	7
A				x			
B			x				
C		x					
D					x		
E						x	
F	x						
G							x

Ex. 2

First employed in the String Quartet op. 20a, this kind of permutational technique is something which, in a variety of developed and modified forms, has been the basis of much of Gilbert's music ever since.

The permutational scheme of the 1972 String Quartet op. 20a (which is also that of Gilbert's next work, the Symphony of 1973) is based on the symmetrical pairing of notes between the two halves (the two hexachords) of a twelve-note set or pitch cycle. Ex. 3 shows these pairings applied to the original version of the twelve-note set. The pairings ensure that any movement *forward* by a note in the first hexachord of the set is mirrored by a similar movement *backward* by its equivalent in the second hexachord.

A	C	D	E♭	G	F#	G#	F	B	E	C#	B♭
1	2	3	4	5	6 ‖	7	8	9	10	11	12

Ex. 3

The most important feature of the permutational system is that the different notes move according to different rules. Although the precise rules which govern these movements are, perhaps, unimportant as far as most readers of this article will be concerned (those interested in such things will find the rules tabulated in footnote 3), it is important to

---

[3] See end of chapter.

notice that (as Ex. 3. demonstrates) notes 1 and 12, the outer notes of the set, stay fixed throughout.

What is vital, however – since it affects both the pitch and rhythmic organization of the work – is the effect that these different rates of progression have upon the resulting sets since, because the permutational rules are different for each pair of notes, there are frequently occasions when two or more notes occupy the same positions while other order numbers remain blank.

Ex. 4, which shows the original row and the first eleven permutations – a 12 x 12 sequence – demonstrates the 'clumping' of notes that results. The progressive application of the same permutational rules produces twelve such 12 x 12 sequences before reproducing the original set.

Sequence I

A

A	C	D	Eb	G	F#	G#	F	B	E	C#	Bb
1	2	3	4	5	6	7	8	9	10	11	12

B

A	G#	C	D	Eb	G	F	B	E	C#	F#	Bb
1	7	2	3	4	5	8	9	10	11	6	12

C

A		F	C,F#	D	Eb	B	E	C#,G#	G		Bb
1		8	2,6	3	4	9	10	11,7	5		12

D

A	G		G#,B	C	D	E	C#	D#,F#		F	Bb
1	5		7,9	2	3	10	11	6,4		8	12

E

A,B	F#			E	C,G	F,C#	D			G#	Eb,Bb
1,9	6			10	2,5	8,11	3			7	12,4

F

A		E,F,Eb			G#,C#	C,F#			D,G,B		Bb
1		10,8,4			7,11	2,6			3,5,9		12

G

A,E,G#	G	C#	Eb	B	C	F	F#,D,B
1,10,7	5	11	4	9	2	8	12,6,3

H

A	D	C#,B	F#	G	F	G#	C#,D#	E	Bb
1	3	11,9	6	5	8	7	2,4	10	12

I

A,B	C#,F,G#	D	E	C,G,F#	Eb,Bb
1,9	11,8,7	3	10	2, 5, 6	12,4

J

A	C#,G	D#,F#	D	E	G#,B	C,F	Bb
1	11,5	4,6	3	10	9,7	2, 8	12

K

A,C#	E,G#	Eb,G	F,B	D,F#	C,Bb
1,11	10,7	4,5	8,9	3,6	12,2

L

AC,F#	E,F	B	Eb	G,D	C#,G#,Bb
1, 2, 6	10, 8	9	4	5,3	12,11,7

Ex. 4

That the notes in the first hexachord are paired with their mirror equivalent in the second hexachord has the effect of ensuring that any one permutation is always symmetrical within itself: that is, that the number of notes that fall in the same position (and hence the number of 'gaps') in one half of the set is always reflected in the other half. Thus, in the final permutation (L) of Ex. 4, both the first and last order numbers consist of three-note collections, the third and tenth of two notes and the fourth and ninth of single notes while order numbers 2, 5 and 6 – and their symmetrical equivalents, order numbers 7, 8 and 11 – remain blank.

. As can be seen most clearly in the concluding *Round* of the op. 20 Quartet, the symmetricality within the permutations has an important effect on both the rhythmic and the textural structure of the work. Discounting the section after letter S (when the movement is interrupted by a reprise of part of Movement I), the *Round* lays out the forty-eight sets of Sequences IX–XII, the last four of the twelve permutation sequences, in a completely systematic and straightforward manner. Every bar consists of one permutation of the series; every bar begins with A natural and ends with B flat (the fixed first and last notes of the set); and every bar reflects the symmetrical nature of each permutation, in that the second half of each bar presents a textural and rhythmic retrograde of the first.[4]

Here, as elsewhere in the work, the presentation of the sequences also determines the length of the formal units. Thus, the 24-bar length of the first main section of the *Round* is determined by the fact that each bar presents one of the twenty-four permutations of Sequences IX and X.

Ex. 5 shows the opening bars of the *Round*, which set out the first permutations of Sequence IX.

One result of the permutational system employed is that the penultimate permutation of the final Sequence XII gives the near retrograde of the original (with notes 2–11 in reverse order), while the last permu-

[4] The rhythmic retrogrades of the *Round* perhaps require further explanation, since Gilbert has not simply written the note durations of the first half of the bar backwards in the second half, and the symmetricality of the bars is therefore not visually obvious in the score.

The following examples show the derivation of the rhythms in bars 2–6 (Ex. 5). In each example, the prime rhythmic pattern (the rhythm of the first half of the bar) is shown on the upper left, its retrograde on the lower left and, on the right, the rhythm that results when the two are juxtaposed. Each symbol represents a quaver's duration with the symbol | representing the point at which a note is attacked and the symbol o representing a held note or a rest.

bar 2   prime | | | | o | }
                                  } together = | | | | o | | o | | | |
        retrograde | o | | | | }

bar 3   prime | o | | | o }
                                  } together = | o | | | o o | | | o |
        retrograde   o | | | o | }

bars 4–5 prime | | o | | | }
                                  } together = | | o | | | | | | o | |
        retrograde | | | o | | }

bar 6   prime | o | o o |}
                                  } together = | o | o o | | o o | o |
        retrograde | o o | o |}

tation presents the original series as two six-note chords. The last section of the work, following the interruption of the return of Movement I, overlays the permutations of Sequence XI with those of Sequence XII until the final bars when the last two permutations are staggered by a bar, quasi-canonically. The last bar thus lays bare the one and only appearance of the two separate six-note 'clumps' and closes the circle by returning to the original series of Sequence I, either in the form of the optional reprise of Movement I or, if the *Ossia* is chosen, in the form of a fleeting statement of the original series on the viola.

Ex. 5

While the *Round* presents a particularly clear example of Gilbert's permutational scheme, it is not difficult to find other passages in the Quartet in which the sequences are presented in an equally clear, straightforward way. At letter P of Movement III, for example, a reworking of the opening of the movement (from letter L onwards) is introduced and accompanied by a new viola figuration which systematically presents all the twelve permutations of Sequence VIII. As in the *Round*, every bar of the viola figuration presents a single permutation of that sequence and every bar consists of a textural and rhythmic palindrome. The passage is preceded by an equally clear statement of the final permutations of Sequence VII.

The fact that this passage is an intricate reworking of something that has already been heard is itself highly characteristic of Gilbert's music – witness the way that, in the *Nine or Ten Osannas*, the *Osanna for the colours about some people* is transformed into *and the nine lost colour years*, the relation between the two *Kumara* movements of *Moonfaring* or the reworking of Encounter I in Encounter II in *The Chakravaka-Bird*. Equally characteristic is the fact that this reworking in the op. 20a quartet presents two kinds of music – music of different character and, effectively, moving at two different tempi – simultaneously: in this case an impassioned, rhythmically free duo in 3/4 at crotchet = 66 on violins 1 and 2, set against the *ritmico* viola in 6/8 at dotted crotchet = 44. The *Chandra* movement of *Moonfaring* and, as Robert Henderson pointed out thirty years ago, the opening of *The Incredible Flute Music* as well as *Spell Respell*, *Mother* and *A Treatment of Silence* similarly explore the possibility of a single piece operating within two different time scales, or, in Gilbert's own words, 'the idea of a composition that could be more than one piece simultaneously'.[5]

The rhythmic structure of tonal music is inextricably linked to tonality and functional harmony. How to forge an equally interdependent relationship between pitch and the rhythmic organization of non-tonal music is a question that has exercised the minds of many composers. Gilbert's music offers a variety of ingenious answers to this problem. The op. 20a String Quartet, in which the rhythmic configurations derive from, and are inherent in, the manipulations of the series, demonstrates one such answer. The opening bars of the *Round* (Ex. 5) give some indication of how this relationship between pitch and rhythm operates. An examination of the opening bars of the work will show more clearly how Gilbert exploits the rhythmic implications of his permutational system.

The first section of the first movement, a set of variations, presents a statement of all twelve permutations of Sequence I. Initially, violin 1 and viola, arco, together unfold the original series (marked I/A in Ex. 6) while violin 2 and cello, pizzicato, unfold the first permutation (I/B in Ex. 6). Since, as the matrix in Ex. 4 shows, neither I/A nor I/B has an empty order number, both are presented as a sequence of regular crotchets, with I/B forming a shadowy, slightly distorted, canonic imitation of I/A. As the sequence progresses, however, the distinction between the arco line and its pizzicato shadow becomes progressively greater.

[5] Robert Henderson, 'Anthony Gilbert', *Music and Musicians*, 20/7 (1971–2), p. 44.

Unlike I/A and I/B, permutations I/C and I/D both contain two points at which two notes occur simultaneously and, thus, two empty order numbers. In the statement of I/C and I/D that follows, the regular crotchet duration established in the opening bars of the piece is maintained but the empty order numbers are represented by crotchet rests, as in Ex. 7.

Ex. 6

Ex.7

Permutations I/E and I/F have an even greater number of empty order numbers, with I/E having four points at which two notes, and I/F two points at which three notes, come together, producing the complex alignment of the two parts seen in Ex. 8. It is against these strictly unfolding permutations of Sequence I that the viola introduces the first free element – a *libero accel.,* which disrupts both the pitch organiza-tion and the regular pulse. The disruption leads to a three-bar interrup-tion (letter A) before the music moves on to Sequence II and the first variation. From this point onwards the piece becomes rhythmically more complicated as the statement of Sequence II/A begins to intro-duce triplets and quintuplets.

The title page of the String Quartet op. 20a describes it as being 'from String Quartet with Piano Pieces op. 20' and the note at the front

Ex. 8

of the score directs that the 'String Quartet may be either performed alone or in combination with the Little Piano Pieces op. 20b'. The Little Piano Pieces op. 20b can also be played separately, independently of the String Quartet. In composing op. 20 Gilbert therefore set himself the problem of writing two works that could be self-contained, individually satisfying pieces and could also be performed together to produce a larger, equally satisfying and coherent musical entity.

An interest in creating such 'variable forms' was, of course, characteristic of much of the music composed in the twenty years from the late 1950s to the early 1970s and, by the time he came to write the Quartet, Gilbert himself had already tackled the question of how to create a music that was both strictly controlled and also allowed for a certain degree of freedom in, among other things, the *Serenade*, *Brighton Piece* and the *Nine or Ten Osannas*. In rising to the challenge in the String Quartet with Little Piano Pieces, Gilbert created a work of characteristic formal ingenuity which triumphantly solves the problems that he set himself.

The movements of the String Quartet version are themselves intricately interdependent. The quartet consist of either five or six movements since, for reasons already discussed, Gilbert allows the performers to choose to end the work either with a *da capo* of Movement I or with the fleeting *pp* viola figure that provides the alternative *ossia* ending.

Whether repeated or not, Movement I is the source of much that happens in the piece and sections of it are constantly recapitulated at various points. Thus, for example, Movement III begins as a continuation of Movement II and leads to a large-scale, reworked, recapitulation of two blocks of Movement I (bars 6–10 after letter E of Movement I returning at letter Q of Movement III, and bars 1–5 after letter E of Movement I returning after letter P of Movement III). Similarly,

Movement IV also consists of a reworking of Movement I bars 1–5 after letter E, while the *Round* of Movement V is interrupted by a section that combines the first three bars of Movement V with material from Movement I letter I. Ex. 9 (in which '+' indicates the number of bars after a rehearsal letter) summarizes the most direct of these reprises.

```
I              II      III                                      IV      V        Round
A–A+1————>1——————————————————————————————>S–S+4
    E–E+5———————————————— >P+9–12—————— >bb. 1–5
    E+5–E+9———————————————>Q+1–9—>R–R+6
        bb.4–5——>b.1
            L–M—>P
                                                         b. 1–2—> S+5–S+7
```

Ex. 9

How, then, to integrate into such an already intricate and self-sufficient form a further collection of pieces for an instrument that is as timbrally different from the strings as the piano?

First, the strings and piano play together only in Movement I and at the beginning of Movements IV and V. Elsewhere the Piano Pieces act as interludes between the Quartet movements, decorating and further reworking the material already heard (or to be heard) on the strings. Gilbert himself has likened the relationship of the Piano Pieces to the Quartet movements to the marginal illuminations on a medieval manuscript.

The Pieces relate to the Quartet movements in various ways. Piano Piece 2, which forms an interlude between Movements I and II of the Quartet (for the sake of clarity I shall use roman numerals to refer to the movements of the Quartet and arabic numerals to refer to the Piano Pieces), begins as a reworking of the opening of Movement I. The first movement of the Quartet begins, as Ex. 6 shows, with a statement of two different, but interrelated, lines of material: a single line *cantabile* arco melody shared between first violin and viola and a pizzicato melody on violin 2 and cello. Piano Piece 2 begins by restating this material in a different form – juxtaposing rather than superimposing the two ideas so that, for example, the first bar of the Piano Piece restates the *cantabile* violin 1 and viola material and the second bar the original violin 2 and cello material.

The toccata-like Piano Piece 3, a reworking of Movement II in retrograde, leads to Movement III, which itself begins with a repetition of
the Movement II material. The end of Piano Piece 2, on the other hand,
prefigures the viola solo at the end of Movement III so that, in this case,
the Quartet becomes a commentary on material already heard on the
piano rather than vice versa. Two performances of Piano Piece 4 sur-
round the performance of Movement IV while Piano Piece 5 – a virtuoso *perpetuum mobile* that extends and develops the material of Pieces
1–4 – is played only when the Piano Pieces are played as a separate
work. When performed as String Quartet with Little Piano Pieces,
Quartet Movement I and Piano Piece 1 are played at the same time.
The pianist starts to play Piano Piece 1 roughly one third of the way
through the Quartet movement and plays a recomposed version of what
the strings are playing at the same point (in this case one might say that
the relation of the piano to the strings is less that of a marginal illumina-
tion to a manuscript than a palimpsest.)

Gilbert allows the pianist considerable freedom in this movement.
Although the superimposition of Quartet Movement I and Piano Piece
1 is devised in such a way that the two are moving at different, albeit
related, speeds (the strings have 76 crotchets at crotchet = 120 while
the piano has 38 crotchets at crotchet = 60) precise synchronization is
unnecessary.

As is clear from Ex. 9, the most important passages in Movement I
are the ten bars that follow letter E (the ten bars that are recapitulated at
various stages throughout the work) and, to a lesser extent, the passage
at letter I, the return of which interrupts the final *Round*. The one essential stipulation in the score is that the pianist stops playing at letter E
(the score says that Piano Piece I 'may' continue at letter F) so that the
E material of the Quartet movement stands alone, thus ensuring that it
will be recognized on further appearances.

What neither the First Sonata nor the op. 20a String Quartet demonstrates (unless one regards the succession of clumping matrices in the
Quartet as an example of varied rhythmic cyclicity) is the use of large-
and small-scale rhythmic cycles that, starting with the Piano Sonata
no. 2 of 1967, developed in Gilbert's music in the 1970s and has become a permanent characteristic of his music. Like Messiaen, Maxwell

Davies and many other composers, Gilbert has been deeply influenced by the rhythmic techniques of Indian classical music, and a feature of much of his music is the extent to which it is controlled by large rhythmic cycles, comparable to the talas which control the larger temporal spans of Indian music.

The second and third movements of *Dream Carousels* (1988) present clear and relatively straightforward examples of Gilbert's use of both pitch and rhythmic cycles. In the second movement of the work, the wind gradually build up a twelve-note cycle, which is firstly superimposed on itself and then extended by the addition of its retrograde inversion to form the following 24-note cycle (which is also joined periodically by its inverted form):

P   RI
G#–A–B–C–D–F#–E–E♭–B♭–D♭–F–G / A♭–B♭–D–F–C–B–A–C#–D#–E–F#–G

The climax of the movement, the 'dream carousel' itself, presents all twelve transpositions of the cycle, with successive statements entering every quaver, in a revolving perpetual canon that gradually crescendos from *p* to *fff* and then fades back to *p*.

The vast cyclic machine that makes up the last movement of *Dream Carousels* is a virtuoso display of Gilbert's rhythmic techniques. In the first section, a long melody on the upper wind is set against two extended rhythmic cycles, each fifteen bars long (presented, in a kind of double hocket, as chords on the horns/trumpets and on saxophones respectively), which repeat against one another and against overlapping versions of themselves. Here and later in the movement the cycles are also subjected to various permutations: thus, for example, on its first repetition the fifteen bars of the original horn/trumpet cycle are presented in the order: bb. 1–5, 11–15, 6–10. The central section of the movement then presents the retrograde forms of the two cycles on percussion and wind as an accompaniment to a new melody on bassoon and horns. Finally, at the climax of the movement, the earlier sections are played simultaneously, with the two melodies together accompanied by both the prime and retrograde forms of the two rhythmic cycles.

 Such constructions in Gilbert's music are not complex rhythmic 'abstractions' divorced from pitch. Nor, despite their relation to the rhythmic cycles of Messiaen, do they represent a suspension of time as a dynamic element, such as one feels in the *Liturgie de cristal* that opens the *Quartet for the End of Time* (a movement that is similarly based on independent rhythmic and pitch cycles). The rhythms that make up the cycles of *Dream Carousels* consist of simple rearrangements of quavers and semiquavers, rather than complex irrational rhythms, and, as in *The Rite of Spring*, are closely linked to fixed pitch areas with the result that they generate enormous, and sometimes almost manic, rhythmic energy. The final movement of *Dream Carousels*, like much of *Igórochki*, the *Biduz* movement of *Moonfaring* and many of his other works, has a rhythmic energy that is peculiarly and characteristically Gilbertian.

These rhythmic techniques, developed in Gilbert's music during the 1970s, are as much indebted to some of the aspects which he discovered in his studies of birdsong as they are to his interest in Indian and Indonesian music. Birdsong, and its implications for the composer, would eventually become the subject of his 1984 MA thesis but had by then been a long-standing interest. Listening to the birdsong of Australia, a continent which he first visited in 1978 and to which he has made many trips since, Gilbert realized that the songs of Australian birds were characterized by 'a predominance of clearly-contrasted, highly characterised trenchant phrases' that embodied a clear periodicity inherent in which was a principal of cyclicity not unlike that found in the rhythmic cycles of Indian classical music.[6] As Gilbert observed in his thesis:

There is a tendency not to sing the phrases in random order but in variants of the same order round and round. Cycles formed by one bird interlock with greater and smaller cycles formed by all the other birds vocal at the same time and overlapping these are longer, diurnal cycles and, of course, even larger seasonal ones.[7]

But Australian birdsong offered not only a rhythmic but also a cohesive harmonic model that 'chimed in well with the echoes of sustained, slowly changing harmonic backgrounds' that Gilbert had already begun to borrow from Indian and Indonesian music.[8]

---

[6] Anthony Gilbert, 'Birdsong: Some Technical Pointers for the Composer', unpublished MA (Composition) dissertation (University of Leeds, 1984), p. 4.
[7] Ibid., p. 42.
[8] Ibid., p. 36.

As early as 1963 Boulez had described a method of chord multiplication in which simple chords could be extended into complex 'combination chords' by adding transpositions of themselves at intervals determined by the constituent intervals of the original chords. It was a
method that Gilbert felt unsatisfactory since, although such transpositions were exact, they destroyed the original character and changed the
tension inherent in the original chord 'in direct ratio to the distance
they [were] removed from their original position … the lower the transposition the stronger the dissonance and the greater the loss of clarity'.[9]
In Australian birdsong Gilbert found a hierarchy of pitch precedence
which embodied 'a clear [background] framework created by the five
pitches of the harmonic series', around which grew a middleground
based on 'a diatonic scale pattern which develop[ed] a tendency to
become slightly less diatonic as it rises' and a background level of 'a
haze of less prominent microtonal activity, whose statistical frequency
increases markedly towards the upper end of the pitch spectrum due to
the preponderance of portamenti and glissandi'.[10]

On this basis, reasoned Gilbert, it should be possible to base a method
of chord multiplication on the 'intervallic characteristics of the natural
harmonic series … which would have the effect of causing the intervals and also the interval of transposition to diminish the higher a chord
is transposed and augment with downward transposition'.[11] Complex
'combination chords' would thus be the result not of a chord and its
superimposed precise transpositions but of a chord and its transposition 'refracted' through the prism of the harmonic series. Such 'refracted' transpositions would, both individually and when superimposed, create combination chords that maintain the 'feel' and the tension of the original.

Most importantly, the chords, their transpositions and the melodic
material derived from them would provide a unified harmonic hierarchy – a background, middleground and foreground – in which a single
procedure could be made to operate at different levels within the same
work. A work such as the op. 24 Concerto of Webern, in which the
structure of the row itself reflects, in microcosm, the larger operations
to which the row is subjected, already demonstrated the possibility of

---

[9] Ibid., p. 39.
[10] Ibid., pp. 13–14.
[11] Ibid., p. 40.

such a procedure in serial music.[12] To Gilbert the harmonic, rhythmic and structural model of birdsong showed a way in which many different kinds of musical ideas, derived from different and apparently antithetical sources and cultures, could be brought into association with the kind of serial/permutational techniques of works such as the First Piano Sonata and the String Quartet and the rhythmic techniques he had been developing since the time of the Second Piano Sonata.

The influence of the rhythmic and harmonic ideas derived from Gilbert's study of birdsong made itself apparent in the work of the mid and late 1970s, first in the radio opera *The Chakravaka-Bird*, many sections of which are based on overlapping short figurations (Gilbert calls them 'mantras') that, like the calls of a large body of different birds singing together, are repeated at measured intervals to produce larger rythmic cycles, and then in *Towards Asâvari*, which was written in Australia in the spring (that is to say the Australian spring – between August and December) of 1978. *Towards Asâvari* was the first work to realize the harmonic ideas that grew out of Gilbert's observation of birdsong. The first movement evolves from the pitches of one fixed chord and a derivative chord based on the inversion of its essential core, against which are set unregulated background string ostinati and 'mantra' figurations that repeat at regulated intervals – some at unchanging fixed time intervals, some according to systematically diminished or alternating time intervals – to produce larger cyclic rhythms. In the last two movements of *Towards Asâvari* the harmonic material of Movement I is subjected to the kind of 'refracted' transpositions described in Gilbert's thesis to produce a series of middleground harmonic blocks.

The working out of the harmonic and rhythmic implications of the ideas derived from Gilbert's study of birdsong is most clearly seen in *Vasanta with Dancing* (1981), a work in which the 'combination chords' developed through the refraction of the harmonic series are combined not only with birdsong-like 'mantras' but also with large-scale tala-like rhythmic cycles derived from Indian classical music. The basis of the work is the six-note chord shown in Ex. 10a and its inversion (Ex. 10b), an inversion at a level at which the two cover all twelve notes of

---

[12] The note row of Webern's Concerto op. 24 is devised in such a way that it contains the prime, inversion, retrograde and retrograde inversion of a single three-note cell.

the chromatic scale. The two chords give rise to two derivative chords through pitch inversion: that is, the pitches of the original chords are written in ascending rather than descending order. Each of the four resulting chords is then subjected to 'refracted' transposition up or down to produce a series of related chord sequences.

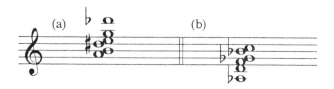

Ex. 10

The result gives Gilbert a hierarchy of material with which to operate, the four chords themselves providing the background level, the series of chord transpositions the middleground level and the harmonic and melodic material derived from the chord transpositions the foreground level. The rhythmic structure of the piece is governed by interacting cyclic 'mantra' figurations and, on a more extended level, by large-scale rhythmic cycles – a 36-crotchet cycle on wind, the two overlapping versions of a cycle of 61 crotchets' length presented by strings and percussion and a cycle of 100 crotchets' length in the harp.

Gilbert's relatively new Third Piano Sonata (he has since completed a Fourth String Quartet) is, in many ways, a summation of the techniques discussed earlier. As the subtitle *autour des palombes / goshawk* suggests, the inspiration for the work reflects Gilbert's ornithological interest – in this case the experience of watching a goshawk flying in Périgord in 1984. Some aspects of the pitch organization of the piece are reminiscent of the kind of permutational system employed in the String Quartet. The work also, however, demonstrates a feature of Gilbert's handling of pitch that has become more important in his more recent music, certain sections being based on what one might, again with reference to Messiaen's use of the term, call modes.

The Sonata is constructed from two distinct groups of material, heard at the very opening of the work: the first consists of predominantly monodic material, characterized by fluttering (*voletant*) birdsong-like figurations around a trill on the notes E and F, and a 'Chant', usually consisting of a single line or two-note chords, that evolves from these figurations. The second group of material consists of a homophonic 'Chorale' which eventually gives rise to the frenetic 'Branle'. The two groups are linked through the note E which, in the form of a trill on the notes E and F, acts as the focal pitch of the birdsong figurations and is also the 'tonic' of the Chorale modes.

Ex. 11 reproduces Gilbert's own handwritten representation of the structure of the piece.[13] In addition to showing the overall formal design of the piece, the sketch also reveals that the larger and smaller temporal structures of the piece are governed by Fibonacci proportions (the golden section point itself, as indicated in the diagram, comes at the end of bar 74 and is marked by a drop from *fff* to *subito pp*). The use of Fibonacci numbers and prime numbers as structural determinants is a recurring feature of Gilbert's more recent music. On the simplest level the work can be described as a series of six variations on this material. The two types of material come together only in Variation 2 (bars 19–61), which presents a version of the Chant of bars 4–14 as a single line weaving between the two hands accompanied by a further single line which will eventually prove to be a retrograde version of the final section of the piece. For the rest the variations and development of the two types of material are not carried out separately but interpenetrate.

Although Gilbert has described the work as being 'not goal oriented',[14] the two different types of material do find some kind of fulfilment in that the Chorale, which is at first presented as fragments that interrupt the Chant and the monodic birdsong, gradually grows in importance and eventually finds a complete statement before being transformed into the final Branle, the function of which is not unlike that of the chorale that closes the *Symphonies of Wind Instruments*.

The two groups of material employ different methods of pitch organization. The birdsong and the Chant sections are based on a twelve-note set which, like the set of the op. 20 String Quartet, is subjected to systematic permutations that constantly generate new pitch arrangements. Since, as in the String Quartet, the set remains untransposed, it

---

[13] Since the example is reduced from its original A4 size the indication 'scale: 20mm = 60 seconds' no longer applies.
[14] Anthony Gilbert, Introductory note to the score of Piano Sonata no. 3.

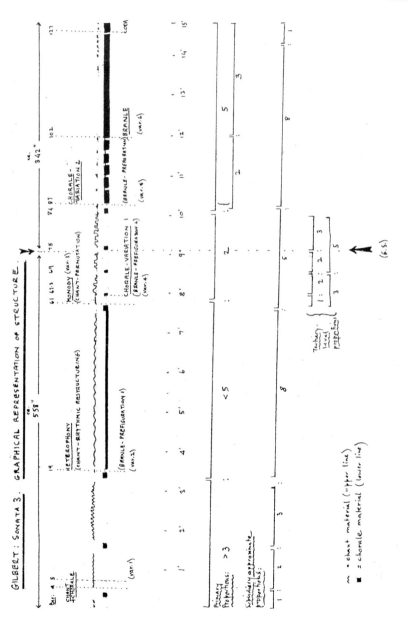

Ex. 11

could perhaps be regarded as mode that happens to cover all twelve pitches of the chromatic scale; certainly, again as in the String Quartet, the lack of transposition generates a strong suggestion of a 'tonic' or focal pitch – an A in the Quartet, an E in the Sonata. The permutational schema, which Gilbert calls a 'shuffle' system, is demonstrated in Ex. 12, which shows the original set and its first three permutations. The numbers below each note indicate its order position in the following permutation; the notes in brackets are optional grace notes.

Sequence Ia

1	2	3	4	5	6	7	8	9	10	11	12
E	F	D#	B	Bb	Ab	A	D	(ab)C	Db	(b)F#	G
8	10	6	2	4	1	3	5	7	9	12	11

Ab	B	A	Bb	D	D#	C	E	Db	F	G	F#
8	10	6	2	4	1	3	5	7	9	12	11

D#	Bb	C	D	E	A	Db	Ab	F	B	(b)F#	G
8	10	6	2	4	1	3	5	7	9	12	11

A	D	Db	E	Ab	C	F	D#	B	Bb	G	F#
8	10	6	2	4	1	3	5	7	9	12	11

Ex. 12

The prime set gives rise to four paired groups of sequences. Sequences I and II apply the permutational system to the traditional four forms (P, I and R, RI) of the set. Thus, the pair of sets that makes up Sequence I consists of:

Ia: the group of ten permutations of the prime form, the opening of which is shown in Ex. 12, all of which hold the notes F sharp and G as notes 11 or 12;

Ib: the group of ten permutations achieved by applying the same system to the inverted form of the set, all of which hold the notes E flat and D as notes 11 and 12.

Ex. 13 shows the original inverted form and the first two permutations of group Ib.

Sequence Ib

1	2	3	4	5	6	7	8	9	10	11	12
F	E	Gb	Bb	B	C#	C	G	A	Ab	Eb	D
8	10	6	2	4	1	3	5	7	9	12	11

C#	Bb	C	B	G	F#	A	F	Ab	E	D	Eb
8	10	6	2	4	1	3	5	7	9	12	11

F#	B	A	G	F	C	Ab	Db	E	Bb	Eb	D
8	10	6	2	4	1	3	5	7	9	12	11

Ex. 13

Sequence II consists of:

IIa: the group that results from applying the same permutational system to the retrograde (R) form of the initial set, and

IIb: the group produced by applying the same system to the retrograde inversion (RI) of the set.

The permutational system ensures that only the starting point of these two groups – the initial R and RI forms – corresponds to any of the sets in Sequence I. In this sequence the all-important E–F, the notes of the recurrent trill, which appeared as the opening E–F of the original P form of Sequence I (Ex. 12) and the opening F–E of the original I form (Ex. 13), become notes 11 and 12 and exchange positions throughout.

Ex. 14 shows the initial set of Sequence IIa and its first permutation; Ex. 15 shows the initial set and the first permutation of Sequence IIb.

Sequence IIa

1	2	3	4	5	6	7	8	9	10	11	12
G	F#	Db	C	D	A	Ab	Bb	B	Eb	F	E
8	10	6	2	4	1	3	5	7	9	12	11

A	C	Ab	D	Bb	Db	B	G	D#	F#	E	F
8	10	6	2	4	1	3	5	7	9	12	11

Ex. 14

Sequence IIb

1	2	3	4	5	6	7	8	9	10	11	12
E♭	D	A♭	A	G	C	D♭	B	B♭	F#	E	F
8	10	6	2	4	1	3	5	7	9	12	11

C	A	D♭	G	B	A♭	B♭	E♭	F#	D	F	E
8	10	6	2	4	1	3	5	7	9	12	11

Ex. 15

In the permutational scheme of the String Quartet op. 20, the first and last notes were fixed. Since in the scheme of the Third Piano Sonata notes 11 and 12 simply exchange positions throughout, the system produces a sequence of ten, rather than twelve, permutations before restoring the original set.

Sequences III and IV are arrived at by applying the retrograde of the permutational system (a 'reverse shuffle') to the four forms of the original set. The opening of Sequence IIIa, with the reverse shuffle applied to the original set, is shown in Ex. 16; Ex. 17 shows the opening of Sequence IIIb when the same procedure is applied to the inversion of the original set.

Sequence IIIa

1	2	3	4	5	6	7	8	9	10	11	12
E	F	D#	B	B♭	A♭	A	D	(a♭)C	D♭	(b)F#G	
11	12	9	7	5	3	1	4	2	6	10	8

A	C	A♭	D	B♭	D♭	B	G	E♭	F#	E	F
11	12	9	7	5	3	1	4	2	6	10	8

Ex. 16

Sequence IIIb

1	2	3	4	5	6	7	8	9	10	11	12
F	E	F#	B♭	B	C#	C	G	A	A♭	E♭	D
11	12	9	7	5	3	1	4	2	6	10	8

C	A	C#	G	B	A♭	B♭	D	F#	E♭	F	E
11	12	9	7	5	3	1	4	2	6	10	8

Ex. 17

Whereas the permutations applied in Sequences I and II produced only ten variants of the set, the application of this reverse shuffle permutation produces eleven variants since neither the opening nor closing pair of notes remains fixed and only note 5 is static throughout.

Sequence IVa and IVb (which are not illustrated) consist of the two groups that result from applying the same reverse shuffle scheme to the initial R and RI forms.

As in the op. 20 Quartet, many of the Chant passages of the Third Sonata systematically lay out the whole of a group or a sequence: thus bars 7–13 present the whole of Sequence IIa in reverse order (i.e. beginning with the final permutation) while the passage from bars 61ff systematically sets out all Sequences Ib, Ia and IIa. In the Sonata, as in the Quartet, Gilbert's permutational system produces a fascinating kaleidoscope of musical patterns – a veritable game with the basic material of the music itself – in which ever-shifting groups of notes gradually evolve, dissolve and reform, change positions and disappear as the work progresses.

Thus, for example – to take only the note groupings presented in the initial prime set of Sequence Ia (shown in Ex. 11) – notes 2–5 of this original set reappear, in a different context, as notes 7–10 of the third permutation of the same sequence and also as notes 8–11 of the final permutation of Sequence IIa, while notes 7–10 of the same set reappear as notes 2–5 of the seventh permutation of the same sequence. Such relationships inevitably hold true for all the different set variants and create an intricate network of motivic links that runs through the piece.

In nature birdsong tends to be either 'closed' (progressing through simple repetition) or 'open' (developing through the addition, subtraction, modification or interpenetration of fragments). In *Towards Asâvari* the harmonic structure ensures that the little 'mantra' figurations evolve and change pitch contour as the harmonic background changes; but Gilbert's permutational schemes, with their constant reshuffling of pitch collections, also lend themselves to the development and variation of material on such an open model. Ex. 18 shows seven tiny birdsong figurations from the opening bars of the Third Sonata, all of which are interrelated and all of which derive from different set variants. Thus (ii) has four of its five notes in common with (i); (iii) begins by repeating the first three notes of (i) an octave higher and then reorders the four final notes; (iv) and (v) are variants of (ii); while the first four notes of (vi) present the opening and closing notes of (i) in reverse order and at the same register before adding two notes that are themselves an inversion of the closing notes of (iv).

Ex. 18

The pitch structure of the Chorale sections and the finale Branle is organized around the three modes shown in Ex. 19; Mode 1 governs the upper voice, Mode 2 the middle and Mode 3 the lower. Although the example shows the notes of the modes at a fixed register, octave displacements are allowed. All three modes are symmetrical. Modes 1 and 2 are complementary in that, together, they cover all twelve notes of the chromatic scale. Mode 3, which is a transposition of Mode 2, shares notes with both 1 and 2 and, most crucially, the three together suggest a 'quasi-tonic' around E, thus linking the modes to the twelve-note sequences discussed above from which derives the fixed F–E dyad which plays so important a referential role in the work as a whole.

Modes

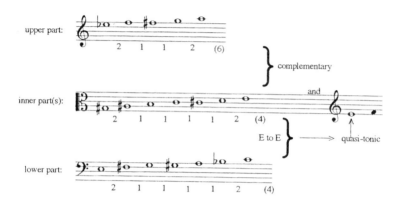

Ex. 19

Rhythmic Evolution

(5 STAGES)

Ex. 20

Rhythmically the material of the opening section of the Sonata, the birdsong figurations and the Chant, is free. The Chorale section is more systematic in its rhythmic organization but here – unlike the String Quartet, in which the series itself gave rise to rhythmic configurations

– the rhythmic structure operates independently of the pitch organization. The Chorale and its later developments are governed by a rhythmic cell that undergoes a series of developments as the work progresses. The basic rhythmic unit – (a) in Ex. 20 – consists of nine durations. It subsequently expands to eleven durations (b), returns to its original nine (c), expands to twelve (d) and then returns to eleven (e).

Ex. 21, which shows the first appearance of the Chorale fragment, illustrates the interaction of the modally organized pitches and the durationally organized rhythmic structure. The five variants of this first rhythmic sequence form the basis of the three appearances of the Chorale fragments at bars 2–18 (variants a, b and c) and the two appearances at bars 58–61 (variants d and e).

Ex. 21

Later, in Chorale Variation 2 (bars 87–101), a derived durational sequence (shown in Ex. 22) undergoes a similar series of expansions (and one contraction). In keeping with the Fibonacci proportions that govern the rest of the work the original rhythmic series and its variants appear five time while the derived series and its variants appear eight times in all. While the pitch material of the Branle derives from the three modes of the Chorale (although the modes periodically change positions, most notably at bar 107), the rhythmic structure is based, not on the extending and contracting rhythmic sequences shown in Exx. 21 and 22, but on the three rhythmic cells shown in Ex. 23, which are developed, varied, extended and reversed throughout this final section. Audibly, the most important of these cells is that labelled III in Ex. 23 which, while it appears in many guises, gradually becomes associated with three fixed harmonic forms during the course of the Branle.

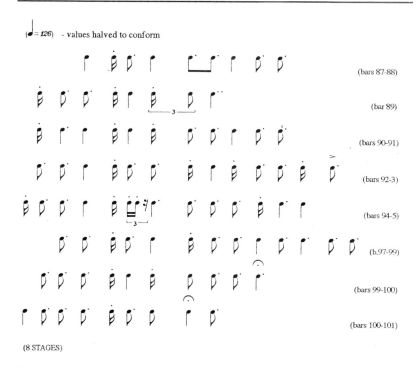

($\bullet$ = *126*)   - values halved to conform

(bars 87-88)

(bar 89)

(bars 90-91)

(bars 92-3)

(bars 94-5)

(b.97-99)

(bars 99-100)

(bars 100-101)

(8 STAGES)

Ex. 22

Structurally the Branle applies the principles of retrograde and inversion, previously applied to the permutational sequences of the Chant series, to large blocks of musical material. The main body of the Branle is built from two blocks (bars 102–6 and bars 108–10), both of which are immediately reversed. Finally, in the last section of the Sonata, the fragmentary return of the Chant melody leads to a series of recapitulations. Earlier, at bars 87–102, Chorale Variation 2 was periodically interrupted by Chant fragments centred on the three notes E–F (the fixed dyad which has dominated the Chant material) and A. In the penultimate section these fragments are reprised in inversion around the notes E–G sharp–A (that is to say, at a level which maintains the centrality of the note E which, as part of the F–E trill of the Chant and the 'tonic' of the modes of the Chorale, links the two groups of material) and leads to the closing Coda which consists of two recapitulations of material in its prime form. The last two bars present a retrograde

Ex. 23

reprise of the figuration of bars 125–6, a reprise which results in the work ending on the all-important E–F dyad. Ex. 24 summarizes the structure of the Branle.

bars 102–6

bars 108–19

bars 112–17	=	bars 102–6	Retrograde
bars 118–20	=	bars 108–10	
bar 122	=	bar 88	
bar 123	=	bars 89–90	Inversion
bar 125	=	bar 97	
bar 126	=	bar 93	

bars 127–8	=	bars 95–7
bars 129–30	=	bar 93

Prime

bars 130–2	=	bars 125–6

Retrograde

Ex. 24

*

It should not be necessary, now – almost eighty years after the composition of Schoenberg's first twelve-note works – to insist on the purely musical nature of the kind of techniques discussed in this article or to have to defend them against the charges of being purely 'mathematical' or 'abstract'. Seventy years ago, in an article on 'Abstraction in Music', Constant Lambert accurately pinpointed the fallacy that lies behind such facile charges when he wrote:

Nothing is more typical of the superficial nature of most modern ... criticism than its slipshod use of the word abstract, particularly as applied to music. We are still apt to regard formalism and emotional expression as opposed interests instead of an insoluble whole. We should realize that a composer ... who uses a carefully wrought and alembicated technique for highly expressive ends, stands nearer to the true tradition of music as represented by the sixteenth and seventeenth-century masters than any of the self-conscious classicists of the eighteenth century, or the self-conscious romanticists of the nineteenth century. Berg's music itself would have sounded strange to seventeenth century ears but his aims were much the same as theirs. At that period there was no divorce between intellectuality and emotionalism.[15]

Although, as I have said, Gilbert's emotional world is far from that of Alban Berg, the observation is as applicable to Gilbert's music as it is to that of the Viennese master. What a discussion of purely technical, compositional matters cannot convey, however – and, happily, what no writing about music can ever convey – is the experience of the works themselves. Only by listening to Gilbert's music can we begin to appreciate the energy, the poetry, the intelligence, integrity and originality of his output. Unfortunately we seem to be living through a period when the work of a whole generation of fine composers is ignored in

---

[15] Constant Lambert, *Music Ho!* (London, 1934), 122.

the interest of populism and the momentarily fashionable. A few of Gilbert's works have been recorded (and are duly listed below); we still need not only recordings but above all an opportunity to hear live performances of many of his major works. The BBC or Schotts presumably have recordings of *The Chakravaka-Bird,* which has not been transmitted since it was broadcast in 1984. Nearer to home, it would be nice to think that the musical establishments in Manchester itself might show their appreciation of what Gilbert has done, for both Manchester and music, by mounting some substantial celebration of his work for his seventieth birthday in July 2004.

ANTHONY GILBERT: CHRONOLOGICAL LIST OF WORKS

Unless otherwise indicated, works written between 1962 and 1994 are available from Schott & Co. Ltd, 48 Great Marlborough Street, London W1V 2BN.
Works written since April 1994 (after *Ziggurat*) are available from University of York Music Press, YO10 5DD. Other works, as indicated, are available from Forsyth Bros. Ltd, Manchester.

1961   *Elegy* for piano (unpublished)
1962   Piano Sonata no. 1
1963   *Duo* for violin and viola (unpublished)
1964   *Missa Brevis* for unaccompanied chorus
       Sinfonia for chamber orchestra
1966   *Regions* for two orchestras (MS in Central Music Library)
       Three War Poems for chorus (unpublished)
       Piano Sonata II for piano 4 hands
1967   *Brighton Piece* for 8 players
       Nine or Ten Osannas for 5 players
1968   *The Incredible Flute Music* for flute and piano (= *Peal I*)
       Peal II for big band
       Shepherd Masque for young voices (Novello)
       Spell Respell for electric bassett clarinet and piano
1969   *A Treatment of Silence* for violin and tape
1970   *Love Poems* for soprano and instrumental ensemble (2 versions)
       The Scene Machine, one-act opera on a libretto by George Macbeth
1971   *O'Grady Music* for clarinet, cello and toy instruments
1972   String Quartet with Piano Pieces, op. 20, comprising
       String Quartet, op. 20a
       Little Piano Pieces, op. 20b
1973   Symphony (revised 1985)
       Canticle I *(Rock-song)* for wind instruments

1974   Canticle II *(Anger)* for 6 male voices
        Ghost and Dream Dancing for orchestra (revised 1981)
1975   *Inscapes* for soprano, speaking voice and small ensemble
        (revised 1981)
1976   *Crow Cry* for chamber orchestra
        Welkin for orchestra
1977   *The Chakravaka-Bird*, radio opera on a libretto translated from
        Indian sources by A.K. Ramanujan, Daniel H.H. Ingalls and the composer
1978   *Towards Asâvari* for piano and chamber orchestra
1979   *Calls around Chungmori* for chamber ensemble and
        participating audience
1980   *Long White Moonlight* for soprano and electric double bass
1981   *Vasanta with Dancing* for chamber ensemble with optional dancer
        Crow Undersongs for solo viola
        Chant of Cockeye Bob for children's voices and instruments
        Koonapippi for youth orchestra
        Sunrising for oboe and piano (Forsyth)
        Little Dance of Barrenjoey for chamber ensemble (unpublished)
1982   *Two Birds by Kuring-Gai* for horn and piano (Forsyth)
1983   *Moonfaring* for cello and percussion (revised 1986)
1984   *Dawnfaring* for viola and piano
        Quartet of Beasts for wind instruments and piano
        Beastly Jingles for soprano and instrumental ensemble
        O alter Duft for piano (withdrawn)
1985   *Six of the Bestiary* for saxophone quartet
        Funtoons, children's pieces for piano (unpublished)
1986   *Fanfarings* for 6 and 8 brass instruments
1987   String Quartet II
        String Quartet III *(super hoqueto David)*
1988   *Peal III* for piano (unpublished)
        Peal IV for organ (unpublished)
        Four Small Farings for sopranino recorder/piccolo and piano (Forsyth)
        Dream Carousels for wind orchestra
1989   *Certain Lights Reflecting*, song cycle for mezzo-soprano and orchestra
        Tree of Singing Names for chamber orchestra
1990   *O alter Duft* for piano duet (withdrawn)
1991   *Upstream River Rewa* for storyteller and Indo-European ensemble
        Mozart Sampler with Ground for orchestra
1992   *Igórochki* for solo recorder and chamber ensemble
        Fanfaring V for brass
        Little Cycle for Elizabeth Yeoman for soprano, cello and piano (unpublished)
1993   *Paluma* for sopranino recorder and piano (arranged from Movement IV of
        Igórochki)
        Trying to make John SLOW DOWN AFTER 50 for sopranino recorder and piano
1994   *Ziggurat* for bass clarinet and marimba
        ... into the Gyre of a Madder Dance for orchestral wind
1995   *Handles to the Invisible* for a-cappella choir, poems by Sarah Day

Stars for treble recorder and guitar
Moon comes up, Pearl Beach (June '79) for alto flute, vibraphone and cello
Flame Robin for sopranino recorder (Forsyth)
Chant-au-Clair for sopranino recorder and piano (Forsyth)

1996   *Midwales Lightwhistle Automatic* for sopranino recorder and piano (Forsyth)
Dancing to the Tune for 4–8 oboes, 2–4 cors anglais, 1 or 2 heckelphones (unpublished)
This Tree (Frances Horovitz) arr. mezzo-soprano and piano (Schott)
Réflexions, Rose nord for bass clarinet and vibraphone

1997   *On Beholding a Rainbow*, concerto for violin and orchestra
Osanna for Lady O for cello and piano

1998   *Ondine – chant au clair de lune* for soprano and recorder (unpublished)

1999   *Vers de Lune* (Aloysius Bertrand) for soprano, flute, cello and percussion (incorporates *Ondine* above)
Os for oboe and vibraphone

2000   *Margareeting* for tenor or descant recorder and piano (unpublished)
Sinfin for vibraphone solo
Sinfin 2 for 4 vibraphones (arrangement of above)
Worldwhorls for bass clarinet
Another Dream Carousel for string orchestra
Photos found at Hukvaldy, August 1928 for oboe solo
Even in flames for variable orchestra
Farings for sopranino recorder and piano (Forsyth)

2001   *Unrise* for 10 wind
Four Seasons for Josca's for young players (variable ensemble)
Sonata III for solo piano
Sinfin parados for two vibraphones (arrangement of *Sinfin*)

2002   String Quartet IV
Kauri for solo tuba

DISCOGRAPHY

Beastly Jingles
Jane Manning (sop), Jane's Minstrels/Montgomery   NMC DO24

Chant-au-Clair
John Turner (rec), Keith Swallow (pf)   Postern PPD 003

Dream Carousels
RNCM Wind Ensemble/Timothy Reynish   NMC DO68

Farings
John Turner (rec), Peter Lawson (pf)   Forsyth FS001/002

Igórochki
John Turner (rec), RNCM New Ensemble/Clark Rundell   NMC DO68

Midwales Lightwhistle Automatic
John Turner (rec), Peter Lawson (pf)   Tabernacle TABIP1

Moonfaring
Psappha: Jennifer Langridge (vlc), Tim Williams (perc)   BML 026

Nine or Ten Osannas
Music Projects London/Richard Bernas   NMC DO14

Quartet of Beasts
Mary Owen (fl), Rachael Ager (ob), Benjamin Hudson (bsn),
Karen Twitchett (pf)   NMC DO68

Six of the Bestiary
Kintamarni Saxophone Quartet   NMC DO68

String Quartet III
Nossek String Quartet   ASC CS CD11

Towards Asâvari
Peter Lawson (pf), RNCM New Ensemble/Clark Rundell   NMC DO68

Footnote 3

[3] The notes move according to the following rules: notes 1 and 12 are fixed and do not move; in each sequence note 2 moves progressively forward (and its partner note 11 moves progressively backwards) one place at each permutation. Thus, the progress of note 2 follows the pattern shown in the following diagram while note 11 has the mirror image of the same pattern:

	1	2	3	4	5	6	7	8	9	10	11	12
A		x										
B			x									
C				x								
D					x							
E						x						
F							x					
G								x				
H									x			
I										x		
J											x	
K												x
L	x											

In each sequence note 3 moves progressively forward (and its partner note 10 moves progressively backwards) one place for permutations B–D and then moves systematically by 2 spaces (i.e. missing a place each time). Thus, the progress of note 3 follows the patterns shown in the following diagram while note 10 has the mirror image of the same pattern:

	1	2	3	4	5	6	7	8	9	10	11	12
A			x									
B				x								
C					x							
D						x						
E								x				
F										x		
G												x
H		x										
I				x								
J						x						
K								x				
L										x		

In each sequence note 4 moves progressively forward (and its partner note 9 moves progressively backwards) one place for permutations B and C and then moves systematically by 3 spaces (i.e. missing two places each time). Thus, the progress of note 4 follows the pattern shown in the following diagram while note 9 has the mirror image of the same pattern:

	1	2	3	4	5	6	7	8	9	10	11	12
A				x								
B					x							
C						x						
D									x			
E												x
F			x									
G						x						
H									x			
I												x
J			x									
K					x							
L								x				

In each sequence note 5 moves progressively forward (and its partner note 8 moves progressively backwards) one place for permutation B and then moves systematically by 4 spaces (missing 3 places each time). Thus, the progress of note 5 follows the pattern shown in the following diagram while note 8 has the mirror image of the same pattern:

	1	2	3	4	5	6	7	8	9	10	11	12
A					x							
B						x						
C										x		
D		x										
E						x						
F										x		
G		x										
H						x						
I										x		
J		x										
K						x						
L										x		

Note 6 moves systematically forward (and its partner note 7 moves systematically backwards) by 5 spaces (missing 4 places each time). Thus, the progress of note 6 follows the pattern shown in the following diagram while note 7 has the mirror image of the same pattern:

	1	2	3	4	5	6	7	8	9	10	11	12
A						x						
B											x	
C				x								
D									x			
E		x										
F							x					
G												x
H				x								
I										x		
J			x									
K								x				
L	x											

There is, therefore, a hierarchy of mobility: the closer a pitch-class is to the centre of the matrix in the prime form of the series, the more drastic its changes of position – the paradoxical result of which is that, as the above charts show, notes 4 and 5 (and their complements, notes 9 and 8) establish a new regularity of pattern.

DOUGLAS JARMAN is Principal Lecturer in Academic Studies at the RNCM and Honorary Professor of Music in the University of Manchester. He is author of three books and some twenty-six articles on the music of Alban Berg and editor of the critical edition of the two Berg concertos for the Berg *Sämtliche Werke*, published by UE, Vienna.

Humphrey Procter-Gregg, 1895–1980: Two Memoirs and a List of Compositions

MICHAEL ALMOND, PETER HOPE AND JOHN TURNER

Humphrey Procter-Gregg (universally known to students and colleagues as P-G) was born on 31 July 1895 at Kirkby Lonsdale, Westmorland. He went to school at King William's College on the Isle of Man, and was Organ Scholar at Peterhouse College, Cambridge, where he read history, graduating Mus.B. and M.A. At the Royal College of Music he was Opera Scholar and a composition scholar under Stanford, and gained a studentship at the opera house of La Scala, Milan.

Humphrey Procter-Gregg, ca. 1955

He became Opera Manager to the Royal College of Music, and was at various times stage manager and producer to the Covent Garden Opera Company, the British National Opera Company, and the Carl Rosa Opera Company, also working in a similar capacity at the Royal Manchester College of Music and the BBC Opera Section. In 1936 he became Reader in Music at the University of Manchester, founding the Music Department, and in 1954 became the university's first Professor of Music. In 1958 he was Director of the Arts Council's Touring Opera, and also of the Carl Rosa Opera Company. In 1962, on leaving the university, he became the first Director of the new London Opera Centre, relinquishing this post in 1964, when he retired to Windermere and devoted himself to composition and opera translation. He was appointed CBE in 1972 and died on 13 April, 1980.[1]

I FIRST MET P-G in the bitter winter of 1954–5 when attending interview at the old Dover Street Music Department of Manchester University, as a result of my application for admission to the joint course at the university and the Royal Manchester College of Music. This was the beginning of a close friendship and working partnership which was to endure until his death twenty-five years later. I was a Yorkshire lad from a mining community background and I had a lot to learn: a good grammar school education, A-levels in French, German and Music, and a passion for the piano and books had in no way prepared me for this whole new world. P-G must have perceived that mere facility at the piano needed broadening to be real musicianship, and I spent hours sight-reading and score-reading at the piano. It is to this, and to the inspiration that Maurice Aitchison[2] afforded me that I owe whatever ability in sight-reading I have: it has stood me in very good stead for half a century.

Under the driving energy of P-G and his staff there were many outstanding concerts in what now appears as the golden age of the 1950s, when one could often see John Ogdon, John McCabe, Peter Maxwell Davies, Elgar Howarth, David Wilde, Harrison Birtwistle and other rising stars regularly traversing Oxford Road between Dover Street and the RMCM in Devas Street.

The Mozart bicentenary of 1956 gave me the enviable opportunity of performing the two-piano Concerto K365 with lecturer Maurice

---

[1] Information from 'Procter-Gregg, Humphrey', *Who Was Who 1971–1980* (London, 1981), p. 643, and Brian Gee, 'Professor Humphrey Procter-Gregg: Some Details of his Career', *Musical Opinion*, 88 (1964–5), pp. 599–601.

[2] Maurice Aitchison, for more than thirty-five years Lecturer and subsequently Reader in Music, University of Manchester. Pianist in the Ad Solem chamber ensemble. Retired in 1981 and died in May 1985 at the age of 59.

Aitchison – a towering presence, literally and figuratively. His hands knew no fear before any virtuoso texture, and I never saw fingerings pencilled into any of his copies: his pianism was immediate and instinctive. P-G conducted the major orchestral concerts at the celebrations, and the *Manchester Guardian* of 24 March 1956 carried a glowing notice by Colin Mason on the previous evening's programme, which consisted of the 'Prague' Symphony and two double concertos (for flute and harp K299 and for two pianos K365) played by the University Orchestra:

He conducts with much intensity and nervous gesture, but with it, he persuaded from the players finely sustained phrasing of unflagging impetus and continuity in its outlines and often very expressive and beautifully polished in its detail. It was a most musical performance in which the sincerity and spontaneity of feeling that is the chief virtue of most amateur music-making was conveyed in playing of an accomplishment that approached the professional.

Other memorable performances under P-G's baton were Beethoven's 'Emperor' Concerto and Violin Concerto, with Maurice Aitchison and Clifford Knowles[3] respectively as soloists, the Mozart and Brahms Requiems, Vaughan Williams's *Toward the Unknown Region*, and Kodály's *Missa brevis*. His conducting was of the inspirational kind, instantly communicating the rhythmic vitality of the music; a lifetime in opera working with singers and years with Beecham gave him a magical touch when shaping a tune.

He invariably conducted the weekly chamber choir rehearsals, in which we performed the standard English madrigal repertoire, as well as motets such as Byrd's *Ave Verum Corpus* and Palestrina's *Stabat Mater*, which we recorded for the BBC Third Programme.

There were frequent departmental solo and chamber music recitals, enhanced by the arrival of the brilliant Canadian pianist Peter Smith on the staff. A close personal friend of Glenn Gould, he had a presence, musicianship and genial, kindly personality that were inspirational to the students and a huge asset to the department. His memorized per-

---

[3] Clifford Knowles, violinist. Born Salford, 1911; studied under Brodsky at the Royal Manchester College of Music. Violinist in the Hallé Orchestra 1927–40, and the BBC Northern Orchestra 1934–40. Sometime member of the Laurance Turner String Quartet and conductor of the Burnley Municipal Orchestra.

formance of Bach's *Goldberg Variations* lives on in my mind.

The professor's kindness to me was invaluable in enriching my education. We went together to hear Cyril Smith play the *Rhapsody on a Theme of Paganini* at the Free Trade Hall. It was an electrifying performance (not without reason had Rachmaninov told Smith that he considered him the best British exponent of his music). Next morning, a Saturday, Cyril Smith was in the department at the invitation of P-G, catching up with news as good friends do, and I was privileged to meet him and play the piano – some Liszt, I seem to remember. Sadly, only a few months later, on a goodwill visit to Russia made by a delegation of English musicians led by Sir Arthur Bliss, Cyril Smith suffered the massive stroke which paralysed his left arm.

My graduation coincided with P-G's absence as director of the Arts Council's Touring Opera of 1958, but we kept in touch as I began a teaching career and married life. Over the years I attended many superb chamber concerts given by Maurice Aitchison and the Ad Solem Ensemble founded by P-G. As well as this ensemble, more than one string quartet owed its success – and, indeed, its existence – to his advice and encouragement.

On retiring from Manchester and leaving the house at 66 Platt Lane, Rusholme, a scene of wonderful music-making over the years, P-G became director of the newly established London Opera Centre, and lived at 37 West Heath Drive, Golders Green. Here his hobby of gardening bore spectacular fruit in the beautiful rose garden. One summer, when I was staying with him at Golders Green, we walked across Hampstead Heath to Kenwood House and stood in front of Frans Hals's *The Laughing Cavalier*. The sudden experience of the real thing, after having seen so many reproductions, made a powerful impression on me – another example of the way in which P-G helped to broaden my awareness.

After this, in 1964, came the Windermere period of so-called retirement at no. 3 Oakland, just up the tree-lined drive opposite the Mountain Ash Hotel. With characteristic energy, he immersed himself in composition of new works, revision of his earlier works, and the preparation of two dozen or so important opera translations for publication by IMC of New York.

Throughout the 1960s and 70s we corresponded regularly and P-G often came to stay with us at our successive homes in Knaresbrough,

Bristol and Salford as a welcome and charming guest. We had count-less musical evenings and recording sessions as I played through the ever-increasing numbers of *Westmoreland Sketches*,[4] studies, suites, preludes and fugues, and sonatas.

One April he invited my wife and me to Windermere for a few days. Joyce had long wished to see Wordsworth's daffodils, so off we drove into the hills in company with P-G, with provisions in the car boot. It was a typical Lakeland April day, with rapid alternation of sun, blue skies and sudden showers. (Did this day, I wonder now, give P-G the inspiration for *Westmoreland Sketches* no. 23, 'A Shower in Spring'?) We sat on fresh green grass in the lee of a dry-stone wall, and gazed on marvellous views as we enjoyed our picnic.

Before I knew him, Procter-Gregg had enjoyed the benefits of being a motorist despite his visual impairment. Luckily for himself, and no doubt others, a car in his control failed to ascend Hard Knott Pass, and the attending inconvenience and distress resulted in his abandoning the vehicle and never driving again.

On another occasion P-G decided on an outing to Blea Tarn at the foot of Wrynose Fell: his idea was to circumnavigate the lake on foot. We parked as near as we could and set off. The going was rough, dense woodland and thicket, with an occasional bog en route. But we com-pleted our mission with a feeling of achievement. It was on this hike that P-G told me about the accident to his right eye. Apparently as a young man he had been caught by a branch that had accidentally whiplashed into his eye from a companion walking in front. The dam-age was so serious that nothing could be done and the sight was quickly lost. When out walking in woodland he was always watchful and so-licitous to others for this reason. The amazing thing to me is that his remaining eye withstood the tremendous strain for half a century. For-tunately his good eye, though I saw it many times succumb to fatigue, did not fail him right to the very end. I remember one afternoon initiat-ing a discussion on Debussy, whose music was absorbing me at that time. On my enthusing over *Prélude à L'Après-midi d'un faune* he played the score at the piano for me. Now, those who know the Jobert miniature score will gasp at this feat. In print much smaller than that of the Eulenburg edition, the notes are no bigger than full stops. How he

---

[4] Procter-Gregg insisted on the older spelling of the name of Westmorland, his native county.

played from this complex score with one eye I shall never compre-
hend.

P-G had a delightful sense of humour and that common touch which
gave him an ease of manner and friendliness with the man in the street.
It was a joy to call in to a remote country pub and see him take country
people to his heart. In restaurants and all manner of eating places he
could invariably charm the staff at least to tone down the background
music if not to erase it completely. I noticed too a remarkable gift with
animals: even the most threatening of farm dogs would usually succumb to his voice and come to lick his hand. He also hand-fed the birds
at the French doors to his music room at Oakland overlooking Lake
Windermere. I much envied him as blue, great and coal tits and robins
quarrelled to come to the peanuts and crumbs in his outstretched palm.

We talked for hours, when not working through his manuscripts or
recording, and I was enthralled by his reminiscences: he met Elgar,
Schoenberg, Delius and Rachmaninov. As a senior composition student at the Royal College of Music he was entrusted to look after
Schoenberg for a whole day: he found him distinctly disagreeable and
bad-tempered, a great contrast to Rachmaninov, who made a powerful
impact on him. P-G refers cryptically to this meeting in his first book
on Beecham.[5] Rachmaninov, as P-G described this episode to me, was
sitting in the wings of a London concert stage, a forbidding, gaunt figure, wrapped in a huge Russian fur coat. He grasped P-G's hand and
held it in both of his for a long time as he looked up intently into his
eyes.

His love of Chopin dated from earlier years: when still only 14 he
possessed the three-volume Klindworth edition of Chopin's complete
works published by Bote and Bock. This had been presented to him by
Trinity College, London, for 'highest honours' in the piano examinations of March 1910. We were discussing Chopin one day and he told
me that he had known an old Scotsman who was once a pupil of Chopin – perhaps this ties in with Chopin's visit to Scotland in 1848–9, and
it might throw light on a very old Fontana edition of Chopin's *Études*
that P-G possessed.

P-G was widely read, and one Christmas many students received

<hr>

[5] Humphrey Procter-Gregg, *Sir Thomas Beecham: Conductor and Impresario* (Kendal,
1973), p. 122.

the same book as a present: *The Life of the Spider* by John Crompton.[6] P-G had read this fascinating account by the South African entomologist in 1955 and had become so enthusiastic that he had immediately ordered a whole batch of them for distribution in the department. He was also very interested in the writer Joseph McCabe, whose *Golden Ages of History* (London, 1940) quickly became a collector's item.[7] He was delighted, in due course, to welcome John McCabe, the author's grandson, as a student in his department. P-G also read widely on gardening, and created a very beautiful display of gentians, on which he was an authority, on the west-facing terrace at Windermere.

He shunned all forms of self-promotion in a life packed with creative activity and achievement; but a singularly selfless act was to come in his final years, when his dedication to the memory of Sir Thomas Beecham led to two books,[8] the proceeds from which went to pay for the commissioning of a bronze bust of Sir Thomas. This was a mammoth task for a man in his early eighties. A long search for a sculptor able to capture the essence of the great man from photographs and recollections by friends resulted in the magnificent bust by Michael Rizzello. The work was crowned by the unveiling and presentation of the bust in Covent Garden Opera House attended by Dame Eva Turner, Sir John Tooley, Eric Fenby, Denham Ford (chairman of the Beecham Society) and many more dignitaries. How I would love to have heard P-G's speech on this occasion; for despite shyness and modesty, blindness in one eye and a speech impediment 'which', as P-G wrote, 'became the bane of my life',[9] his was a commanding presence.

He died on 13 April 1980; a kindly, courageous and generous man who left no immediate family, but a host of indebted colleagues, former students and friends – and a legacy of music with which to enrich and beautify our lives.

---

[6] John Crompton, *The Life of the Spider* (London, 1950). John Crompton went on to write many absorbing accounts of the insect world, notably *The Hunting Wasp*, *Ways of an Ant* and *The Hive*.
[7] A former Roman Catholic priest, McCabe was known for his unorthodox blend of history and philosophy.
[8] *Sir Thomas Beecham: Conductor and Impresario* (Kendal, 1973) and its successor *Beecham Remembered* (London, 1976).
[9] Unpublished autobiographical notes in the Procter-Gregg Archive, Henry Watson Music Library. Procter-Gregg attributed the speech defect to mustard poultices administered as a cure for a childhood illness.

THE COMPOSITIONS span sixty years – some early études and sketches date from 1916–17. A newspaper report of a piano recital given by P-G in Douglas, Isle of Man, in 1916, mentions the inclusion of three, at least, of his own *Sketches*.

The audience at Mr H. Procter-Gregg's pianoforte recital in Villa Marina Hall, on Thursday afternoon, was fairly large but nothing like so large as the occasion merited. For the most part, those present were people of musical taste, but, unfortunately, the bulk of Manx folk are not yet educated up to the class of music which was interpreted by Mr Procter-Gregg. Lady Raglan was there, as were many people of social prominence in the Island. The financial proceeds were in aid of the Children's War-time Club and the Y.M.C.A. Huts. There was a very fine programme, and every number of it was a great musical treat. Mr Procter-Gregg has a mastery of the pianoforte such as is achieved by few, and as he is young in years, and is still an ardent student, he should go far. To a perfect touch he unites marvellous technique, the artistic sense, and a complete appreciation of his subject. Indeed his chiaroscuro is delightful – his soul is in his playing, and he speaks, as it were, to his hearers in the strains he evolves. On Thursday, he played all his numbers from memory, which is in itself no mean feat. Altogether, his performance thrilled and enchanted an audience which included a goodly number of people of musicianly attainments. Mr Procter-Gregg rendered the following compositions: – in 'Fantasia in C minor' (Mozart); 'Prelude and Fugue in C sharp' (Bach); 'Grand Humoreske in B flat' (Schumann); 'Two sketches' (H. Procter-Gregg); and a Chopin group consisting of 'Three studies (in A flat, G flat, and C minor'), 'Impromptu in F sharp,' and 'Polonaise in A major.' Very acceptable in all these, he particularly excelled in the Humoreske, which was something to give thanks for. The audience would fain have had him do much more, but he wisely declined all encores with one exception – it was impossible for him to resist the rapturous recall which followed his interpretation of his own sketches, and, responding, he played 'Dream Song' from 'Pianoforte Sketch Book no 2.' This dainty composition by himself had but one fault – it was all too short. The sketches proclaim that Mr Procter-Gregg is as original and graceful in composition as he is brilliant in execution. In the course of the afternoon he rendered good service to those members of his audience who intend competing in the pianoforte solo (open) class at the next Musical festival, by prefacing the Chopin group with the playing of the 'Berceuse in D flat' (Chopin), which is the subject selected for competition. The hints derivable from Mr Procter-Gregg's treatment of the subject should prove of high value.[10]

Once P-G had established his high standard of composition in his early twenties, he rarely fell below it. Good music is an inspirational fusion of melody, harmony and rhythm in a balanced, satisfying framework. P-G's tunes are memorable and beautifully crafted; his harmonies and progressions masterly and his rhythms vital, subtle and playful. There are sonatas for violin (four), viola, oboe, horn, clarinet (for the latter also a concerto); well over a hundred piano pieces; twenty or thirty unaccompanied choral pieces (*Tune thy Music to thy Heart*, to a poem of Thomas Campion, is a gem for SATB); half a dozen large-scale pieces for chorus and orchestra; incidental music to *Le Malade imaginaire*,[11] and more than seventy solo songs with piano.

Ex. 1

[10] *Isle of Man Examiner*, 9 September 1916.
[11] Procter-Gregg was the mastermind behind this projected production of *Le Malade imaginaire*, acting as producer, stage-director, musical director, and composer of the music. Auditions and rehearsals began in October 1948, with a projected performance date of 7 March 1949. By the end of 1948, however, P-G had realized that this was over-ambitious, and was suggesting postponement until the autumn of 1949. Whether a performance ever took place is not clear from the papers in the Procter-Gregg collection.

The corpus of songs is a treasure trove for the singer, embracing settings of Burns, Byron, Campion, Congreve, Housman, Masefield, Shakespeare, Shelley, Stevenson, Tennyson and others. Humour abounds in his choice of text: in Violet Jacob's *The Gowk*, a servant girl is oppressed by a tyrannical housekeeper, lashed by 'the clash o' her tongue'. But unknown to all she is meeting her lover, Jimmie, in the orchard under the apple tree where sits the cuckoo. She comforts herself gleefully as they plan to run away:

> And the wise-like bird in the aipple-tree – he winna tell!
> She may rin an' glower – what care I?
> We'll be far awa!
> Let her seek the lee-long day.
> Wha's to tell her the road we'll gae … (Ex. 1).

In Ravenscroft's *In Despite of a Country Life* the singer bemoans the drudgery of a farmer's wife:

> The milkmaid sings beneath the cow
> The sheep do bleat, the oxen low.

She is tired of dogs, turkey cocks, jackdaws, magpies, ducks, crows and the ploughman:

> If these be comforts for a wife (Ex. 2).

Ex. 2

The compositions for piano are at the core of P-G's musical output, and the *Westmoreland Sketches* were composed over a number of years, though mostly in Windermere. One or two come from a much earlier time; for example the happy, carefree A major piece no. 14. The collection comprises twenty-six pieces in all (arranged in four books of 6, 7, 7 and 6), which encapsulate his outstanding melodic and harmonic gifts. The inspiration for these sketches can be found in the scenery of the Lake District with its ever-changing faces: sky and lakes take on different hues as clouds roll over fells and mountains, and each piece reflects this transient nature of the countryside: it might be the visual impact of a landscape, a lake, a mountain; or the recollection in tranquillity of the mood and atmosphere evoked by a particular location; or, more subtly, an expression of innermost feelings, of happiness, of longing, of nostalgia as the composer viewed a scene in retrospect. As Maurice Aitchison wrote in his foreword to the published collection (Manchester, 1983):

P-G always was content to write what he knew and what he felt; the essential sadness (sad because transient) of natural beauty, regrets for the passing of the old order and the old traditions – these mark him out as a late Romantic, and it is entirely understandable that he insisted on the old, traditional spelling of his home county, in giving the title 'Westmoreland Sketches' to these sets of piano miniatures which reflect his reactions to the ever-changing colours and moods of his beloved Lakeland landscape. For the most part, these pieces were written between 1964 and 1968, and in a very real sense they celebrate his homecoming, the return of the native after a lifetime spent largely elsewhere. An initial stimulus to their composition already lay to hand in the one or two pieces which, the composer tells us, had been completed previously. The original scheme seems to have been for four self-contained cycles of four numbers each. But such preconceived schemes can rarely be adhered to in practice, and as new numbers were written, the vein appeared still to go on, yielding eventually the twenty-seven pieces which now make up the whole collection. For this, the composer's growing interest in freer metrical schemes may have been partly responsible, such numbers generally having been written at a later stage (see the alternative no.8). The cyclic idea does, however, appear strongly in the group of pieces in Book 4 with seasonal titles. In a letter to a friend, the composer suggests that these pieces might well be played in a different order, starting with another 'season' and letting the others follow in natural sequence, thus giving the possibility of a choice of four quite distinct emotional schemes from the endless 'da capo' procession of the seasons.

The heart is seldom worn on the sleeve, and only the last four pieces – *A Shower in Spring, Summer Dreams, Autumn Reflections* and *Winter Elegy* – reveal a programmatic intent. The imaginative range of keyboard textures in these four miniatures is immense: from the hovering, ephemeral, seemingly timeless, caressing arabesques of *Summer* so wonderfully suggestive of heat-haze (Ex. 3) to the hard, crisp, percussive outbursts of *Winter*, with notes that crack like breaking icicles (Ex. 4).

Ex. 3

Ex. 4

In *A Shower in Spring* threatening clouds roll across the sky with E minor thirds, followed by raindrops which soon develop into torrential hail and driving rain. The fury peaks and the rain eases as the E minor clouds roll away, changing to E major as the sun is revealed once more. A tonic major triad ushers in birdsong (Ex. 5). Anyone who has seen the sun reappear like this after a sudden shower in late April in the Lakes will immediately recognize the scene depicted here. *Autumn* gives us the swirl of dry, wind-blown leaves as syncopated quavers twist and

Ex. 5

Ex. 6

writhe in a fountain of dead foliage, before ushering in a reprise of the opening theme (Ex. 6).

Sketch no. 19 is a miniature whirlwind – a *moto perpetuo* (apart from two chordal bars at the start of the coda) that sings its song defiantly as it rushes headlong to slam the door shut! A decorated E flat minor chord writhes in anger for one bar before the theme is stated with great insistence, and with an emphasis on its second beat that is to recur. As in the B minor *Etude* (considered later), the right hand carries the tune as well as taking a fair share of the fiery, accompanying semiquavers. The tune shifts to the tenor register, taken mostly by the left thumb, as the music modulates to G flat major. Bars 13 and 14 plunge into D major briefly (giving extra importance to the second beat). But by bar 21 we are wrenched back into E flat minor and the opening tune, though this is suddenly cut short after five bars, interrupted by the two bars of chords. But impetuous octave semiquavers are resumed to hurtle pell-mell to the final cadence (Ex. 7).

Ex. 7

P-G composed effortlessly and with very little reworking: there were one or two pocket-sized manuscript books for use when travelling, but mostly he just sat at his desk looking out over Windermere across to the Langdale Pikes, with an occasional move to the piano, more to confirm his first thoughts than anything else. Just occasionally he would feel the frustration of capturing what he wanted in musical notation, which many composers have experienced. Once or twice he had a better thought, such as the ending of the beautiful Sketch no. 13 in E flat minor (Ex. 8).

Ex. 8

Ex. 9

In the case of no. 8 he felt the need to provide an alternative to the original *Allegretto scherzando* (8a). The replacement, Sketch 8b, is a beautiful *Andante ben mosso* (Ex. 9). It has a lovely *grazioso* middle section which subtly shifts the main accent on the barline in 11/4 to the middle of the bar in 5/4 (Ex. 10). The original piece in E minor has a palindromic ABCBA form, and an effective canon between soprano and tenor in the 'C' section, which is sandwiched between peaceful 'B' sections, themselves a contrast to the outer *scherzando* 'A' sections in E minor (Ex. 11).

Ex.10

Ex. 11

Ex. 12

The introduction to the first movement of the piano sonata in C minor was added in the early 1970s, many years after composition of the sonata, and is an inspired afterthought. It represents a huge wave that crashes ashore, throwing up a mighty spray with its foaming crest (right-hand chromatic double thirds) before ebbing to give way to the relentless rhythm of the sea (Ex. 12). The sonata as a whole is impelled forward by the sea as a motivic force, in particular the notorious tides and currents around the Isle of Man. This was Procter-Gregg's intention, and the fugato finale especially portrays the sea at its most dangerous and threatening.

The beautiful B major slow movement sings of a calm day at sea under blue skies, with rhythmic motifs of three quavers and of three crotchets (Ex. 13). The ensuing dozen bars or so rework these ideas until a sequence of diminished sevenths achieves its purpose of unsettling the tonality. The last chord, at a moment of great beauty, over a B double-flat bass, glides into a restatement of the main theme, now in D flat. This raising of the pitch of the key of the movement by a tone, along with effortless, dreamy, wide-spaced arpeggios, brings great serenity. The melody has powerful elegance and climaxes at bar 53; note the inversion here of the first three notes of the movement, ascending instead of descending (Ex. 14). The chord at this high point in the movement (in pitch and intensity) is basically a diminished seventh on F with appoggiaturas C sharp and E gliding upwards to D and F respectively, into a beautiful B flat major 6-4 chord in the next bar (Ex. 15). The establishment of this chord (bar 54) prepares the way for the final presentation of the melody in the tenor register (Ex. 16). Those first three quaver notes are now revealed as a horn call, and what a beautiful horn tune this is!

Ex. 13

The melody is briefly enticed to revisit the D flat major world of tranquillity before accepting the home polarity of B major. Bewitching chromatic harmony clothes a brief coda motivated by hints of the tune. The last eight bars or so are on a tonic pedal supporting a progression that attest to P-G's complete mastery of harmony. Analysis does not

Ex.14

Ex. 15

Ex. 16

reveal the magic, but the bare bones are shown in Ex. 17. Through the middle of this passage, until the very end, wander echoes of the main theme; and the important three-quaver figure closes the door on an idyll that is perfect in itself and in its setting in the sonata structure, between two movements of intense dynamic power.

Ex. 17

There are eight piano studies spanning half a century:
G major   1918–19
F major   1919
E flat minor   1937
B major   1938
A flat major   1964
C major   1965
A major   June 1966
B minor   December 1966

Space precludes an assessment of this important collection but I would like to take a brief look at the last. (The mid 1960s, when P-G was in his seventies, were a particularly fertile period for composition.)

The B minor study displays a level of athletic activity naturally found in the traditional étude, and, as in much of P-G's music, the texture reveals implied polyphonic movement even in what at first sight appears as a single line of semiquavers.

The opening (right hand staff) combines an insistent melodic motif of a dotted figure and two crotchets, with accompanying arpeggios (Ex. 18). The left hand surges upwards emphasizing the rhythmic figure until a high point at bar 9 leads to a temporary subsiding of passion. A varied resurgence of the opening texture achieves a wonderful climax with the D major chord at bar 17. This opening section has tremendous drive and concentration of material. The relaxation that accompanies the allargando at bar 17 ushers in a *poco piu tranquillo, legato e dolce*. The middle section in this ternary structure is ingenious in its rhythmical subtlety and effectiveness. The serene melody (ignoring barlines) appears to be in 6/8 time: the rest of the right hand providing an internal counterpoint so that again we have a two-part texture. The left hand has quaver triplets in 4/4 time (12 to a bar), providing a three-against-two cross rhythm to the inner right-hand part (Ex. 19).

Ex. 18

Ex. 19

None of this dissection explains the complete ease and natural flow of this piece. The tune after eight bars increases in urgency by compression (at the 3/2 bar) into crochet beats. The melody soars aloft, building up in intensity now with chords emphasizing the tune with syncopated accompaniment (Ex.20) until a re-emergence of furious semiquavers (bar 43) produces a masterly lead into a reprise of the opening. A three-fold insistence on the original dotted motif (bars 47–51) explodes into an ecstatic phrase, bars 51–3 (Ex. 21). Syncopated crashing chromatic chords in quaver triplets, with alternating hands, lead to a final four-bar plagal cadence of Rachmaninovian grandeur though with characteristic P-G chromatic harmonies (Ex. 22: pianists with Rachmaninov's hand-stretch can fill in the harmony notes with all five fingers of the right hand in the last two bars).

Ex. 20

Ex. 21

Ex. 22

This is composition of the highest order – melodic inspiration allied to complete command of harmony within a framework that evolves out of its very content. Thus it meets the criterion of all artistic creation, whether it be sculpture, painting or architecture: no vital work of art can be 'poured' into a predetermined mould. The piece is fairly difficult to play, but once the notes have been deciphered and the fingering allocated, it is a warhorse that is indeed thrilling to ride. As Ravel would say to his composition students: 'Complexe, mais pas compliqué!'

I wish I had quizzed P-G about his mentors in composition:. certainly C.H. Kitson was a tutor and friend at the RCM in the 1920s (his professorship at Dublin did not impose mandatory residence), and there is a charming letter from Kitson while on a walking holiday with his wife in Champéry (near Chamonix and Mont-Blanc) in Switzerland asking P-G for news of his scholarship application. (This would be for La Scala, Milan, which P-G was eventually awarded.) And his library included all the books on harmony and counterpoint that Kitson wrote. But I think P-G had a natural facility for composition and that he must have spent years as a youth studying the great masters before ever getting to Cambridge and the RCM. (There was a well-thumbed Czerny edition of Bach's '48' in his library.)

My graduation year, 1958, saw H.K. Andrews as external examiner. He was the author of volume 2 of the *Oxford Harmony* (London, 1950), which dealt with chromatic harmony and modulation. Volume 2 was certainly my vade mecum as a student but I don't think P-G ever thought of chords as having labels like French, German, Italian or Neapolitan 6ths for example. He just knew unerringly how to keep a melody afloat and not let it come to rest until it was really time for it to do so. Since Andrews stayed with P-G in Platt Lane one wonders at the after-dinner conversation!

The chamber sonatas are very much duos in the sense that demands on technical and expressive powers are of the highest order for both performers, though the nature and eloquence of the writing for solo instrument is more than enough to counterbalance the piano part.

P-G wrote the F major violin sonata (no. 3) for Thomas Matthews.[12] This work is a masterpiece of unity and melodic and harmonic invention. At the opening (Ex. 23) a two-bar melodic outline on piano, by way of introduction, contains much that drives the whole sonata forward. The violin enters darkly and hesitantly in bar 3, but it only needs a seven-bar exploratory phrase to launch into a carefree swinging tune, (Ex. 24) with piano joining in happily. The movement heading is *allegretto lusingando* – the latter term a favourite with P-G. The opening piano phrase, in various guises, unifies all three movements and provides an exciting peroration to the whole sonata (Ex. 25). The gentle descending D minor 7 arpeggio of the very first bar of the sonata is now asserted triumphantly. Ex. 26 gives the basic harmonic structure of the last six bars. Sometimes, unavoidably, one is caught up emotionally in a work when performing – though it is better to preserve some degree of detachment in order to secure the notes. But I have never failed to be intensely moved by this sonata.

Ex. 23

P-G's last major work was a heroic horn sonata, first performed by Robert Ashworth (then a student at the RMCM, now Principal Horn of Opera North) on 31 October 1975 at the Eightieth Birthday Concert in the Denmark Road Faculty of Music, a former cinema converted to P-G's

---

[12] Thomas Matthews, born Birkenhead, 1907. By the age of 15 a violinist in the Royal Liverpool Philharmonic Orchestra. Later leader of the Hallé Orchestra. By 1947, he was Head Professor of violin at the RMCM. He formed a close friendship with Procter-Gregg, who wrote the third violin sonata for him in 1947–8.

design to house the university's music. Acoustically, the hall of this

Ex. 24

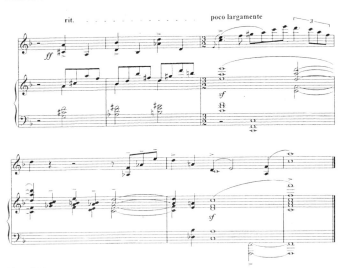

Ex. 25

Ex. 26

building was one of the best for chamber music in the north of England. This programme was repeated a few months later in March at the
Theatre in the Forest, Grizedale, Hawkshead. Paul Cropper and Maurice
played the Viola Sonata; Maurice accompanied Clifford Knowles in

the C major Violin Sonata no. 2; I played four études and some *Westmoreland Sketches* and partnered Robert in the Horn Sonata. In his programme note for this concert, P-G wrote of the Horn Sonata:

The horn, with its lovely sound and huge compass nevertheless has intrinsic difficulties (imperceptible in the orchestra) which in chamber music set problems pneumatic and hydraulic for writer and performer; audiences should wisely ignore them, realizing that its eloquence must be shaped in shorter, separate periods than that of most wind instruments. In the first movement of this work (early 1975) the mood is cheerful and lyrical: the customary two themes are developed with the help of an opening rhythmic figure: the close is contented and serene. The second movement is nostalgic – it might recall De Vigny's

Dieu! Que le son du Cor est triste au fond des bois!

The last movement cheers up considerably in a fugal style which is almost jocular: it plays at solemnity in the middle, and ends in a burst of gaiety.

This sonata is a substantial and important contribution to the growing repertoire of sonatas for this instrument. The opening eighteen-bar tune soars aloft in an extended arc only coming down to rest after a climax on a high A in bar 17. The tune is at once taken up by the piano and followed in canon at the half-bar by the horn. This melodic and contrapuntal invention allied to a characteristic dynamic harmonic drive impels the music forward through a skilfully managed sonata-form structure that features an effective and telling F major start to the recapitulation. The coda harks back to earlier tunes, with shimmering internal piano trills, and brings the movement, after considerable heroics on both instruments, to a *calmato* close, echoing the opening three-note motif.

The second movement indeed does reflect De Vigny's words, but a *poco più mosso* soon incites the solo instrument to reach ever upwards out of the depths. A further *più mosso* brings a less troubled tune, with an occasional subtle 5/4 bar that imparts rhythmic lilt. A return to the home tonic of F minor brings back the opening sombre mood, though a change to the tonic major lightens the darkness with a plagal cadence.

The finale is a *fugato* romp full of fireworks for both instruments, with contrapuntal wizardry that is exciting though never academic to play. The final thrilling climax puts both players on their mettle, and the last few bars masterfully round off the whole work with the recall of the opening three-note motif.

It is only after much familiarity that the interdependence of P-G's tunes is revealed. As in Haydn, the melodies sometimes seem elusively related, as if deriving from some unheard common source, and, as a result, pervade the whole work with a hint of monothematicism that gives the sonata great unity.

MICHAEL ALMOND

MICHAEL ALMOND was educated at Barnsley Grammar School and then at Manchester University and the Royal Manchester College of Music. At the two latter institutions he followed the Joint Honours course in music, studying the piano under Claud Biggs, and graduating Mus. B. and ARMCM in 1958. He taught music in secondary schools and at a teacher training college before becoming a lecturer in music at Salford University, where, until his retirement, he was also pianist and concert organiser in Peel Hall.

I FIRST MET P-G in 1949. I had had no response to my application to the Music Department of Manchester University, so one Saturday morning in early summer I summoned up the courage to go into the department, which was then in Dover Street, to enquire if my application had been received. The department seemed deserted, but ahead was a glass door, clearly an office. Nervously I knocked, and saw inside a tall, very thin man whom I took to be the secretary. I explained my predicament and, leading me along the corridor, he said, 'Come in, and I'll interview you now.' To my horror I realized that this was Procter-Gregg, and that this was going to be a serious interview for which I felt totally unprepared. Somehow I survived, and later, after I'd sent him some compositions, I was accepted for the course.

It was a small department. There were six in my year, and only about twenty of us in all doing the Mus.B., plus a number of others taking music as part of a mixed BA. Most of the teaching was done by P-G (as we were instructed to call him) and by Maurice Aitchison, who had just joined the department from Cambridge and who was only three or four years older than I. Not only did the students all know each other well, but we spent a lot of time with both Maurice and P-G because, in addition to attending all the classes, we were expected to go to

The old Manchester University Department of Music in Dover Street

as many of the concerts in Manchester as possible. This was important, as opportunities to hear music in the late 1940s and early 50s were very limited.

P-G's dark, greying hair was always cut short and he was blind in one eye, though this was not at all obvious. He told me it had been caused by looking up at the lighting when he was working at Covent Garden. He also had an occasional stutter which he had had from childhood. Though slightly disconcerting when you first met him, one soon got used to it and it never seemed to trouble him. He mostly wore suits of a conventional, even drab sort, or else a cardigan instead of a jacket.

P-G's musical tastes were notoriously conservative. There was little written after 1918 that he really enjoyed. His intolerance of modern music became a problem for some later students (famously in the case of Peter Maxwell Davies), but I found I could learn a lot from his extensive knowledge of the Classical and late Romantic repertoire and of opera in particular. In composition classes I found him very good at suggesting music I should study to overcome specific problems I might have. It also helped that Maurice Aitchison was prepared to introduce us to at least slightly more up-to-date music – Hindemith, Bartók, Shostakovich, and so on. I vividly remember Maurice's impeccable sight-reading of *Ludus tonalis* for us, and he and Clifford Knowles playing through the Walton Violin Concerto.

Not surprisingly, P-G was an excellent judge of performers, both instrumentalists and singers, and was unstinting in his praise of those with talent. He was especially devoted to Sir Thomas Beecham, with whom he had worked closely in the British National Opera Company seasons at Covent Garden in the late 1920s. After Beecham died, P-G wrote two fine books about this great conductor and commissioned a magnificent bronze bust from Michael Rizzello to be placed in Covent Garden. I went to several Beecham concerts with P-G, and I remember with particular pleasure a performance of Delius's *Irmelin* in Oxford that a number of us attended – Maurice and I travelling back to Manchester on a late-night, almost empty train.

P-G composed throughout his adult life. He insisted that his students should write at least a few bars every day, sound advice which he himself followed. But he refused to promote his work or seek its publication. There is a significant body of work which merits an in-depth study, and indeed there is much that I have neither seen nor heard. But a number of pieces I remember with pleasure. The first is a group of part-songs on words by Sir Walter Scott, written for our university madrigal group in 1951. His fine vocal writing and sensitivity for the words also informed his setting of the Jean Ingelow poem 'High tide on the coast of Lincolnshire' for choir and orchestra, which we performed in 1953. I also heard, while I was still a student, Clifford Knowles and Maurice Aitchison play at least two of the four violin sonatas, and, in the later 1950s, a very good performance of the Clarinet Sonata.

Although there was little in P-G's music that could not have been written in the earliest years of the twentieth century, it has its own individual sound world. Late romantic harmonies are often tempered by intricate contrapuntal writing. Much of his music is infused with a sense of sadness and loss, exactly reflecting P-G's own pessimistic view of life, and regret for the passing of an older order. The music is always restrained and elegant; drama and 'effects' are avoided. Perhaps for these reasons, this music does not always yield up all its treasures at first hearing. P-G was always changing his mind about exactly how his music should be performed, which must have been frustrating for the performers! But I remember how Maurice, Clifford Knowles and Paul Cropper among others took great pains to create P-G's ideal performance. And I also know from what he told me how much he appreciated their efforts.

P-G made a significant contribution to musical life in Manchester through the many fine concerts he organized in the university. He went to great trouble to form a chamber music group for the Music Department, a project that came to fruition with the establishment of the Ad Solem ensemble in the year after I left.

In 1953, during my final year, P-G introduced me to Ernest Tomlinson, who had graduated a few years before I arrived in Manchester. Ernest was now the arranger at Mills Music in London, and in the late summer of that year he wrote to me to offer me a job as his assistant and copyist. It was the first step, and a most valuable one, in my career as arranger and composer. P-G very kindly let me board at his London house in Golders Green until I could establish myself. Because P-G usually came to London once a fortnight, I saw him frequently in the six months or so that I stayed there. On those occasions he took me to innumerable concerts, operas, plays and art exhibitions. Despite four years at university I was at that time still culturally naive, and P-G broadened my horizons enormously in this period. We also talked for hours, about philosophy, art, politics, religion and so on. He told me a little of his earlier life. He was born in Kirkby Lonsdale of a reasonably well-to-do county family; his father he described as 'all hunting, shooting and fishing'. He had obviously flourished at Cambridge, and then studied further at the Royal College of Music. Clearly very much part of the musical establishment of post First World War London, he told me of the glittering musical soirées of Lady Cunard, which were attended by all the well-known composers and performers of that time. He clearly regretted the passing of that era, and greatly disliked most of what had happened in England since 1945. Since I came from a very different background and another era, there were many things that we didn't agree on at all. But somehow he survived my left-of-centre politics, and my – to him – eccentric view that things were getting better, and we remained good friends through the many years that followed. I think we shared a sense of humour, so we could laugh together about our significant differences. I certainly learned a great deal from him in those formative years.

After I moved into my own flat I went back to Manchester to see P-G and Maurice Aitchison a number of times, and P-G put on my Trumpet Concerto at a university concert with Elgar Howarth as the soloist. My mother and stepfather then moved to Westmorland, so I went less often. I left Mills Music after about eighteen months, to be a freelance arranger and composer, and soon after that I married for the first time. Though there were fewer opportunities to meet, P-G and I still kept in touch. All his many friends will remember those closely written postcards, often witty, always informative. P-G even came to see my children; although he thought that children were a hindrance to a life in music, he accepted that this was right for me.

After leaving the university in 1962, he became the first director of the London Opera Centre, newly formed by Covent Garden and the Arts Council. This involved him in a great deal of travel, and I remember receiving cards from all over the world. I think he found the travelling quite arduous, but he withstood it with his characteristic stoicism.

In 1964 P-G finally retired and chose to return to Westmorland, where he had been born. He bought a fine house in Windermere with splendid views over the lake to the Langdales. Now he could devote much more time to his composition, and it was in the years 1964–8 that most of the *Westmoreland Sketches* were written. He also pursued his hobbies of painting and gardening, both of which had been part of his life through all the years I knew him. He mostly painted in watercolours, his subjects landscapes and especially the mountains of the Lake District and Scotland.

I was able to visit him a number of times during his retirement, and in addition to playing for me what he had written, he also felt a need to discuss what should happen to his house and other belongings after his death, and also what should be done with his music. In 1972 he was appointed CBE for his contribution to music. When I offered my congratulations, he was characteristically modest about his achievements.

Through to his mid seventies he continued to visit London, his energy apparently undiminished. We saw less of each other in this period,

largely because of the pressure of my work, but when we did, his conversation and intellect remained as sharp as ever. Inevitably, as he reached
his eighties, physical ailments gradually took their toll, and he told me
a number of times that he was quite ready to die. A staunch atheist, he
faced death calmly, and the process with the same stoicism that he had
manifested all his life. As he saw death approaching, he moved into a
nursing home and died quietly in his eighty-fifth year.

At one of our meetings in his later years, P-G told me that he had
lived for art, and that art, in all its forms, had sustained and nourished
him throughout his life. He shared this enthusiasm with his friends, and
I am sure that I am only one of many who benefited from his well-
informed, intellectually sharp love of all things beautiful. There were
many things over which we disagreed, but our thirty-year friendship
both changed and enhanced my life, and I know now that fortune smiled
on me that Saturday morning fifty-three years ago, when I timidly opened
the door to the Music Department of the university in Dover Street.

PETER HOPE

PETER HOPE was born in Stockport in 1930. He studied at Manchester University
and the Royal Manchester College of Music before moving to London work as
a freelance composer and arranger. His works include the Momentum Suite for
string orchestra (1959), the orchestral suite The Ring of Kerry (1968), and the
Concertino for bassoon and orchestra (2000).

Humphrey Procter-Gregg: List of Compositions

DRAMATIC
The Pied Piper: A Dramatic Parable (1920)
Le Malade imaginaire (incidental music; includes Three Dances for small orchestra)

ORCHESTRAL
Concerto in A for clarinet and orchestra
Pastoral Dance for small orchestra (piano score, and unfinished short score with details
of orchestration)
Variations on an Air from Aberdeenshire (violin and orchestra)

*In addition, the Procter-Gregg Archive contains sketches for both a piano concerto and
a violin concerto.*

VOICE AND ORCHESTRA
The Danube to the Severn (Tennyson)
In the Highlands (Stevenson)
The Land of Lost Content (Houseman)
Spring Wakens (Tennyson)

SONGS WITH PIANO
Paul Bewsher: In an Aeroplane (1921)
Rupert Brooke: All suddenly the wind comes soft (c. 1940)
T.E. Brown: The Bough of May
Robert Burns: I dreamed I lay; Bonny Lesley; Guid Ale (1922); Bonny Wee Thing; O my
    luve's like a red, red rose; Duncan Gray*; The Farewell; Out over the Forth; The
    Dusty Miller*; The Lady Mary Ann; I dreamed I lay where flowers were springing;
    The Farewell
Byron: There be none of Beauty's daughters; The Evening Star*
Thomas Campbell: A wet sheet and a flowing sea
Sheila Fox-Smith: Steel Rails; So Long (1930); The Wine of Life;
    Limehouse Reach*
James Hogg: A Boy's Song
A.E. Housman: The Land of Lost Content; With rue my heart is laden (1920/1930)
Leigh Hunt: Jenny kissed me
Violet Jacob: Tam i' the Kirk; The Wild Geese (1941); The Water Hen; The Gowk
    (1941); The Licht Nichts; The Banks o' the Esk
John Masefield: Trade Winds; The West Wind
Alice Meynell: Renouncement
Christina Rossetti: Uphill (1932); O Roses
William Shakespeare: Casket Song (1945); I know a bank; O Mistress Myne (arrangement)
P.B. Shelley: The Widow Bird; One word is too often profaned; Music when soft voices die
R.L. Stevenson: In the Highlands*; Blows the wind today; Requiem; The Unforgotten;
    Half the World Apart (1940); Canadian Boat Song; The Stormy Evening*
Wyndham Tennant: The Freedom of the Downs
Tennyson: Old Yew; Wild Bird [2 settings]; I envy not in any moods; The Danube to the

Severn goes*; Ring out Wild Bells; O that 'twere possible; There rolls the deep (1941)
17th century and earlier: I loved a lass (Withers); Carol: I sing of a mayden (Anon.); He
that loves a rosy cheek (Carew); Out upon it! I have loved (Suckling); Follow your
Saint (Campion); Tune thy music to thy heart (Campion); Never weather-beaten sail
(Campion); Fain would I change that note (Anon.); To Julia (Herrick); Spring the
sweet spring (Nashe); Go, lovely rose (Waller); Love is a sickness (Daniel); In Despite of a
Country Life (Ravenscroft) (?c.1934); Love is but the frailty of the mind (Congreve)
(1922); Believe not him (Anon.); Sleep (Fletcher)
Anon.: The Ploughman (1945); I have friends among the dead (1922); La Mort du Roi
    Renaud (1920)
School Song for King William's College, Castletown, Isle of Man: Insulae Collegium
    (K.A.R. Sugden) (unison voices with chorus, piano and optional bugle)

Notes

1. This list follows but expands the composer's own handwritten list of songs.
Dates have been added where these appear on the manuscripts.

2. The songs marked with an asterisk were published by Boosey & Co. in the
1930s. *I know a bank* was published in 2000 in the Boosey & Hawkes 20th
Century Easy Song Collection.

3. The composer envisaged many of the songs as collected into cycles, but the
gathering was usually well after the songs were composed individually, and he
clearly changed his mind on numerous occasions as to both the contents of the
collections and the number of songs in each cycle. Projected cycles include *Three
Songs of Fine Ladies* (Love is but the frailty of the mind; Believe not him; In
Despite of a Country Life), *Five Songs from In Memoriam* (The Old Yew; The
Danube to the Severn goes; I envy not; Wild Bird; Ring out Wild Bells), *Songs
from Burns*, *Five Songs of Angus* (Tam i' the Kirk; The Water Hen; The Wild
Geese; The Gowk; The Licht Nichts), *Five Sailor Songs* (The Wine of Life; Steel
Rails; Memories; So Long; Limehouse Reach), *Songs from Stevenson* (In the
Highlands; Blows the Wind Today; Half the World Apart; The Unforgotten;
Requiem; The Stormy Evening).

RECITATION WITH PIANO
Home Thoughts in Laventie (1916)

CHORUS
A Case – Catch (1959): SSTB
Two Choral Amens (1933): SATB
Daffodils (Herrick): SSATB
Fain would I change that note: ATBB
Five Songs for Chorus (Scott) (1952) (Coronach; Lucy Ashton's Song; Song in Waverley;
    Rangers' Song; True Love's the Gift): various combinations
Joly Joly Wat (1933): SATB

Magnificat (1919) and Nunc Dimittis: SSATB and organ
Motet: O Lord turn thy wrath away from us: SATB
Motet: The Revival (Vaughan) (1968): SSAATT
Motet: The Sun and Stars (Whitmore): SATB
Motet on Webbe's Morning Hymn (Keble) (1943): SSATTBB
Three Madrigals (Love is a Sickness; To Blossoms (1959); Cupid and Campaspe
Tune thy music to thy heart (Campion) (1971): SATB
To Violets (Herrick) (1935): SATB
Many other shorter pieces

CHORUS AND ORCHESTRA
High Tide on the Coast of Lincolnshire (Jean Ingelow)
Jerusalem (Blake)
Kubla Khan (Coleridge)

PIANO
Berceuse and Tarantelle
A Book of Waltzes (1931)
Gay Variations and Finale on an Original Theme (dedicated to R.J. Forbes)
[24] Preludes, in two books
[5] Preludes and Fugues
Rhapsody (1916–17)
Scherzo in F sharp minor (1927/1937/1971)
Seven Pieces without Purpose (1924)
Sonata in C minor
Suite of Eighteenth Century Dance Forms (1941)
Second Suite of Eighteenth Dance Forms (1958)
Theme, Variations and Tarantella
Two Fantastic Waltzes (1930)
Two Little Sketches (1911–13)
Westmoreland Sketches, vols. 1–4 (26 [actually 27] Pieces), 1964–8,
    Forsyth, 1986 (edition includes a substantial editor's preface, with biographical
    information, by Maurice Aitchison)
*Many shorter pieces, including mazurkas, tangos, inventions, waltzes, studies, etc. Also
cadenzas to Mozart's Piano Concerto in D minor K466*

ORGAN
Processional for a Festival Organ (1937)
Three Chorale Preludes

CHAMBER MUSIC
Canzona (horn and piano) (and two other unfinished horn pieces)
Country Tune (cello and piano) (1977)
[5] Pieces for Paul (violin and piano) (1972–7)
A Rustic Suite (two recorders and piano), Arnold, nd
Sonata no 1 in A minor (violin and piano), Boosey, 1936 (dedicated to Albert Sammons)
Sonata no. 2 in C (violin and piano)

Sonata no. 3 in F (violin and piano) (1947–8)
Sonata no. 4 in D (violin and piano)
Sonata in F sharp minor (viola and piano) (1969)
Sonata no. 1 in E (cello and piano)
Sonata no. 2 in D minor (cello and piano) (1977)
Sonata (flute and piano) (fragment only)
Sonata in A (horn and piano)
Sonata in G minor (clarinet and piano)
Sonata in E minor (oboe and piano) (1970–1)
String Quartet in G minor (first three movements only extant)
String Quartet no. 1 in F sharp minor
String Quartet no. 2 in D minor
String Trio in G major
Variations on an Air from Aberdeenshire (violin and piano)
Several other shorter pieces for violin and piano

This catalogue has been compiled from the manuscripts, working copies and sketches housed at the Henry Watson Music Library, where they were deposited by Michael Almond, one of the musical executors of the late Humphrey Procter-Gregg, who carried out some initial sorting and arrangement of the collection by genre, and to whom I owe a great debt for his organization of the material and his comments on this list. It should be regarded as a preliminary working draft only, as considerable research will be needed to identify and where possible date much of the material in the collection. Procter-Gregg rarely dated his manuscripts, and most works exist in several versions, often differing substantially from each other. He often omitted details of the author of the text for his songs, and even the titles of songs are frequently inconsistent between different copies of the same work. Often there are indications of (usually chamber) instrumentation of songs, but this appears hardly ever to have been carried through, even where the reference is to a scored original version! And the collection contains many untitled works and fragmentary scores, which need collation and identification.

JOHN TURNER

Recollections of Humphrey Procter-Gregg, 1932–1937

DOUGLAS STEELE

The life and character of Douglas Steele (1910–99) are described in *Manchester Sounds*, 1 (2000), 93–112. What follows is based on tape-recordings made in March 1985, largely on the initiative of Ian Kemp, then Professor of Music at the University of Manchester, in order to have some record of musical study in Manchester in the 1930s. This transcript retains the informal tone of Steele's narrative.

I JUST WONDERED if I could convey something of what it was like to be at the University when I worked with Humphrey Procter-Gregg, at Wright Street. Wright Street was always spelt by us music students as R-I-G-H-T, because it was a most wonderful place. It was a large, ramshackle tall building next to a kind of drill hall and in that drill hall there were the performances by the University Chorus. You climbed up stairs, twisting stairs, and you came down a corridor into Humphrey Procter-Gregg's room.

'Well, my boy, how are you this morning?' That was the greeting. And he would sprawl with his long legs in a chair and he would say, 'How's little Douglas this morning?' Well, those were great mornings. On pouring wet days there was always something exciting to hear about. Humphrey would take out Aldous Huxley's book *Do What You Will* and read a section of it, just to be listened to. Then he would say, 'But we'll go over to the hall, my boy, and you will be able to hear the Taylor Quartet rehearsing the Ravel quartet. I must take my little miniature score with me. Where is it? Where is it, my boy? Oh, here it is, yes. Now we must go.' We all gathered round him and trooped across to the hall and there was the Charlie Taylor Quartet, a splendid team that Procter-Gregg had adopted and was training. He had trained many quartets in his time and was an expert. They were expecting a visit from the Léner Quartet. Well, we were absorbed in this because he was such an extraordinarily good coach. He would patiently tell them what to do and make them go over it again. He was an absolute perfectionist. We listened enthralled. There would be, I should think, about eight of us then.

Humphrey Procter-Gregg, ca. 1918

Humphrey Procter-Gregg used to keep his contacts with London and opera and the BBC so that you never knew quite where you were or where he would be. He'd be taking taxis here there and everywhere. Going to London to do a rehearsal for the BBC broadcast which Beecham was doing of *Tristan* and he would vanish, leaving me to take charge and to take control of the University Madrigal Society, which had at its head a wonderful person, Jo Watterson, who had the gift of gathering people together.[1] I would be left to look after the Madrigal Society at about 5 o'clock on a Friday afternoon. I would let myself out somewhere about half past six or something like that, lock the place up, and go back home. Sometimes I wouldn't go home on the days when Humphrey was there. He would say:

Come, my boy, to Lancaster Road and sit and have a lesson with me in the evening. Bring your work with you and I've got something for you to do. I want you to write in a translation of *Falstaff* which I'm making. I want you to write it in my score. We're going to do it together. We're going to do the last chorus when they all appear in front of the curtain and they all line up and we're going to put 'Life's but a jest, we're in it.' So come and we'll do that.

Well, they were wonderful evenings. We went on and on, talking and talking and he would go and strum on the piano and play, talk and get me to paste little pieces of paper over things he'd written – piano preludes. They would have bulging bits of paper in which various things had been tried and so they all mounted up into a great pile on the top of the manuscript. And one would have to paste over ideas which quite often returned to the very first thing that he had put down. Most extraordinary.

Humphrey made me secretary of the University Music Club. We had Professor Hartree, who was Dean of the Faculty of Music, and he was a most musical man. He was Professor of Applied Mathematics and had invented the differential analyser. His wife Elaine Hartree was an absolutely superb person, who would gather up, like Jo Watterson, a crowd of people together and inspire them all to gather round Humphrey and form the University Chorus. Humphrey said I was certainly the worst secretary they'd ever had because I would not and could not stand the business of writing up the minutes. So I got behind with that and he used to say, 'My boy, you're the worst, you know. You really are the worst.' However, I struggled on and I took down the minutes as best I could.

Professor Hartree had gathered together in the University Orchestra all kinds of people. There was Arnold Cooke, a pupil of Hindemith; he

---

[1] Jo Watterson was a Levenshulme-resident soprano, a stalwart of the Manchester Cathedral Voluntary Choir.

played the cello. There was Professor Hartree himself, who played the timps. There was Dr Brunner; he played the flute. There was Mary Fleur, the daughter of Professor Fleur, the great French Professor. They were wonderful people. George, who was Procter-Gregg's manservant, used to put out all the stands and the music desks for the orchestra. And I would help him to do that. When the rehearsal was over Humphrey would vanish quickly like a vampire bat – gone! – leaving George and myself to clear up all the stands and all the music.

Procter-Gregg with Beecham at the recording of Tristan und Isolde

We did a performance of the *Christmas Oratorio* at Holy Innocents' Church, where I was organist. This is in Fallowfield and it is a beautiful church. It then had no carpets, so it had wonderful resonance. I had three choirs to look after – a ladies' choir, a men's choir and a boys' choir, very big – and it was a top-hatted sort of congregation. Great people like C.P. Scott[2] would go to it and Miss Heertz who had heard Brahms conduct the Fourth Symphony in Hamburg. They were all in the congregation. Wonderful people.

---

[2] Editor of the *Manchester Guardian*.

Well, Humphrey decided he would do the Bach *Christmas Oratorio* with the University Chorus and Orchestra and he had a policeman who sang the bass. He was known as the 'Policeman bass'. Humphrey discovered him. But the extraordinary thing was that Humphrey disliked the recits. He wouldn't do them. He simply wouldn't do them. 'My boy, I can't stand it.' And he said, 'So many of these choruses with Bach, they trundle so. They trundle. Oh, my boy, they trundle so much we can't do these terrible recits. So I'm going to ask somebody to read the recits while we sing the music.'

Next morning we got an absolute slanging report by Cardus[3] saying, 'This is truly a case of something in which the University Chorus can do better.' And the next morning Humphrey was lying in bed saying, 'Look at this, my boy, look at this. Look what they've said.' Well, of course, it was a rather deplorable performance really because it was so awful that those superb recits were left out and then the speaking voice coming in and then the chorus making interjections. It was all quite wrong but he would have it that way and, of course, that's what happened. And he was particularly upset because Cardus had given him a brilliant review of his Second Violin Sonata, which Forbes[4] played with Henry Holst. Then Humphrey said to me the next morning, 'People will think I've been taking him out to dinner, you know, my boy. They will think I've been taking Cardus out to dinner.'

He was no conductor. He had a flimsy, dancing sort of beat that you could hardly follow and he used to kind of dance when he conducted. It was most extraordinary. There was no sense of control at all. We sang as best we could because we all liked him and he had this highly infectious and attractive stammer, which was not at all disturbing and really after a time one got used to it and it became very attractive.

I was also involved in playing for the Convocations. Humphrey had been, in his earlier days, an organist but he declined to play any more and left it to me. 'You play, my boy. You play for the Convocations, and Mr Walton[5] will give you a signal when to start.' And I used to go

---

[3] Neville Cardus, music critic of the *Manchester Guardian*.
[4] R.J. Forbes, Principal of the RMCM.
[5] Frank Walton, who retired in 1963, was the Deputy Registrar of the university and instigated the transition of the Music Department to a full Faculty. His son Robin Walton was a pupil of Steele at Stockport Grammar School and took private composition lessons with Procter-Gregg. He later became senior lecturer in music at the University of Witwatersrand.

up, and Humphrey used to come and sit on the organ stool with me, with his long legs, and look down, and peer down, and Mr Walton would give me the signal, and I would play the great *grave* section of the Fantasia in G major.[6]

Humphrey was paralysed with interest over this *grave* section and decided that he would write a playing-out processional piece of music. He set to, and he made the most prefabricated imitation of it, of the great Bach piece. It was badly laid out for the instrument; it really was a thing that certainly did not sound inevitable at all. It was very unpleasant to play, but of course I had to play it and, I remember, he did it in pencil and I had the penance of having to ink this in first of all over his pencil, and then play from the manuscript. This went on and on and on, every time I played – that was the exit piece – and I got to detest it very much.

On one of the occasions when I was playing there for Convocation, Beecham came up to Manchester and he had agreed to have a Doctorate of Music given to him. He'd refused it before and simply turned it down very briefly without answering the university's letter; and he had then been approached by Humphrey, who knew him very well because Humphrey had produced operas for him, and he decided to come and take his degree. And I had to play. Now this was an extraordinary experience because Humphrey said to the Vice-Chancellor, 'I think what we'll do is we'll secrete some of the University Chorus behind bowers of flowers in the Whitworth Hall, and they will then, when Beecham comes up, spring out and give the great acclamation to Hans Sachs from the Mastersingers last act.' Well, the Vice-Chancellor simply smiled and said, 'I don't really think, Mr Procter-Gregg, we can do that, you know.' So he came back to me and said, 'That's a wonderful idea gone by the board, my boy, gone by the board.' Well, Beecham came, and as I played the great introduction to Act III of the Mastersingers, in an arrangement of my own, Humphrey said, 'He's smiling. He's smiling. He's pleased. He's coming up. He's looking pleased.'

I believe I was the first person to do his new syllabus, which contained performance and conducting. He said, 'My boy, I think you ought to do that. And you must give up your reading of medieval history. You

---

[6] By J.S. Bach, BWV572.

must give that up.' I was reading *Burying History for Fun* on the side because I had got into the university by one of those extraordinary back entries of the mature matric. And the time came, of course, when final exams were being approached and all this exciting time became more serious when I realized that I was going to have to do conducting in the RMCM hall with an orchestra and that I should have to do accompanying for the examination. They insisted, Humphrey and the others who were examining, that I should play four organ pieces on the Whitworth Hall organ; and, of course, there was the written paper to be done as well. It was an all-round kind of thing. And I was the first, as I say. So I had to work very hard, and Forbes said, 'You're going to do the Fourth Symphony of Beethoven. It's going to be a small section of the Hallé and a small section of the Chorus of the Hallé, and we're going to do the Brahms *Song of Destiny* again for your finals, and you'll have to sight-conduct the piece which we will give to you.'

The time came in my examination for the conducting test. Forbes played the harp, or the piano, on the platform, and Humphrey Procter-Gregg played the timps, and a section of the Hallé played, and a section of the Hallé Chorus sang, and I started off by doing the Beethoven Fourth, and they were all wonderfully helpful, wonderfully helpful. And I got through it, and then the big test came, the sight-playing piece. They had concealed from me what they were going to do, and they opened their parts, and Forbes marched to the desk and put in front of me Debussy's *Prélude à L'Après-midi d'un faune*. I was terrified. I didn't know what to do. I knew *L'Après-midi* from hearing it many times, but it changes time in the most extraordinary way. I felt I was making an awful mess of it, but they were all so good, and the solo flute player was so wonderful: he gave me absolute latitude and allowed me to wander gently through it. And at the section changes everybody was so helpful. Well, the result of it all was that I went to Humphrey Procter-Gregg that night and I almost broke down in tears. I said, 'I've made an awful mess of *L'Après-midi*.' He said:

No, my boy, you didn't. No, no, no, no you didn't. Now don't say that, you didn't, no. You did it very well, you managed it very well. It's a difficult piece, my boy, it's a difficult text. Now, let me make you some coffee now, and I'll show you what I want you to do.

And so it went on. He was astonishingly good. He helped me in so many ways.

One weekend, Humphrey suggested that five of us should go with him by car, and he would drive, and we would go to Alderley Edge for the afternoon. Now, I don't know how long it had been since he'd driven, but he'd got this old car and we all piled into it. And it was the most hair-raising expedition because the car was swerving and this was really unnerving. It was the most terrible driving, the most erratic driving. And it was a marvellous afternoon, a sunny summer after-noon. We climbed from Alderley village up to the Edge, and there we all sat looking out over the great plain, right over. And there he sat. And then he started. He worshipped Delius, and he gave the most wonder-ful talk to us about the music of Delius. This was a wonderful excur-sion, and a wonderful exposition of the music of Delius. Then we had a splendid tea and came home in the same hair-raising way we had gone. A very memorable occasion, but that wonderful talk was some-thing that made history for me.

William Hardwick: Organist, St Ann's Church, Manchester, 1936–1969

STUART SCOTT

WILLIAM HARDWICK, known as Bill to all his friends, was born at Bolton, Lancashire, on 25 January 1910. His family was not particularly musical, but his leanings towards music were in evidence from the age of four, when he began learning the piano at a preparatory school in his home town. His only recollection of those early lessons was of the occasion he got his knuckles rapped for making a mistake in 'We are little children'. His final school days were spent at the Municipal Secondary School, Bolton. Years later, he gave the inaugural recital on the new organ when the school became a county grammar school.

More rigorous training followed with T.H. Ingham of Southport, with whom he studied piano and entered local music festivals, winning a number of classes. Later, he was to gain an LRAM (Piano Performer) and ARCM (Piano Accompaniment), along with the ARCO diploma, obtaining these within the space of thirteen months. (He had been encouraged to take up the organ by W.J. Lancaster of Bolton Parish Church). Continuing his studies with Dr F.H. Wood, organist of Blackpool Parish Church, he gained his FRCO two years later.

At the age of 13 or so, Bill had become organist at the Church of St James, Breightmet, Bolton. Around that time Sir Walter Alcock, organist of Salisbury Cathedral, gave a recital at nearby Market Street Congregational Church, Farnworth, a musical experience which persuaded Bill to become organist there in 1928. He was to maintain close contact with Alcock at Salisbury Cathedral during his wartime service in the south of England. Although Salisbury was out of bounds to soldiers, Bill used to go to the Cathedral to hear Alcock – and sometimes to play there himself, getting caught out on one occasion. He remained in his post at Farnworth for six or seven years during which time he gave organ recitals throughout the north-west of England and as far afield as Frome, Somerset, giving his first recital there at the Methodist Church in 1928.

Although now very busy as an organist, Bill found time to continue playing the piano. He took part in a concert with the Northern Studio Orchestra broadcast live on the BBC North Regional Programme, at 1.45 on 17 February 1933, taking two solo spots interspersed between orchestral items conducted by John Bridge.[1] The solos he offered the listeners on that occasion are suitable for only the most technically well equipped of pianists. Opening with Brahms's *Rhapsody* in G minor (op. 79 no. 2) and Poulenc's *Deux Novelettes*, he went on to conclude with Chopin's Polonaise in A flat (op. 53), followed by the 'Black Key' Étude (op. 10 no. 5) and the 'Butterfly' Étude (op. 25 no. 9).

Recital tours continued, but in 1935 he was appointed organist at Christ Church, Walmesley, Bolton, and the following year at St Ann's Church, Manchester, where he had already given recitals and had lessons with the previous organist, George Pritchard. Other Manchester engagements included broadcasts for the BBC, one of the first being a recital from the Manchester College of Technology on 3 August 1937. On that occasion the *Radio Times* described him as an infant prodigy[2] and the *Daily Herald* reported that he had given a good account of himself.[3] Even though busy in the city, he still made time for recitals on his home patch, playing in a Bolton Musical Artists' Recital at St George's Church that same year.

The approaching war years and wartime itself did nothing to diminish Hardwick's recital appearances. In 1938 the *Musical Opinion* critic wrote of his recital at St John's, Smith Square, that

His programme served to demonstrate the beauties of St John's organ … the exceptionally fine flutes on the swell and choir were heard to advantage in a prelude of Vierne; the full ensembles on great and swell … were used at length in Moussorgsky's 'Kieff Processional' and the 'Postludio Festivo' from Karg-Elert's *Sempre Semplice* pieces; and the *timbre* of the swell célestes suited the string texture of Herbert Howells's first *Rhapsody*.[4]

Hardwick knew Howells well through his work at the Blackpool Music Festival, where he often accompanied and adjudicated piano classes. Indeed, it was on one such occasion that Dr Howells, as adjudicator, paid tribute to Hardwick in saying that, perhaps more than anyone else, the accompanist deserved to be the winner. Others recognized his qualities as accompanist too, and after the Music Festival at Lytham St Anne's in June 1948, the *Blackpool Gazette and Herald* quoted Dr Northcote

[1] *Radio Times*, 17 February 1933.
[2] *Radio Times*, 3 August 1937.
[3] *Daily Herald*, 3 August 1937.
[4] *Musical Opinion*, 61 (1937–8), 546.

as having described him as 'an immaculate accompanist'.

During the war years, Bill served in the Royal Armoured Corps, stationed at Bovington in Dorset, but maintained his interest in music through performances with the Southern Command Dance Band, for which he was pianist, and where he exercised his talent for interpreting lighter music. There were also annual summer organ recitals at Bath Abbey and at St Mary's, Redcliffe, Bristol, which continued along with visits to Winchester; and throughout the 1940s his music-making brought him an enhanced reputation as a recitalist and much praise from critics too.

After a recital at Carnforth Parish Church in 1946, one reporter wrote that 'those who attended were held spellbound by a magnificent performance full of interest throughout. It was quite astonishing what he could produce from our small organ.'[5] Two years later the critic for the *Skegness Standard* hailed him as a distinguished organist:

Mr. Hardwick revealed his masterly playing during the course of a virtuoso programme, which included one of the most technically difficult works ever written for the organ, the *Étude Symphonique* by Bossi, which makes the utmost demands on the recitalist's pedalling and general command of the instrument ... Mr. Hardwick's performance of the *Fantasia in F minor and major* by Mozart was considered by more than one authority to be the finest organ playing ever heard in St Matthew's Church ... in addition to these outstanding performances the resources of the fine organ in St Matthew's were displayed with the utmost variety and purpose, and in so doing Mr. Hardwick paid the highest tribute to the organ builder's art.[6]

During that period, Hardwick did not neglect his duties in Manchester and there were memorable performances of *Messiah* at St Paul's Methodist Church, Swinton, in December 1949 and 1950 under the direction of G.W. Gaythorpe. At the first of these, the soloists included Isobel Baillie, Bernadine Lees, Cyril Hornby and Norman Walker, all of whom were praised for their performance along with Hardwick, who according to the writer in the *Swinton Journal* showed a deep insight into the composer's music as accompanist.[7] The same critic

[5] *Carnforth Parish Church Magazine*, March 1946.
[6] *Skegness Standard*, 4 August 1948.
[7] *Swinton Journal*, 9 December 1949.

reviewed the *Messiah* performance of the following year, again prais-
ing the soloists Doris Gambell, Gladys Ripley, Conrad Gyves and Norman Walker, and adding that 'For his work at the organ, Mr. William
Hardwick was not one jot overpaid by the ovation he received at the
end. Chorus and soloists owed him a great deal.'[8]

Throughout the 1950s the BBC Home Service continued to record
and to broadcast Hardwick's recitals from Manchester Town Hall, and
no doubt one particularly tedious recording session there, later broadcast at 9.15 am on Whit Sunday 1953, remained in his mind for some
time after.[9] Not only was the programme difficult, but the recording
engineers had difficulties too, as they had to suspend recording and Bill
had to stop playing every time the Town Hall clock chimed. However,
another performance broadcast on the Home Service in February 1958[10]
brought appreciative letters from listeners Nigel Cook, who praised the
balance between the baroque and more traditional registrations, and
82-year-old retired recitalist Guy Michell, a pupil of Lemare, who noted
how well the pedal part came over in Bach's Dorian Toccata and Fugue,
the full organ being magnificent at the close.[11]

In later years recital tours included the Isle of Wight and Liverpool
where, in February 1964, Bill gave a recital at St George's Hall. The
programme included what had become rather a speciality of his – Bach's
Fantasia and Fugue in G minor – and the following day the *Liverpool
Echo* noted that the fugue was splendidly phrased and articulated, the
performance as a whole being brilliant.[12] The writer in the *Liverpool
Post* joined in the praise: 'his programme was not only admirably chosen and arranged, but played with exemplary differentiation of style,
technical resource and command of the instrument.'[13] His exceptionally clear phrasing, neat pedalling and wise registration were also noted
on this occasion.

The first major concert of the Salford Choral Society took place on
18 December 1948, and consisted of a performance of Handel's *Messiah* accompanied by Hardwick on the organ of the Great Hall, Royal
Technical College, Salford (now Peel Hall, University of Salford). From

[8] *Swinton Journal*, 8 December 1950.
[9] *Radio Times*, 24 May 1953.
[10] *Radio Times*, 3 February 1958.
[11] Letters in the collection of Ruth Gee.
[12] *Liverpool Echo*, 4 February 1964.
[13] *Liverpool Post*, 4 February 1964.

that date he took part in *Messiah* performances with the society every year until 1963, and routinely at the end of each performance the audience stamped in appreciation of his artistry. Of the many notable *Messiah* performances at Salford in which Hardwick was involved, the one on 3 December 1960 stands out as having a most distinguished cast of soloists in Elizabeth Harwood, Janet Baker, John Kentish and Norman Lumsden. The Paul Ward Small Orchestra accompanied, augmented by Hardwick at the organ, although he had accompanied alone for many earlier performances. The *Messiah* concert on 7 December 1963 was to be his last for Salford Choral Society, where he was well liked by all the choir members. One, Sam Gee, remembered that 'he gave me organ lessons, but he never gave me an account. He taught me for free.'

In the mid 1960s, when he was lecturer in organ studies at the Northern School of Music and music master at Stretford Grammar School, Bill took me into his GCE music class; even though I wasn't at that time (or indeed at any other time) a pupil at the school, I was given special dispensation to attend the class. I remember that it concerned itself mainly with four-part harmony and the analysis of such set works as Beethoven's 'Pathétique' Sonata, which Bill played to us over and over again on an upright piano that had seen better days. His performances were always listened to in silence and watched by fascinated eyes. Analytical discussion was never allowed to dominate his comments, and looking back one realizes how his enthusiasm and performance technique gained our interest, respect and admiration.

Classes had to finish at 12 noon precisely or even slightly earlier on occasion, as Bill gave his regular Tuesday Mid-Day Recitals at St Ann's,[14] and it was a great treat to be taken by car into the city centre to hear him play. Afterwards, he would return us to school for what was left of the afternoon session, when all that remained in our minds were the exciting memories of performances which included such works as Mendelssohn's first sonata, Parry's Fantasia and Fugue in G, Franck's A minor Chorale, Vierne's *Carillon de Westminster*, and preludes and fugues by Bach. His repertoire was eclectic and all-embracing, and his programmes featured much twentieth-century and contemporary music, including Messiaen, Howells, Britten, Kelly, Harus, Whitlock, Karg-Elert, Bairstow, Vierne, Widor, Dyson, Lloyd Webber, Edmunsen,

---

[14] The tradition of these Tuesday recitals, continued in so distinguished a manner by Ronald Frost, is believed to date from the early years of the twentieth century.

Gigout and W.H. Harris. He also introduced music by the American composers Clokey and Nevin. One always came away from his recitals with a sense of joy.

Hardwick was a true musician who inspired others and was thoroughly well liked by his pupils. Colleagues too were always willing to pay tribute, one such being Douglas Steele, who wrote some delightful organ pieces for Hardwick to use in recital. They were personal friends for many years, and when Douglas was assistant at Manchester Cathedral, Bill would play services for him when he was indisposed. Whether in recital or church service, his playing style was distinctive in its imaginative registration, energetic rhythm, intelligent phrasing and flawless manual and pedal technique.

During the annual carol service at St Ann's in December 1968, he was taken ill and rushed to hospital, where he died early in the New Year. His talent and friendliness were missed by all who knew him or heard him play.

Hardwick's memorial is in St Ann's Church for all to see and hear – the fine Jardine organ, which in 1953–5 was rebuilt, and the choir organ extended, to his design. For some time before his death he had been working on plans to add a positif organ as a separate department to the existing instrument. In the 1996 rebuild this was executed to his original design, with one or two additions, and a fourth manual put on.

The author wishes to acknowledge the valuable assistance offered by Ruth Gee, who made available her personal collection of press cuttings and other material.

STUART SCOTT was born in Stretford in 1949 and studied composition with Sir Lennox Berkeley. At the age of 21 he was awarded a prize at the Stroud Festival International Composers' Competition for his wind trio Conversations, op. 30; and since then his music has been performed and broadcast in the UK, USA, Germany, Scandinavia and Japan. He is a member of the Royal Society of Musicians of Great Britain and has helped promote the music of other British composers through lectures and publications.

Eric Fogg, 1903–1939
LEWIS FOREMAN

CENTENARY CELEBRATIONS are wonderful occasions for reassessment, and when we have a forgotten but once almost-popular composer whose music is now completely unknown, this cries out for performances. One such composer is Charles William Eric Fogg – Eric Fogg – who was born in 1903 and was closely associated with Manchester music, laying the foundations of his musicianship while a chorister at Manchester Cathedral. His parents were both well known in the city, his father, Charles H. Fogg, being organist to the Hallé Orchestra and his mother, as Mme Sadler, a soprano and teacher.

Fogg's father was also a composer, two of whose works (an orchestral adagio *In Sombre Woods* and an Overture in D minor) had been played by Dan Godfrey at Bournemouth in 1910,[1] and who in due time was able to effect an introduction for his son to the Bournemouth conductor. Unfortunately Fogg senior appears not to have published widely: a search on the Copac website[2] reveals only one item by C.H. Fogg, a substantial piano solo *Theme with Variations* published by Chappell around 1904.

Eric Fogg was known as a precocious pianist as well as a composer. By the age of 15 he had been appointed organist at St John's Church, Deansgate, Manchester. He started composing when very young, and his *Idyll* for orchestra (possibly the work later called *Sea Sheen*) was heard at Bournemouth on 24 March 1919, when he was 16. Eighteen months later (by which time he had reached op. 57!) he conducted a performance of his own orchestral ballet music *A Golden Butterfly* on 21 September 1920 at Queen's Hall. Fogg was, of course, his father's pupil, and Sir Henry Wood admits in his autobiography[3] that parental contacts were necessary to arrange such a first hearing at a Queen's Hall Promenade Concert, though presumably Wood assessed the music on its merit, for he repeated it in the 1924 season.

It was only at this point that Fogg went to study at Birmingham with Granville Bantock, a teacher whose ready fluency and colourful orchestral palette Fogg inherited. We may get a feel for Fogg's extensive output by taking a quick chronological journey through his main works. The ballet score *The Golden Butterfly* was to a scenario by Leigh Henry

---

[1] Thanks to Stephen Lloyd for his unpublished catalogue of performances of British music at Bournemouth.
[2] <www.copac.ac.uk>
[3] *My Life of Music* (London, 1938), 404.

F. Sancha

Caricature of Leigh Henry from Y Cerddor Newidd, May 1922

(then recently back from internment at Ruhleben, the prisoner-of-war camp on a Berlin racecourse where Germany kept artistic foreigners during the First World War). Henry also provided the words for Fogg's *Three Chinese Songs* of 1920. (Is Leigh Henry another forgotten would-be modernist composer of the period or, with his monocle and waxed moustache, merely the poseur many thought him to be at the time – one whose extravagant pro-German stance during the Second World War underlined his extreme tendencies earlier? In the absence of most of the music we do not know, yet he certainly enjoyed a brief, high-profile career as a writer and impinged on the young Fogg in this capacity.)

Fogg's music was first published when he was only 15 (a song 'Someone to love'), and at the same age he won a Cobbett Prize for his *Dance Fantasy* for piano and strings. Much of his success in the 1920s came with his chamber music and songs, including three string quartets, works for cello and piano, and a quintet for piano and wind that Cardus described as 'luscious' when it was given in March 1930. In Cobbett's view, the Quartet in A flat (published by Elkin)

belongs to the new school of musical thought, but one in which clarity is not sacrificed to modernity. His quartet is far from easy to play, the scherzo especially needing the co-operation of first rate artists to make it effective. The composer, therefore, has been fortunate in securing performances at Manchester by the Catterall and Edith Robinson Quartets, who have placed this clever work in a favourable light.[4]

It is possibly the chamber music which will bring Fogg's name before a wider audience. Central to his achievement is a quite gorgeous extended setting of Keats's *Ode to a Nightingale* for baritone, string quartet and harp, with a running time of some 15 minutes. I remember that I found it very striking when I heard a BBC performance in the early 1960s. Indeed it was one of the things that made me go out to buy a tape recorder, but I have never encountered it again and no one – not even the BBC – seems to have preserved it. The cover for the full score of the *Ode*, published by Elkin, was designed and calligraphed by Fogg's friend and erstwhile pupil Thomas Pitfield, who was frequently employed by Elkin as a music cover designer.

As we have seen, Fogg was fully launched on the musical scene when very young, and works poured from his pen; by the age of 21 he had a good spread of publications already available. His orchestral works tended to be short and fairly lightweight: the overture *Comedy of Errors* (1922), an orchestral evocation *June Twilight* (1928), another overture *Song of Myself*, performed at Bournemouth in 1929, the Bassoon

[4] W.W. Cobbett, ed., *Cobbett's Cyclopedic Survey of Chamber Music* (London, 1929–1930), vol. 1, p. 409.

II. RHAPSODY (quasi recitativo.)

Opening of the second movement of Fogg's String Quartet in A flat, (published by Elkin & Co., 1925)

Concerto at the Proms in August 1931, and the atmospheric Fantasy Overture *September Night* at the Proms on 17 August 1935. Clifton

Helliwell remembered that this orchestral score was much admired at the time.[5] Fogg himself conducted the concert, and as he left the rostrum Henry Wood was heard to remark: 'Heard every note – takes eighteen minutes.' This is one of the works we can unfortunately no longer trace. Much of Fogg's orchestral music has so far proved impossible to locate, and it would be appreciated if any readers having knowledge of the Fogg family or the composer's estate would contact the author.[6]

Of the orchestral music that is easily available the Bassoon Concerto remained silent for far too long after Archie Camden's broadcast with the BBC Welsh Orchestra on the BBC Home Service in February 1952; Rachel Gough's revival of the concerto at Eton in 1988 may have been the first performance for thirty-five years. It is now recorded,[7] however, and Fogg would surely have been delighted that the soloist is the principal bassoonist of the Hallé, Graham Salvage. The work is a notable addition to the literature of concertos for the bassoon and, with its clear textures, lyrical and bitter-sweet slow movement and jolly outer movements, shows a delightful French sensibility one might not have suspected from Fogg's other music.

Two of the shorter orchestral works were fortunately printed with piano–conductor scores, available with parts through public libraries. Of these the delightfully atmospheric orchestral idyll *Sea Sheen* (wind 1 1 1 1, brass 2 0 0 0, timpani, percussion, harp, strings) dating from 1920 would be well received in any programme, and orchestral societies might do worse than celebrate the Fogg centenary by borrowing the material from a local public library: it will probably cost nothing but the reservation fee, and the music is a joy. Speaking personally, a performance of the other short orchestral piece available via this route – *Merok*, a later work dating from 1931 – would be even more desirable in the centenary year, as I have never heard it![8]

Fogg was first associated with the BBC when he joined the North-

---

[5] Clifton Helliwell, *Music in the Air* (Padstow, 1989), pp. 79–80.
[6] Please contact the author by e-mail at *lforeman@nildram.co.uk*
[7] ASV White Line Light Classics WHL 2132 (reviewed in *Manchester Sounds* 3, pp. 175–6).
[8] A search on the Encore! database gives both held in the Lancashire County Library collection, while the Birmingham Conservatoire also holds *Sea Sheen*.

ern Station (then known as 2ZY) in Manchester in 1924.[9] In the manner of early broadcasting he was the anonymous staff pianist and was billed as 'Keyboard Kitty'. He became known to a wide audience as one of the best-loved 'uncles' on Children's Hour from Manchester after 1929, and as such became a popular humorist, celebrated particularly for his imaginary nursery world among whose inhabitants were an earwig christened Montgomery that supposedly lived in a matchbox in Fogg's breast pocket. He was also the voice of Grizzle, a fictitious dragon kept in the dungeons of the BBC in Manchester. So popular did the latter become that the little song *The Grizzle Grumble* that Fogg wrote for him quickly found a publisher.

BBC 2ZY Aunties and Uncles: Uncle Eric is in the front row, second from right

In 1931 he was appointed official accompanist at the BBC's Manchester studios. When the Daventry transmitters closed in October 1934 as new facilities at Droitwich came on stream, the BBC was able to develop its short-wave services to the British Empire, and one facet of the enhanced service was music. For this the BBC Empire Orchestra was

[9] See Ian Hartley, *2ZY to NBH: An Informal History of the BBC in Manchester and the North West* (Timperley: Willow Publishing, 1987).

established under the direction of Eric Fogg. Although it brought him to London, he remained comparatively little known to his colleagues or the public as he had to work mainly at night, conducting live broadcasts aimed at time zones up to twelve hours away and unheard in the UK.

The orchestra at first consisted of only sixteen players. Its pianist was Clifton Helliwell, who later became Fogg's deputy as assistant conductor. He remembered how 'four or five concerts each week disrupted normal daily life. No two days followed any recognizable pattern. Occasionally we saw the sun rise, now and again we saw it set. In the middle of the night we walked to the studios through deserted streets.'[10] One recording of the Empire Orchestra playing under Fogg survives in the Leech Collection in the British Library, which includes two acetate sides of Elgarian miniatures, *Mazurka* and *Sérénade mauresque* op. 10, recorded off air on 1 June 1938.

Fogg's connections with Manchester musicians at this time were many and varied. In particular, he knew Walter Carroll well and supported him in his educational work in the city. In 1933 Fogg succeeded Archie Camden as conductor of the Manchester Schoolchildren's Orchestra (founded by Carroll in 1923), for which the magically orchestrated *Seascape*, a suite for small orchestra taken from Carroll's piano miniatures for children, was probably intended. This work, published by Forsyth in 1930, shows to the full his sensitivity and skill in drawing beguiling colours from a small ensemble. In addition Fogg arranged *Six Gypsy Songs* by Brahms for the Manchester Elementary Schools Choir (also founded by Carroll), which sang them with the Hallé under Hamilton Harty on 4 March 1929, just before the famous 'Nymphs and Shepherds' recording.[11] Another eminent Manchester musician who received encouragement and hospitality from Fogg and his cellist wife Kathleen Moorhouse was Thomas Pitfield; before he became a student at the RMCM he had advice on composition from Fogg as well as occasional cello lessons with Moorhouse.[12]

Fogg wrote two works for chorus and orchestra, both published in

---

[10] Helliwell, p. 77.
[11] See Anthony Walker, *Walter Carroll, the Children's Composer* (Manchester: Forsyth, 1989). *Seascape* has been recorded by the Northern Chamber Orchestra directed by Nicholas Ward on *Manchester Accents*, ASC CS CD45 (reviewed in *Manchester Sounds* 3, p. 174).
[12] See Thomas Pitfield, *A Song after Supper* (London: Thames Publishing, 1990) and Thomas Pitfield, *A Cotton Town Boyhood* (Altrincham: the Author, 1993).

vocal score by Elkin. Regrettably, the orchestral full scores and all the parts are lost. The earlier piece, *The Hillside*, was described by the composer as a 'ballade'. It is set for soprano and baritone soloists, chorus and orchestra and plays for about 27 minutes. The published vocal score is dated 1921 (i.e. when Fogg was still only 18), but the work was not performed until 21 November 1927, in the Free Trade Hall under the composer's baton; it was repeated in London on 1 February 1929. The words are from the then very influential *The Gardener* of the Bengali poet Rabindranath Tagore, who in 1913 had been the first Asian to win a Nobel Prize for literature. Tagore enjoyed a wide popular success at about the time of the First World War and was set by composers as different as Bridge, Janáček, Stenhammar, Szymanowski and Zemlinsky, so Fogg was in good company.

The poem is an allegory of death in the Indian hills ('One evening a stranger came down from the cloud-hidden peak; his locks were tangled like drowsy snakes'). A BBC official reporting on the first performance noted that

Fogg has very wisely not attempted to invest the Eastern words with any pseudo-Eastern local colour, interpreting the rather mystic legend as if it had been an episode of English country life. This was the impression it gave me and on mentioning it to him he confirmed that that was his intention.[13]

The Hillside opens with an orchestral prelude whose lyrical second theme underlines Fogg's debt to his teacher Bantock: its tone colours the whole work. There is no attempt at descriptive motifs other than a succession of accentuated harmonies which characterize Death, the stranger. In the first part the stranger arrives and a girl disappears; in the second the music takes on a warmer tone as May comes and the women speculate on the girl's fate and the existence of a land beyond their hills. Thus far the story is told by the chorus, but then, in one of Fogg's most affecting passages, his baritone soloist takes the voice of the poet and launches into an atmospheric solo: its wistful and tender sense of mystery is a remarkable achievement for a boy of 17. Altogether this is a colourful and beautiful work that merits inclusion in choral society programmes.

---

[13] BBC Written Archives, Caversham – Eric Fogg composer file.

For the Broadheath Singers' revival[14] at Eton in September 1988, Robert Tucker commissioned Rodney Newton to re-orchestrate the work, a remarkably successful exercise. Newton set himself the task of producing as authentic a version as possible, but without available models of Fogg's orchestral style he had to conjure a sound world from the piano reduction in the vocal score. Occasionally this meant he was faced with creative artistic decisions, and he remarks:

there was one isolated moment when I took the liberty of adding something not in Fogg's score but of which I hope he would have approved. One bar before before fig 20 in the vocal score Fogg writes a very dramatic F-minor-6 chord on the second beat of the bar marked *ffff*. This occurs in the treble clef and is doubled an octave above. I could not help feeling that this very dramatic gesture would sound a trifle odd on the orchestra without something below to support it. I therefore added an F in the bass trombone, timpani, cellos, and double basses on the first beat, plus a bass drum for good measure. The dramatic F-minor-6 chord is given to brass and wind with the addition of the tam-tam … and I must say I thought the effect came off very well in performance.[15]

In 1926 Fogg married the cellist Kathleen Moorhouse, for whom he wrote the *Poem* for cello and piano,[16] and while the couple lived in Manchester all seemed to be well. One suspects it was the move to London and then his appallingly unsocial working hours that caused the marriage to fail. It ended in divorce at a time when BBC people did not do such things. With the outbreak of war in September 1939 the Empire Orchestra was disbanded, an event which caused Fogg considerable depression. We cannot know how good a conductor he was, but he apparently adopted an autocratic style which did not go down well with the players, though it is reported that he brought off some excellent programmes with limited forces. In December 1939, on the way to his second wedding (to a Bournemouth woman, Elsie Percival), Eric Fogg was killed under a tube train at Waterloo Station. He was 36.

---

[14] At Eton the Broadheath Singers and the Windsor Sinfonia were conducted by Robert Tucker, with soloists Richard Campbell and the late Tracey Chadwell.

[15] David J. Brown, ed., *before … Elgar … and after: 25 Years of the Broadheath Singers 1971–1995* (Iver, Bucks, 1995), p. 28.

[16] An earlier cello and piano piece is the substantial four-movement *Phantasy* op. 48, dedicated to Vyvyan Lewis; it was composed in 1919 and published the following year by Bosworth.

Clifton Helliwell remembers Fogg as 'witty, amusing and the best of good company' but significantly adds that 'his changes of mood were frequent, abrupt and quite unpredictable'.[17] Could it have been a sudden impulse or was it a tragic accident that resulted in his falling under a tube train? An open verdict was recorded. But whatever the reason for Fogg's demise, we certainly lost an interesting musical figure who had already achieved a distinctive voice.

Critical reception of Fogg's music during his lifetime was at first hostile on account of his presumed 'modernism'; later there were complaints that he did not wholeheartedly encompass modernism on the one hand or traditionalism on the other. He first claimed attention as a bold young revolutionary, yet Neville Cardus remarked after his death that 'he kept faith to the end to the Strauss–Bantock vein of a ripe lyricism … he loved to make lovely and uninhibited sounds – and he knew how to make them'.[18] His brilliant youthful works are undeniably derivative: *The Golden Butterfly*, for example, with which he made his Prom debut at the age of 17, was said to take its cue from early Stravinsky.

Fogg wrote a number of songs that were widely sung in their time; 'Peace' (from the cycle *Songs of Love and Life*), with its slow, haunting cadences, was a particular favourite. Like the choral work *The Hillside*, this cycle sets words by Rabindranath Tagore. It is unfortunate that so many of Fogg's orchestral works seem to be lost, but his facility in orchestral writing contributed to the survival of one or two pieces which were occasionally heard on BBC radio programmes of lighter music until quite recently and which, if not great music, are charming and worthy of revival; among these may be singled out the short tone poem *Sea Sheen*. Fogg died just as he was coming into maturity as a composer, but his centenary is an anniversary that should be observed, and while one would not make extravagant claims for him, his works are immediately attractive and deserve at least a hearing.

Fogg's second more complex choral work, *The Seasons*, setting poems by William Blake, was composed for the 1931 Leeds Triennial Festival but suffered from having its first performance in the same programme as the première of Walton's *Belshazzar's Feast*. In the blaze of

---

[17] Helliwell, p. 79.
[18] *Manchester Guardian*, 20 December 1939, 3.

Advertisement published in 1927 for Elkin's list of Fogg's music

Walton's masterpiece there was no possibility of Fogg's lesser score being given adequate assessment, and it was never played again. In September this 2003, however, it was revived in Slough by the Broadheath Singers and the Windsor Sinfonia under Garry Humphreys. In this case it is fortunate that the printed vocal score is heavily cued with details of the orchestration, and another distinguished Manchester composer, David Ellis, completed a re-orchestration (with support from the Ida Carroll Trust and the Pitfield Trust) which enabled the work to be sung with full orchestral accompaniment.

Fogg's 'Carol of the Little King' and 'Jesukin', both adapted for choir (unaccompanied or with organ) from his song cycle *The Little Folk* op. 34, were for a long time in the repertoire of most good choirs in the country, and for many years the 'Carol of the Little King' was performed each Christmas at Manchester Cathedral. It is a gem of a song, and we must hope that this centenary year will bring it back into use. For that and the Bassoon Concerto alone, Fogg deserves not to be forgotten.

Ode to a Nightingale was performed at the Royal Northern College of Music on 12 November 2003 by Henry Herford (baritone) with the Navarra String Quartet and Louise Thompson (harp) in a concert to celebrate the life and work of Anthony Hodges, former librarian of the RNCM. The programme included other works with a local connection, by Rawsthorne, Pitfield, Manduell and Ernest Tomlinson.

LEWIS FOREMAN was formerly Librarian of the Foreign and Commonwealth Office, having previously worked in HMSO, the Department of Trade and Industry, and in public libraries. His interest in British music has been lifelong, and he has written or edited books on Elgar, Grainger, Havergal Brian, Vaughan Williams, Rubbra and others as well as the standard biography of Sir Arnold Bax. He is Chairman of the Council of the Central Music Library Ltd.

Thomas Pitfield: A Personal Memoir
NORMA PITFIELD

Thomas Pitfield as a young man

BEREAVEMENT BRINGS in its train confusing and contradictory emotions and memories. Sorrow and relief were strong in me when my uncle, Thomas Pitfield, died. There was relief that the waiting had ended for my aunt and for myself, but much greater was the relief I felt for my uncle, who had believed for some time that his real life was over. His infirmities in the last few years had made it impossible for him to continue his extraordinarily varied artistic output as composer, artist and writer.

My grief at his loss was shared, in part, with all the people who had moved in his orbit, friends, musical colleagues and the hundreds of music students he had taught, so many of whom became friends or interpreters of his work, or both. My own particular sorrow was that a beloved relative who had been as significant a figure in my life as my parents had gone. He played a paramount role in forming and encouraging my interests, attitudes and beliefs.

Aged four I was taken to his wedding at the Unitarian Chapel in Bank Street, Bolton. The many steps leading to the entrance made a strong impression as they increased in length to the right-hand side as we approached the door, owing to the steepness of the street. Inside was cool and bare. My parents and I sat behind my uncle. He was about 30 then, small, neat with a little moustache and dressed in one of the faintly tweedy suits he always favoured and whose texture was, even then, familiar to me. Then my aunt appeared, incredibly slender and elegant in her simple coat.

Alice Pitfield, by Thomas Pitfield, February 1947

Because of this marriage my life changed radically. Alice and Tom were moving away from Bolton to the Midlands. This meant that Tom was leaving the house in Bury New Road where he had lived all his life. His mother remained. My father, mother and I left our home be-hind and above our shop to live with an increasingly helpless and disa--

greeable elderly woman. I calculate that she can have been only a year or two older than I am now, 71. She resembled Queen Victoria in her last years, dressed in black and unsmiling.

The tormented relationship my uncle suffered with his mother is well documented in his various autobiographical books. I can confirm her profound philistinism and lack of any ordinary affection. A less loving mother or grandmother cannot be imagined. I was forbidden to play any games on Sunday, or any music other than hymn tunes. Fortunately I had caring parents who whenever possible took me on expeditions on the Sabbath. In dry weather we would take a tram or bus to its terminus in some moorland village, then, carrying our thermos and sandwiches for a picnic, walk to another terminus, returning to the centre of Bolton and the ten-minute walk home to 57 Bury New Road, the house my great-grandfather built. On these walks my mother often talked of my uncle. When she married she had left her Buckinghamshire village to live in the Pitfield household for a few years, while she and my father saved up enough to buy their shop. Tom had taken my mother under his wing, making drawings of her, giving her piano lessons, introducing her to books, most memorably *The Mill on the Floss* and *Middlemarch*. I still have the copies he gave her. Best of all though, he took her for long walks over the moors to alleviate her homesickness. Later I too was to experience this kindness and consideration.

Alice and Tom were regular visitors to our house. I was always excited on these occasions knowing how special my uncle was, not only to me, but to my parents as well. My one quarrel with my uncle's autobiographies is that he showed no sense of the admiration in which he was held by our family. Even his own, terrible, mother had been overheard to boast of his achievements for by this time his music was starting to be published and there were occasional broadcasts on the Third Programme. We would sit in the kitchen and listen in silence, incredulous that anyone connected with us could have achieved such fame. The admiration we felt extended to my father's cousins and their families and to my mother's family. Before and after his marriage Tom had spent holidays with my mother's family in Sherington, near Newport Pagnell. Tom was friendly with my mother's sister Florence, who had seven children, so stayed with her brother Albert and his wife Elsie, who had none.

From Albert's house he explored the nearby villages, the fields and the river, carrying his canvas shoulder-bag holding paper, watercolours, pastels and a folding stool. Years afterwards people in the village would ask me about my uncle and his paintings, describing his fast, purposeful gait, and how they caught sight of him hard at work down by the river or up on a hill. I often wonder if his love of trees was engendered by these holidays. Of course there are trees in Lancashire, but that part of north Buckinghamshire was generously wooded at the time and the variety of species was immense. His fine linocut of a willow by water always makes me think of Sherington and the river Ouse.

Many of the local people who remembered him spoke with admiration of him and his work. He always made a deep impression on those with whom he made even fleeting contact. His seriousness of purpose, his urgency in capturing experiences both heard and seen, and his overriding need to translate them into musical composition, drawing, painting and writing were tangible to everyone he met. As a result he was able to bring out the best in even chance acquaintances. I have been with him when he has asked a passer-by about the provenance of a building that had caught his interest. The question would spark off a long conversation. My uncle's demeanour drew from others a store of memory and a desire to give something to this man which, in turn, engendered new ideas in my uncle's mind. An invaluable aid to all this intensity of vision and purpose were my uncle's sketch books. These he kept throughout his life to the time when he could no longer see. He would often jump up in the middle of a conversation about a piece of his work to fetch one of the sketch books which were all dated, and return with the original drawing, quotation or bars of music.

As in all families there were some problems. My father and uncle were diametrically opposed politically, so politics were never on the conversational agenda. The main criticisms I can remember were to do with dress and diet. Both my aunt and uncle were what were then called 'dress and food reformists'. Clothes should be made of natural fibres, hygienic and suitable for a person's lifestyle, not used to display wealth, status or sexual charms. My mother loved clothes and was a very fine, and trained, tailor. Much as she loved my uncle she was hurt by his sometimes tart remarks and could not forget them. In those days Tom refused to wear a formal suit when he made appearances on concert platforms. My parents were mortified when all around were in tails and we had worn our best for the occasion.

Perhaps more problematic was my aunt and uncle's vegetarianism, a rare phenomenon in those days. Before their visits to us my mother agonized over the menu. If they came for tea all would be well. She would make delicate sandwiches, cakes and a trifle. A midday meal was difficult. My mother was an excellent and traditional cook, who loved to provide meals. She was always at a loss to find a vegetarian savoury and hit on the idea of cheese soufflé. For years the cheese soufflé appeared with embarrassing regularity until, after years of spending holidays at Alice and Tom's home, I was able to teach her a few alternatives.

When I was about eight my parents could no longer leave my grandmother alone, nor could they find anyone willing to stay with her while we had our annual seaside holiday. Alice and Tom suggested that, to help the situation, I should spend some weeks of my summer school holidays with them. This I did every summer and spring holiday until I was 17, and beyond when at university. Before this happened my parents and I had had short stays with Alice and Tom first of all in the house they rented in Wolverhampton when Alice's father was still alive. (Tom did not immediately escape from filial duties after his marriage.) I was enchanted by this house. It had a sunken garden where lived a tortoise. After the death of Alice's father they moved to a house on what I think was a council estate. The house was tiny. Alice embroidered a huge hanging, designed by Tom, to hide the sink and cooker, drawn in the evenings to transform the back kitchen into a sitting room. My uncle used the front room as his study. To me this house was equally lovely, with the garden beautifully covered in marigolds and nasturtiums, for I saw my aunt and uncle as exotic creatures. They lived their lives in such a totally different way from my parents.

Alice and Tom's days were carefully planned to be regular and purposeful; the house was always full of music and fascinating people. Once when I was staying there Walter Wilkinson, the famous puppeteer, and his wife came and did a show for us over the top of the open door in my uncle's workroom. My uncle, who had become interested in puppetry through his friendship with Walter, gave me two glove puppets he had made, with carved wooden heads.

These must have been hard times for Alice and Tom. The war was on and my uncle was involved in helping conscientious objectors with their tribunals, having been through the procedure himself. This was another bone of contention between my father, since he had served in WW1, and my uncle. Some of Tom's employment had lessened because of the war. Alice took on more piano pupils and taught Russian in a school and to private pupils. But I heard about their difficulties only later. At the time I was fascinated by everything about them and assumed that all was well.

In all the years I knew them their routine never changed. They rose early and ate home-made muesli, Russian style, as taught to my aunt, who was born in Russia and lived there until the Revolution when she was 14. With our toast we had home-made jam or Yeastrel, a kind of Marmite for which I developed a strong passion. During the war they drank acorn coffee, to which I developed a strong antipathy. After breakfast Tom disappeared into his study until lunchtime at 12.30. My aunt and I could hear the piano from time to time, different tunes in snatches, different chord combinations, until the whole piece finally emerged. Lunch was cooked and substantial, nut-roast or rissoles, stuffed cabbage leaves, *kasha*, vegetable hotpot, or pie, then for dessert usually a fruit pie or crumble. All was appetizing and full of, to me, different tastes.

After lunch Tom would return to his work; Alice and I would wash up and put everything away. Soon there was at least an hour-long walk at too brisk a pace for me. I was chided and by the end of the first week was able to keep up. In one respect, though, I never caught up. Tom would point out the types of trees, plants and flowers en route and draw my attention to the different birdcalls, telling me how he had annotated all those he heard in the garden. I wish I could claim to have acquired his encyclopaedic knowledge, but there was so much information at such speed that my mind panicked and I retained very little. Back home Tom worked again until supper at 6.30, a salad and maybe cake with stewed fruit or the moist and tasty malt loaf made by my aunt.

Often Tom would disappear once more, leaving us to read or mend or, maybe, embroider. When Tom was with us for the evening we would listen to a concert, talk or play on the radio. When the *Radio Times* arrived each week Tom would carefully go through all the programmes on the Home Service and Third Programme starring those of interest. Listening was by firelight only. My aunt and uncle believed in concentrating without distraction, whatever the activity.

At some point Tom must have decided that my powers of concentration were good enough to invite me to work with him in his workroom, though not on music. My musical capacities did not impress, though he taught me how to play the beautiful harpsichord he possessed at one time, and he had recommended my lovable and very capable piano teacher, Matthew Hernan. It was my artistic prowess that he so generously encouraged and developed. However, this invitation may have coincided with a commission he had been given to write and illustrate a series of booklets on teaching art in schools. I was taught many of the techniques and media featured in the course. They included simple bookbinding. As well as the construction of the book other skills and techniques were brought into it such as illustration, and the designing and printing of cover and endpapers. For these we used potato prints, or the five-point pen needed for ruling manuscript paper, or another technique which involved scraping through colour mixed with a mild solution of wallpaper paste with a 'comb' cut from card. Tom taught me some calligraphy, at which he was an expert, so I could design titles for the books. Also a large linocut of a capering clown was achieved, an oil painting done on piece of board of a tree trunk, 'shut eye' drawings which consisted of pressing the palms of the hand on the closed eye lids, then remembering a pattern thus seen and drawing it on small squares of black paper with pastel crayons. I was also taken out on watercolouring expeditions. From this time on I was allowed to work in his room every morning as long as I kept quite quiet. Later on he always looked at my work, giving helpful and encouraging advice.

I proved useful to him in regard to another commission. In the mid 1940s he was asked to write music for the Royal Academy of Dancing's 'Ballet in Education Children's Examinations'. When I was four, after a bout of rheumatic fever, my mother was advised by the doctors to send me to dancing classes. Subsequently I took all the ballet exams up to the Advance Grade. So I was roped in for the whole of one summer to try doing the exercises to my uncle's tunes. Later on he gave me the manuscript of this work with its many pastings over and tempo changes, rather more untidy than his usual elegantly and immaculately penned scores. This reminds me that once Alice and I stayed up nearly all night copying out scores for a concert. I was never asked to undertake this chore again and can only hope it was not because there were too many wrong notes at the performance.

From my earliest childhood Tom gave me carefully chosen books. *Alice in Wonderland* and *Through the Looking Glass*, both beautifully bound, Lewis Carroll's nonsense verse, stories and poetry by his friend Walter de la Mare, for example, all are still treasured possessions. Of course their library was available to me. I remember reading, on my uncle's advice, *The Ragged Trousered Philanthropists*, *The Diary of a Nobody*, various books by George Orwell, Arthur Koestler and William Blake, the latter a passion I grew to share with my uncle. Both he and my aunt cultivated my taste in music, taking me to concerts, and playing on the piano music that they both valued highly. As a result music has always played a vital part in my life. Because my uncle wrote poems, composed, did wood-carving, I too tried my hand. Those things I could not do I abandoned, then found other art and craft activities to try. The biggest lesson learnt was that I saw these activities as worthwhile and natural things to do.

Early on in these enchanted times my aunt and uncle asked me to drop the prefixes and address them as Alice and Tom. I was surprised and delighted and did so from then on. I was nine at the time. It took some time for my parents to accept what they may have interpreted as lack of respect on my part. When I explained that it was at Alice and Tom's request they no doubt thought of it as another of 'our Tom's' eccentricities.

Later on when my uncle moved to Macclesfield and began to teach harmony and composition at the Royal Manchester College of Music, there were visits to their home at Broken Cross of small groups of his students. My memory of these events was of their easeful nature. Alice would make a huge afternoon tea, there would be endless talk and laughter and music. Tom would do his party trick playing the piano with two hands and one foot, quite an athletic accomplishment, and very funny. Once when I was there John Ogdon was one of the group. He resembled a huge and hairy overgrown schoolboy, with enormous hands and fingers, seemingly almost as large as my aunt's beautifully toned Grotrian–Steinweg as he coaxed out of it the most astonishing sounds.

When a person dies it takes a long time and an effort of will to forget the images of the last, sometimes painful, years, and get back to the vibrancy of the life. My experience of the vibrancy of my uncle's life lasted the whole of mine until he died in my 68th year. All that time he was ever present, whether in person, in my thoughts or in the evidence of most of the best aspects of my life. The time of my most intense contact with Tom was in the formative years of childhood and late adolescence. Later, as my life became more centred on my own career, our relationship changed. I visited them two or three times a year and they occasionally stayed in my various London homes. Later they visited more frequently in my Suffolk homes. The tables were turned in some ways. I took pleasure in showing them East Anglia as they had once introduced me to Shropshire and then Cheshire.

This memoir started with a comment on the complexities of emotion experienced when a person dies. I miss Tom more than ever as time goes on, but what also remains is a strong sense of regret. I do regret that in the middle part of my life I saw so much less of him and Alice, but that was inevitable. What I truly regret is that I didn't take more notice of all the things my uncle said, played and made, careless of the uniqueness of the man and his works, lazily relying on my now imperfect memory to conjure up his essence for other people.

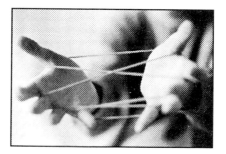

Random Recollections of Thomas Pitfield: Tettenhall College, 1935–1945

L.N. CHOWN

MY MEMORIES of TBP are slight in quantity and faded in vividness after more than sixty years. He came to Tettenhall College in May 1935 to help in the Junior School, whose numbers were growing: the school magazine, *The Tettenhallian*, noted that 'some of us listened in to a broadcast of Mr. Pitfield's songs at the end of last term' (i.e. March 1935), but whether, as a small boy of eight who seldom sang anything in tune, I belonged to that particular audience is doubtful. The previous autumn four new wireless sets had been presented to the school by kind parents connected with the electrical trade – these gave as much pleasure, to boarders especially, as the arrival of four new computers today – so reception would have been clear and made Pitfield's introduction to the school community easier.

I remember his first lesson with us in form 1A (year 5 in modern terminology). He took us for art and, a bit later, nature study. Linocutting is the branch of art or handicraft, however you want to describe it, with which he is indelibly associated, in my mind, from day one. The imprints, in black ink on a white background, made as permanent an impression on my mind as they did on the paper. In late spring or early summer he led us members of his set on foot from school to Castlecroft Lane – a tidy step even for regular walkers – and spent the afternoon pointing out the features of some fine trees in that area before it was developed to the extent you would find today. Pitfield was acutely sensitive to nature's artistry and believed in sharing his awareness with young and old alike.

As in art, so also in music: he used every available means of marketing his talents with a diligence driven by a determination to lift himself and Alice out of the discomforts they put up with through being short of money. Our school carol service at the end of the autumn term 1935 (Pitfield's second term) included his carol 'The Song of the Christmas Waits'. His steady output caused at least one of his more knowledgeable colleagues to remark, half jokingly, that 'the only composers to have written words to their music are Wagner, Berlioz and Mr Pitfield'. When our long-established music master, Alfred E. Hunt, became too ill to continue, in 1940, Pitfield stepped into his shoes and remained on the staff for the next five years. Of his music lessons – we had one or possibly two a week – I can remember precious little; they usually took place in chapel which, in addition to the organ, contained a reasonable piano. Pitfield never played the organ, not even during services; true, it was not in a good state of repair, but my distinct impression was that he had no interest in ever doing so. Organs and organ music lay outside his sphere. I do recall references to Vaughan Williams and his ingenious methods of extracting folksongs from all and sundry, for this was so akin to Pitfield's own major line of business, or one of them.

At lunch in the school dining hall he made no secret of his ardent vegetarianism, although meat rationing in the years 1940–54 effectively prevented anyone from over-indulging in that source of protein. When a colleague sitting by him once remarked that God made eggs for us to eat (factory farming had scarcely begun) he replied 'I disagree with God, then.' Like many an art teacher, his taste for colour in shirts and ties contrasted noticeably with the more conservative, subdued choice of clothing worn by other members of staff. Curiously, when Peter Donohoe – whom I had never seen before – sat at the grand piano on the stage in Tettenhall Towers to play Pitfield's Second Piano Concerto, his profile immediately brought back memories of Pitfield's own: the medium-brown hair brushed back beneath a balding pate, the prominent eyes and general physiognomy seemed like an enlarged replica of Tom's, although Peter was taller and broader in body.

In August 1942 Alice and Tom cycled out to our school scout camp at Hinnington Farm, Shifnal, about ten miles north of Wolverhampton. I had completed two terms of Russian at Wolverhampton Technical College (now a university), so Alice tried out my oral skills with a few sentences. My confidence plummeted when I could not understand a word of what she said. The pathos of that incident has remained with me always: I salute TBP and the wonderful way he used his gifts but am far more thrilled by listening, on Radio 4, to foreigners who speak nearly perfect English.

During his last two years at Tettenhall College, 1943–5, I was at Balliol and then at Bletchley Park, so lost direct touch with Pitfield's ongoing contributions to the life of the school. We were privileged to have him among us for so long and glad he was able to settle at the Royal Manchester College of Music where he could fully spread his wings.

L.N. CHOWN was a pupil at Tettenhall College, 1934–43.

The Music of Thomas Pitfield:
A Working Catalogue

JOHN TURNER

Thomas Pitfield: self-portrait

INEVITABLY, the listing that follows will contain numerous omissions and inaccuracies. The sheer welter of music that Tom Pitfield composed during his long lifetime beggars belief. There still exist his lists of submissions to publishers from March 1935 to October 1993, a period of nearly sixty years, and they make fascinating reading. In one year alone, 1937, the submissions total no fewer than 148 works – though a few of these are of artwork (including his linocuts of Ross-on-Wye and Ludlow to the Great Western Railways – what evocative posters those would have made!) and poetry (including limericks sent to Basil Blackwell). Among the plethora of workaday part-songs submitted to a multitude of publishers we find his now lost String Quartet (sent first to OUP, and then successively to Curwen, Augener, Boosey and the Cecilian Press – Tom was nothing if not persistent!), and the early (also lost) Piano Concerto, sent to the Hallé, the BBC (no less than four times), Louis Cohen and Sir Henry Wood.

No serious attempt has been made to identify all items in these submissions lists, as the information given is so sketchy, intended purely as an aide-mémoire for the composer. This catalogue has therefore been prepared from the collection of manuscripts housed at the Royal Northern College of Music (and I am greatly indebted to Sarah Wickham, the College's Archivist, for her ready assistance), and from available published copies, together with information from Tom's own collection of programmes, also housed at the College. The collection of manuscripts is however far from complete. In an age without ready access to the photocopying machine, submissions to publishers and prospective performers would usually have been of the original manuscript, and on many occasions these would not be returned (no doubt many Pitfield manuscripts still languish in publishers' vaults or were destroyed on periodical clear-outs at a time when the value of manuscripts was not so much appreciated as today), and frequently the only manuscript of a piece would be given or lent to a performer and retained; it is probably in this way that the manuscripts of both the bassoon and horn Sonatinas have been mislaid.

But the composer himself was probably the worst culprit of all. Tom would frequently lose interest in a work after several rejections from publishers and would either destroy the manuscript (if he thought that the piece had no future or he was depressed about it), or recycle the material into other works, often by mutilating the original manuscript. For example, the *Concerto Lirico* for violin and orchestra – one of the composer's most memorable works, in the opinion of both Peter Mountain, its first and only (so far) soloist, and Tom's pupil John McCabe, who heard the broadcast – was destroyed by the composer himself tearing up both score and orchestral parts, after a particularly painful experience at the broadcast première. And the first work that he wrote for me, *Dancery*, for recorder and harpsichord or piano (which recycles material from early piano pieces and the Sinfonietta, though I did not know it at the time), after being submitted to many publishers and rejected, was then reworked and extended to become the Recorder Concerto, the original manuscript being cut to shreds in an abortive attempt to produce some pieces for euphonium and piano! Fortunately I had copied the original manuscript.

I have also appended a list of music (other than his own) for which Tom Pitfield designed the covers. By far the most significant of these is that for the first publication of Britten's *Simple Symphony*. He also designed a cover for the *Sinfonia da Requiem*, but this was never used – the original artwork for it is now in the Britten–Pears library at Aldeburgh. A rather crestfallen Tom would frequently tell the story of how he had been asked to design an alphabet for use on Britten's music covers, but that Britten had failed to turn up at a planned meeting at Boosey and Hawkes to discuss this and afterwards disclaimed any knowledge of the request.

Sadly, towards the end of his life, Pitfield embarked on a series of clear-outs, probably at the instigation of his wife Alice, and he told me that one of the casualties had been his collection of the covers that he had designed. These covers were in general paid hack-work for him, commissioned by particularly OUP, Curwen, Elkin and Lengnick, so he did not think them of interest. The list provided has therefore been compiled by chance and serendipity, and I would greatly welcome any more information from readers – and indeed any corrections and additions to the list of works.

Note. (1) Items marked * are included in a typewritten early programme, without date or venue but probably mid to late 1920s, in the RNCM Archive. The performers were Alice M. Astbury (piano; later to become Alice Pitfield), Stephanie Baker (mezzo-contralto), William H. Bushell (viola), Marion Crompton (violin II), Harry Eckersley (piano), Stanley Horridge (violin I), Nellie Partington (piano) and Thomas B. Pitfield (cello). Only one movement each from the Piano Quartet and the Violin Sonata was played. All MSS are presumed lost or destroyed.

(2) Items marked † are included in a programme dated 11 May 1929 of

the Bolton Musical Artists' Association, held in 'the Dining Hall, Hulton Steelworks'. The pianist was Thomas B. Pitfield, the singer Stephanie Baker. All MSS are presumed lost or destroyed.

FP – first performance   TBP – Thomas B. Pitfield

OPERA AND STAGE WORKS

Adam and the Creatures (TBP). A Morality with Music, for narrators, chorus (SATB), organ and percussion (Sam Fox, 1972)
Ded. 'To Maurice H. Ridgway'. FP 29 Feb 1968, Bowdon Parish Church; Longford Singers (Ronald Frost), Simon Wright (organ), Stuart Pedlar, Terry Gare, TBP (percussion)

The Barnyard Singers (A Serenade for Robbers) (Roberta Foster): A Children's Opera in 2 acts, for treble and non-treble voices, piano duet and percussion (Hinrichsen, 1954)
Ded. 'To Doris Staton'. FP March 1953, Crewe County Grammar School

Broom Beast and Boggart (TBP). An Entertainment for Halloween, for 2-part voices, piano and percussion [Introduction; A Haunted Place (spoken); Cauldron Song and Dance; A Ghost Story (spoken); Epitaph for Nantwich (A Round); Witches' Midnight Song; The Nocturnals; Bat's Song; Interlude; Bat's Autumn Song; Witches' Chant; Conclusion]
MS at RNCM (part photocopy and part original, incorporating pages from The Nocturnals, a Churchyard Comedy (play with music) for piano, voices and percussion)

Columba of Iona (TBP). A Play with Music intended for performance in church, for soloists, chorus, organ, clarsach (or harp) and percussion
MS location unknown (photocopy at RNCM)

Coney Warren (TBP). A Comic Opera for the Young, in one act, for 6 singers, chorus and youth orchestra (Seesaw, 1979)
FP 25 Nov [year unknown], Didsbury College, Manchester

The Devil in White (TBP), composed 1939: A Morality in One Act, with music for mixed voices/organ/strings
MS at RNCM

The Elm Spirit. Ballet, composed 1933
FP Liverpool Ballet Club; also perf. 5 July 1934 in Examination Concert at RMCM (arr. for flute, oboe, bassoon, string quartet, double bass, piano)
MS assumed lost or destroyed; orchestral parts destroyed by composer

Everyman. Morality Play with chorus and orchestra
MS lost

The Hallowed Manger (TBP). A Nativity Play with Music, for 3-part women's voices, one optional male voice, string quartet and optional tambourine (Cramer, 1951)
Ded. 'To Walter de la Mare'
Revised edition (Cramer, 1969), for SATB and SSA choirs, with optional TBB, baritone solo and percussion
Ded. 'To Sheila Barlow'. FP 23 Dec 1951, Parish Churches of Prestbury and Blackrod

The Hare's Bride. 'A Ballet composed for Quintet'
FP 9 March 1929, Miss Atkinson's Studio, Deansgate, Manchester

MS assumed lost or destroyed

Harry the Hare (TBP). Comic Opera for Children in One Act, for treble/female voices, piano, violin, cello and optional percussion
Ded. 'To Margaret John, & the Children's Opera Group'. FP 4 May 1957, Royal Academy of Music Theatre
MS lost (microfilm at RNCM)

The Holly and the Ivy. A Christmas Play in two scenes, with music for mixed choir/ quartet, two guitars, and glockenspiel
MS lost or destroyed, but photocopies survive

Maid of Hearts. Ballet
FP 22 Feb 1937, Crane Hall, Liverpool; Ballet Club of Liverpool, Merseyside Chamber Orchestra, Louis Cohen
MS lost, but pp. 21–42 of full score (Dance of Kitchenmaids) survive in RNCM

Pageant of Peace
FP 18 April 1929, Women's Peacemakers' Council, Bolton
MS lost or destroyed

A Princess in Tartary. 'Fantasy with music, written by Daniel Varé and composed by Thomas B. Pitfield'
BBC recording broadcast 13 July 1945; London Chamber Players, Anthony Bernard

The Rejected Pieman. Ballet
FP Jan 1936, Crane Hall, Liverpool; Butterworth School of Dancing, Merseyside Chamber Orchestra, Louis Cohen
MS lost or destroyed

Tansy (original title Autumn Nocturne) (TBP). An Operatic Fable, for voices, violin, cello, piano duet, and percussion
FP 22 March 1956, Wirral County Grammar School for Girls, Bebington
MS mutilated: RNCM has pp. 13–24 and 59–64 and microfilms of full score and short score

SOLO AND ORCHESTRA

Concertino for percussion and full orchestra [Two Interwoven Folktunes; Canzonetta; Russian Tunes and Doubles] (OUP, 1962)
Ded. 'To Vilem Tausky'
MS location unknown (MS of version by composer for percussion and piano, Trafford Libraries)

Concerto for piano and string orchestra, composed 1937
FP Merseyside Concerts, Liverpool. Later arr. as ballet music (see *Hallé Magazine*, June–July 1947)
Lost

Concerto (no. 1 in E minor) for piano and orchestra [Allegro risoluto; Grave; Allegro gaiamente], composed 1946–7 (Hinrichsen, nd; version for 2 pianos, Hinrichsen, 1981)
Ded. 'To Stephen Wearing'. FP 12 Nov 1949, Liverpool Philharmonic Hall; Stephen Wearing, Liverpool Philharmonic Orchestra, Hugo Rignold
MS at RNCM; MS of 2-piano version location unknown (copy in RNCM)

Concerto no. 2 'The Student' (formerly Concerto Academico) for piano and full orchestra [Dance-Prologue; Interlude on White Keys; Air and Variations (The Oak and the Ash)] (Hinrichsen, 1960; version for two pianos also published)

Prefaced by the following quotation from Milton: '... and bring with thee / Jest and youthful jollity'

Concerto for recorder (SopDTrT) and string orchestra [Allegro risoluto; Melody and Variant (Andante piacevole); Rondo alla tarantella (Allegro giocoso)] (Bardic, 1994) Ded. 'To John Turner'. FP 15 June 1986, Bowdon Festival; John Turner, Goldberg Ensemble

  MS at RNCM

Concerto Lirico, for violin and orchestra, composed 1958 [Allegro apprensivo/Molto allegro grazioso/Allegro giocoso – Elegy – Allegro ('Release')]

The Elegy ('In Memoriam: Albert Hardie (Aug. 2nd 1958)') may be played separately with leader playing solo part; this section survives in the mutilated full score (see below)

  MS at RNCM (mutilated full score and autograph solo part, ed. Clifford Knowles, with complete microfilm), and photocopies of pp. 1 and 33 of full score

Concertino Accademica, for cello and orchestra, composed 1979 [Allegro grazioso; Andante con dignita; Variants on Jenny Pluck Pears] (Piper, 1981)

Conversations, for clarinet, string orchestra and harp [Response; Children Dancing; Dirge at Night; Melody and Deviations] (Leeds, 1970)

FP 9 July 1978, King's School, Macclesfield; Neville Duckworth, Northern Chamber Orchestra, Nicholas Smith

See also CLARINET AND PIANO

Fantasia on an Old Staffordshire Tune, for violin and orchestra, composed 1950 (Hinrichsen, nd)

Ded. 'To Laurance Turner'. FP 9 Aug 1951, Liverpool Philharmonic Hall; Laurance Turner, Hallé Orchestra, John Barbirolli

MS location unknown (copy full score, piano reduction [with MS amendments] and solo part at RNCM)

Into the Ark (TBP), for speaker, string orchestra, piano and percussion (Mostyn Music) Also version with piano: see below

Kitchenmaids' Dance (from the ballet 'Maid of Hearts') for piano and strings (Cramer, 1938)

Ruminations: Folk Song Studies for string orchestra and piano

[Preamble; Transformation 1 (Homage to Percy Grainger); Interlaced Melody (I live not where I love); Transformation 2 (On Faithful Johnny); Variants on 'Jenny Pluck Pears'] (Roberton, nd)

Ded. (movements) 1 'To Christian Blackshaw', 2 'To Ronald Stevenson', 3 'To David Ellis', 4 'To John Ogdon', 5 'To John McCabe'

MS piano and violin I parts at RNCM (with all other parts in another hand)

St Melangell and the Hare (TBP), for female narrator, string orchestra and percussion (Mostyn Music)

Also version with piano: see below

A Shropshire Lass: Song Cycle for medium voice and orchestra on poems by Mary Webb [Introduction; Hunger; The Little Sorrow; Safe; The Happy Life], composed 1984

MS at RNCM

Also version with piano: see below

Three Nautical Sketches. Recorder (D) (or piccolo) and string orchestra [arrangement of Three Nautical Sketches for recorder and piano: Quodlibet; Meditation on Tom

Bowling; The Keel Reel], MS
Ded. 'To John Turner'. FP 28 Oct 2000, Macclesfield Heritage Centre; John Turner,
Northern Chamber Orchestra, Nicholas Smith
Variegations for orchestra and concertante piano [Varied Theme; Little Nocturne;
Scherzino; Noel] (Chappell, 1968; Piper, 1983)
MS damaged in fire at Chappell's; MS (title in composer's hand) and photocopy of
recopied score at RNCM

ORCHESTRA
Arietta for string orchestra
Ded. 'To Malcolm Layfield and the Goldberg Ensemble'
MS at RNCM
Bucolics (Folk Song Studies), for orchestra [Two Scottish Tunes; Where are you Going
to my Pretty Maid; So Far from my Country; Gathering Peascods; The Little Room;
Carrion Crow]
MS at RNCM
Concert Interlude for string orchestra
Ded. 'To Kenneth Wilmott (commissioned by the Altrincham Concerts Society 1968)'
MS at RNCM
Concert Overture, composed 1950–1 (original title Concert-Piece in C)
MS at RNCM
See also PIANO DUET
Concert Piece (NCM), MS
FP 16 Oct 1973, RNCM; RNCM Symphony Orchestra, David Jordan
Epitaph for string orchestra, composed 1981 (Roberton, nd)
Prefaced by the following quotation: 'The village ancients lie / Each under leaning
stone, / With graven legends dimmed, / Moss-overgrown.'
MS full score and sketch score at RNCM
The House that Jack Built. In 1958 catalogue, annotated as 'with speaking part'
A Keele Garland: Suite for string orchestra [Motley; Passacaglia on a French Tune; Three
Interlinked Celtic Tunes; Scots Reel] (Mills, 1957)
Lyric Waltz, for string orchestra (Bardic, nd)
MS at RNCM
Mancunian Heralds, for full orchestra, composed 1978
Ded. 'A Signature Tune for Young Manchester Schools' Musicians'
Material used in finale of Recorder Concerto
MS location unknown (copy score and orchestral parts at RNCM)
See also BRASS/WIND BAND and TWO PIANOS
Overture on North Country Tunes, composed 1953, 'Commissioned by BBC for per-
formance May 28th 1953, North Region' (Hinrichsen, nd; Banks, nd)
See also PIANO DUET
Processional March (Francis, Day & Hunter, 1950)
Russian Interlude (OUP)
FP 4 Feb 1946, Wolverhampton Civic Hall; Hallé Orchestra, John Barbirolli
Sinfonietta, for orchestra [Introduction and Dance-Variants; Polka; Pavan; Jig; Finale],
composed 1946, MS (formerly OUP)
Ded. 'To John Barbirolli'. FP 23 April 1947, Albert Hall, Manchester; Hallé Orchestra,

John Barbirolli
The Polka and Pavan were subsequently performed separately with altered
orchestration; the Polka was later adapted for oboe and piano, and the Pavan used in
Dancery for recorder and piano]
MS full score, and MS sketch for Polka and Pavan (with title Dance Variants), at
RNCM
Theme and Variations for string orchestra [Larghetto flessibile e contemplativo; Var. 1
(Minuet and Trio); Var. 2 (Air and Canon); Var. 3 (Mazurka); Var. 4 (Hymn); Var. 5
(Finale)] (Augener, 1951)
Ded. 'To John F. Russell'

BRASS/WIND BAND
Fanfare for brass and percussion (Hinrichsen, 1961) on the letters ACCEFED (part of the
name Macclesfield)
FP 12 Oct 1961, King's School, Macclesfield; Charter Festival concert, cond. Paul
Ward
MS at RNCM (full score and short score arr. for piano)
Fantasia on Edwardian Music-Hall Songs (Mostyn Music, 1993), scored for and at the
request of the composer by Tony Cresswell
Lightweight Suite, for wind band (2 flutes, oboe, 2 clarinets 2 bassoons, horn) [Pas de
deux; Foxtrot; Polka; Promenade; Doubles]
Ded. 'To Timothy Reynish'
MS at RNCM
Mancunian Heralds, for brass band, composed 1978
Ded. 'A Signature tune for young Manchester School Musicians'
MS at RNCM
Material used in finale of Recorder Concerto
See also ORCHESTRA and TWO PIANOS
Noels and Canons, for wind band, composed 1984
Ded. 'To Timothy Reynish'
Suite in B flat for brass band (Everyman Suite) [Passepied; Solemn Processional;
Country Dance and March], composed 1954 (Mostyn Music)
Ded. 'To John Golland'. FP 5 Feb 1957, Ulster Hall Belfast; Northern Ireland Concert
Brass Band, Eric Ball
MS at RNCM (sketch score)
Two Short Pieces for brass band [Solemnity; Solace]
MS at RNCM (sketch score and fair copy)

PIANO SOLO
Air and Canon (same as last movement of Themes for string quartet)
MS at RNCM
Alla Marcia (Cramer, 1943)
Allegro Giocoso, for small spinet, harpsichord or piano, etc. (Hinrichsen, 1962)
Ded. 'To Joseph Saxby'
MS (entitled 'Piece for virginals') at Trafford Libraries
Alphabetics: Three Ostinato Studies [A Allegretto (based on contours of Russian Easter
Hymn); B Poco meno mosso; C Moderato]

MS at RNCM
Andante Pensivo (Cramer)
Arietta & Finale (Augener, 1932)
Bagatelle in C (Augener, 1952)
Ded. 'To Michael Mullinar'
Bagatelle in E flat (Augener, 1950)
Ded. 'To Beatrice Tange'
Bagatelle no. 3 in F
Ded. 'To Keith Swallow'
Bagatelle. Incomplete sketch of piece in C major dated 3 Oct 1994
MS at RNCM
Ballet in Education: Children's Examinations. Royal Academy of Dancing, 1947, revised edition 1960
Bits and Pieces [Short Preamble; Dance-Piece; Repose; White-Key Piece; Gopak; Hymn] (Forsyth, 1972)
Bucolics [Two Scottish Folk Songs; Where are you Going to my Pretty Fair Maid; So Far from my Country; Gathering Peascods; The Little Room; Carrion Crow]
Cameo and Variant, composed July 1993
MS at RNCM (with composer's workings for string arrangement)
Canzonetta
MS at RNCM
Arr. for strings as Arietta
Capriccio (Augener, 1932)
The Chimes Minuet (Cramer, 1955)
The Circle Suite [Bourrée for H.E.; Minuet for G.H.; Pavan for S.H.; Jig for A.S.] (Augener, 1938)
Ded. 'To my friends, Harry Eckersley, Gladys Horridge, Stanley Horridge, Alice Shepherd'
Comedy Interlude (from The Rhyming Shopman)
MS at RNCM
Country Dance (previous title Schoolchildren's Dance)
MS at RNCM (pp. 5–8 of a larger score: p. 5 scored for 3-part children's voices and piano)
Crooning†
Diversions on a Russian Air (The Blacksmith) (OUP, 1959)
Ded. 'for John Ogdon'
English Suite [Preludial March; Barbara Allen's Shadows; Folk Dance; Variations and Theme (Bonny Sweet Robin); Reel] (Chappell, 1962)
Fantasia on Edwardian Music-Hall Songs (Mostyn Music)
Five Short Pieces, composed Sept. 1932 [Prelude; Dance-Miniature; Bagatelle; Crooning; Merry-Go-Round] (Augener, 1932)
Folksongs in Two Parts, with optional notes [Soul-Caking Song; The Cheshire Man; Johnny Todd; Two Street Tunes (Election Song and Mock Mayday Song); O When I was a Schoolgirl; Oldham Rant; There Was a Pig Went Out to Dig] (Bardic, nd)
MS at RNCM
Foxtrot
MS at RNCM

Grades: Set 1, Book 1 [Song Tune; Distant Bells; Borrowed Rhythm; Marching Song; Solemn Pavan; Variations; Slavonic 1; Slavonic 2; Ostinato and Canon; Waltz Song; Chasing Barbara Allen's Shadow; Ostinato] (Music Exchange, 1981)
Heritage: a muster of folk tunes, composed June–July 1994
    MS at RNCM
Homage to Percy Grainger
    Ded. 'to Ronald Stevenson'
    MS at RNCM
Homage to Tchaikovsky (OUP, 1963)
Homecoming (previous title Salutation)
    Ded. 'For Alice'
    MS at RNCM (2 copies)
Humoresque (Augener, 1957)
    Ded. 'To Iris Loveridge'
Impromptu on a Tyrolean Tune (Augener, 1957)
    Ded. 'To Nina Walker'
The Innocent, composed Feb. 1991
    Ded. 'To Robert Keys'
    MS at RNCM (organ pedal part added in another ink by the composer)
Intermezzo, perf. 21 Nov 1931, Bolton Musical Artists' Association
    MS lost or destroyed
The Keel Reel, composed Aug 1980
    Ded. 'For Peter and Elaine Donohoe'
    MS at RNCM
    Other versions for guitar, recorder and piano, recorder and strings, recorder and guitar
Little French Suite [First Variations; Air; Noël; La Pastourelle; Berceuse; Variations (Finale)] (Chappell, 1961)
Little Nocturne
    MS at RNCM
Little Russian Suite [From the Steppes; Bells; Cossack Choir; For Russian Dancers] (Ascherberg, 1962)
    Ded. 'To David Lloyd'
A Little Song (Cramer, 1952)
A Little Suite [Prelude (Three-Note Tune); Sarabande; Russian Dance; Jig; Ostinato; March] (Elkin, 1951)
    Material used in Dancery and Three Pieces (recorder and piano)
The Lonely Shepherd†
Lulling Song
Lyric Waltz, composed 1988 (Bardic, 1989)
    MS at RNCM
March (Election Song)
    MS at RNCM
Mazurka (Bardic, 1989)
    Ded. 'for Ronald Stevenson'. FP 30 April 1983, Eddisbury Hall, Macclesfield; Stephen Reynolds
Miniature*†
Minuetto (Augener, 1933)

Novelette in F (no. 1) (Cramer, 1953)
   Ded. 'To Stephen Wearing'
Nursery Song (on a Russian Folk Tune) (Banks, 1964)
   Ded. 'To Albert Griffiths'
Pavan in Old English Style†
Persistencies: Five Studies in Ostinato [Molto allegro giocoso; Andante tranquillo;
   Allegro alla marcia; Adagio teneramente; Vivace e gaiamente] (Schott, 1936)
Peter's Puckish Piece, composed Feb 1990
   MS at RNCM
   The 'Peter' in the title is Peter Lawson
Polka
   MS at RNCM
Prelude in C major†
Prelude in D major†
Prelude in D minor (Doubt and Decision)*
Prelude in E minor*†
Prelude in E minor (Defiance)*†
Prelude in G minor*
Prelude*
Prelude, Minuet and Reel, composed 1931 (OUP, 1932)
Promenade
   MS at RNCM
Quiet Melody
   MS at RNCM
   Used in comic opera Coney Warren; see also PIANO DUET (Canzone)
Radetzky March (Johann Strauss, arr. TBP) (Music Exchange, 1981)
Reel Tune*†
Rigaudon (Cramer, 1961)
   Ded. 'To Iso and Hedwig Elinson'
Short Prelude and Sarabande (Augener, 1935)
Singing Tune (title whited out; version of Carol-Lullaby)
   MS at RNCM
So Far from my Country. Irish folk tune collected and arr. by TBP
   MS at RNCM
Solemn Pavan (OUP, 1940)
   Ded. 'To Michael Mullinar'
Sonata
   One movement (Allegro quasi allegretto) perf. 21 Nov 1931, Bolton Musical Artists'
   Association, TBP
   MS lost or destroyed
Sonatina
   FP 17 Feb 1932, OUP concert, Hubert J. Foss (deputizing for Arthur Benjamin)
   MS lost or destroyed
Sonatina in A minor [Allegro articulato; Larghetto espressivo/Allegro minaccevole;
   Allegro gaiamente e grazioso], composed 1942 (Francis, Day & Hunter, 1948)
   Ded. 'To Gordon Green'
Sonatina in C [Canon; March] (Augener, Freeman, 1971)

Sonatina no. 2 [Allegro poco serioso; Threnody; Finale] (Bardic, nd)
    MS at RNCM
Sonatina for octavina spinet [Allegro; Theme on Three Notes; Scherzo; Allegro],
    composed 1953
    FP 16 Dec 1957, Henry Watson Music Library, Manchester; Geoffrey Buckley
    MS lost (the Allegro Giocoso [see above] may be a surviving movement)
Song Without Words (Cramer, 1952)
Studies on an English Dance Tune [Bi-tonal; Seven-eight, Dorian; Cantabile Melody;
    Major-Minor; Three-two-three; Octaves] (Elkin, 1964)
    Ded. 'To John McCabe'
Ten Short Dance Movements [Passepied; Minuet; Solemn Dance; Gay Dance; Quick
    Gavotte; Slow Jig; Tyrolean Dance; Polka; March; Tarantella] (Augener, 1948)
    Ded. 'To Mrs. Kentish Barnes'
Theme and Hymn†
Three Little Pieces [Prelude; Merry-Go-Round; Miniature]
    Perf. 21 Nov 1931, Bolton Musical Artists' Association
    MS lost or destroyed
Three Short Rhythm Studies for piano [Allegretto piacevole; Moderato lusingando;
    Allegro moderato giocoso]
Toccata (Augener, 1953)
    Ded. 'To Lucy Pierce'
Toccatina (The Birds), for harpsichord or piano (Banks, 1971)
Two Little Dances (in Old Style) [Minuet; Gavotte] (Augener, 1936)
Two Russian Tunes [Nursery Song; Cossack Cradle Song] (OUP, 1948)
    Ded. respectively 'To Douglas Miller', 'To Dorothy Miller'
Two Traditional Airs†
Variant on Couperin's Soeur Monique (previous titles Soeur Frederique and Meditation)
    MS at RNCM
Variants, composed June 1972 [Moderato piacevole; Andante sereno; Allegro, poco pesante
    ma articolato]
    MS at RNCM
    Movement 1 uses the same material as the second movement of the Recorder
    Concerto

PIANO DUET
Canzone
    MS at RNCM
    Used in comic opera Coney Warren; see also PIANO SOLO (Quiet Melody)
Concert Overture, arr. TBP
    MS at RNCM
Dance for Two (Pas de deux)
Dance of the Wedding Guests (from ballet 'The Rejected Pieman'), arr. TBP (Cramer,
    1937)
Interlude (from 'A Sketchbook of Women'), arr. TBP, composed 1952 (Hinrichsen)
Kitchenmaids' Dance (from ballet 'Maid of Hearts'), arr. TBP (Cramer, 1954)
    Ded. 'To Albert Howdie'
Lyric Waltz, composed 1988

MS at RNCM
Minors, Dance Suite [Galliard; Sarabande (In Memoriam Iso Elinson); Sinister Dance; Rigaudon (arr. from piano solo] (Cramer, 1965)
Ded. 'For Hedwig Stein and Iso Elinson'
Overture on North Country Tunes, arr. TBP
MS at RNCM (orchestral version published by Banks)
Scottish Suite [Reel (based on Miss Forbes's Reel); Three Interlaced Tunes (Ye Banks and Braes, Leezie Lindsay, The Siller Crown); Scottish March (based on Tillie Fowler)]
MS at RNCM
Two-Way Tunes, A Second Term Music Book (with Duets) [Singing Fingers; A Musical Walk; Dancing Fingers; Nestlings' Lullaby; Up and Down; Wistful Waltz; Tunes with Variations] (Elkin, 1946)
Ded. 'For my wife and her young pupils'

TWO PIANOS
Dance of the Wedding Guests (from ballet 'The Rejected Pieman'), arr. TBP (Cramer, 1949)
Mancunian Heralds, composed 1978)
MS at RNCM (sketch score laid out for two pianos)
See also ORCHESTRA and BRASS BAND
Three Movements from 'The Rhyming Shopman', arr. TBP [Introduction; Lullaby; Wedding Song]
MS at RNCM

ORGAN
Bridal Processional (Oecumuse, 1986)
Ded. 'For Judith, on her wedding day (August 30th 1986) from her mother and father' (commissioned by Mary and Robert Peers)
Epithalamion, composed 1988
Ded. 'For John and Margaret'
MS with JohnTurner
Meditation: see ACCOMPANIED CHORUS (Triptych)
MS at RNCM
Postlude on 'Hymn of Penitence' (Oecumuse, 1989)
Based on 'Hymn of Penitence'; previously part of A Short Community Service
Prelude on 'Hymn of Trust' (Oecumuse, 1989)
Based on 'Hymn of Trust'; previously part of A Short Community Service (as Postlude on Hymn of Penitence)
Short Sonata (Cramer, 1939) [Larghetto serioso e sostenuto; Allegro moderato, poco maestoso]
Originally called 'Sonatina', a title to which the composer reverted after later revisions

VIOLIN AND PIANO
Fantasia (Associated Board, 1975, in The Well-Tuned Fiddle, book 3)
In Minuet Style (Augener)
Kitchenmaids' Dance, arr. TBP from the ballet 'Maid of Hearts' (Cramer, 1967)
Miniature*

Sonata*
Sonata no. 1 in A [Allegretto articulato; Ostinato; Scherzo; Cyclic Variations], composed
1939 (Francis, Day & Hunter, 1947; Forsyth, 1968)
Ded. 'To R.J. Forbes'
Sonata no. 2 [Appositions (Allegro con brio); Mulatto (Andantino elegante); Scherzo &
Trio; Chiaroscuro (Allegro con brio)]
Ded. 'To Dennis & Penny Simons'
Sonatina [Allegro semplice ma gaiamente; Sarabande; Scherzo; Allegro giocoso] (Cramer,
1950)
Ded. 'To Clifford Knowles'
Sonatina Accademica [Allegretto commodo; Canzonetta (Andante semplice); Scherzo –
Passepied (Allegretto giocoso); Theme and Variations]
MS lost (RNCM has photostat of score and MS violin part)

VIOLA AND PIANO
Introduction and Meditation (on a Theme by Couperin)
Ded. 'for Elizabeth Holbrook and Keith Bond'
MS location unknown (photocopy in RNCM)
Sonata in One Movement, composed c.1931
MS lost or destroyed
Sonatina [Lento – Andante grazioso; Allegro con spirito] (Cramer, 1947)
Ded. 'for Maurice Ward'. FP 12 May 1945, Bolton; Leila Hall, TBP
Sonatina Arr. of Sonatina for cello and piano; the MS omits the Arietta, but this is
within the viola range in the original
MS (viola part) at RNCM

CELLO AND PIANO
Celtic Tunes [Miss Oswale of Auchincruive; So Far from my Country; The Gentle Dove;
The Belfast Almanack] (Forsyth, 1969)
Ded. 'To Dorothea Campey'
Evening Song (Lullaby)
Arr. of Candle Vesper
MS at RNCM
Five Scottish Tunes [The Shepherd's Wife; Comin' Through the Rye; The Silver Crown;
Leezie Lindsay; Miss Forbes's Reel] (Bayley & Ferguson, 1967)
Ded. 'To Paul Ward'
Pavan, composed 1929 (Augener, 1934)
Perf. 21 Nov 1931, Bolton Musical Artists' Association
Reel, composed 1928 (Augener, 1934)
Perf. 21 Nov 1931, Bolton Musical Artists' Association
Sonata in D minor [Variations; Pastoral Interlude; Epilogue], composed Dec 1937–Feb
1938 (Francis, Day & Hunter, 1949)
Sonatina [Preludio; Arietta; Scherzino; Toccatina] (Cramer, 1955; Bardic, 1996)
Ded. 'To Oliver and Sheila Vella'
Two Linked Tunes (in 1958 catalogue: no further information)
Waltz. Perf. 21 Nov 1931, Bolton Musical Artists' Association
MS lost or destroyed

DOUBLE BASS AND PIANO
Sonatina [Poco allegro; Quodlibet; Allegro grazioso] (Yorke, 1974)

VIOLA DA GAMBA AND PIANO
Variant, for viola da gamba and harpsichord or piano
Ded. 'For Oliver Brookes'
MS at RNCM

SOLO RECORDER
Sonatina Pastorale [Toccatina; Canzonetta; Cadenza; Giga], for treble+sop recorder
(Forsyth, 1993, in Pieces for Solo Recorder, vol. 2)
Ded. 'To John Turner'
MS at RNCM
Waving Corn, for treble recorder
MS with John Turner

RECORDER AND PIANO
Three Nautical Sketches, for descant recorder/piccolo and harpsichord/piano [Quodlibet;
Meditation on Tom Bowling; The Keel Reel] (Piper, 1983)
Ded. 'To John Turner'
See also SOLO AND ORCHESTRA
Dancery (SopDTrTB) [March; Pavan on Three Notes; Dorian Gavotte; Bergamasque;
Second Pavan; Little Tarantella]
Ded. 'for John Turner'
MS destroyed by composer to use in other works (only fragments survive); photo-
copy in possession of John Turner, who also owns a separate MS of the Little
Tarantella
A Little Caribbean (Tr) (Piper, 1984)
This is a transcription of Conversation Piece for clarinet and piano.
Lyric Waltz (D) (Bardic, nd)
There are other versions for string orchestra; piano; piano duet; recorder and piano;
cello and piano; clarinet and piano; flute and piano; recorder, cello and piano
Miniature (T)
This is a version of the Wordless Song: see CHORUS A CAPPELLA (Three Choral
Miniatures)
MS with John Turner
Three Pieces (Tr) (Forsyth, 1987, in 'A Birthday Album For The Society of Recorder
Players')
Ded. 'for members of the Society of Recorder Players'
MS at RNCM (not the fair copy used for publication)

FLUTE AND PIANO
Lyric Waltz (Bardic, nd)
Morning Song
MS at RNCM
Sonatina [Allegro giocoso; Scherzo (Allegro); Andante tranquillo; Allegro],
composed 1948 (OUP, 1949; Piper, 1983)

Ded: 'For Gareth Morris'
MS at RNCM (presented by Gareth Morris)

OBOE AND PIANO
Polka (Forsyth, 1985, in Modern Wind Music, vol. 2)
Rondo Lirico (OUP, 1947; Thames, 1986)
Ded. 'To Leon Goossens'
Sonata in A minor [Allegro moderato; Air and Variations] (Augener, 1948; Piper, 1983)
Ded. 'To Evelyn Rothwell'. FP 14 June 1947, Houldsworth Hall, Manchester; Evelyn
Rothwell, R.J. Forbes
Two Dance Pieces [Pavan; Polka]
Ded. 'for Leon Goossens'
MS at RNCM (Pavan only, with title 'Two Dance-Pieces' struck out and the
dedication to Goossens whited out; the Polka is presumably the same as that
published by Forsyth, above)

CLARINET (B flat unless otherwise stated) **AND PIANO**
Conversation Piece (OUP, 1960)
Later transcribed as 'A Little Caribbean' for recorder and piano
Conversations, Suite for clarinet and piano [Response; Children Dancing; Dirge at Night;
Melody & Deviations] (Leeds, 1970)
FP 28 Sept 1969, Altrincham; Janet Hilton, Margaret Brownbridge
See also SOLO AND ORCHESTRA
Graceful Dance (OUP, 1966)
Ded. 'To Janet Hilton'
MS at RNCM (sketch score, with clarinet part worked in pencil)
Lyric Waltz (Bardic, nd)
Melody in Sevens, for clarinet in A and piano
Sonatina [Counter-Rhythms; Paean; Elegy; Fives and Sevens] (Elkin,1966; Thames, 1986)
Sonatina no. 2 [Allegretto commodo; Canzonetta; Passepied; Theme and Variations],
composed 1976
MS at RNCM

BASSOON AND PIANO
Sonatina
MS lost (no copies known to survive); in 1958 catalogue

HORN AND PIANO
A Folkish Tune (British & Continental, 1975)
Originally second movement of Sonatina: see below
Sonatina
MS lost (copy with Anthony Halstead)

EUPHONIUM AND PIANO
Doubles (on folk tune Carrion Crow)
Evening Song (Lullaby)
Same as Evening Song for cello and piano

RECORDER ENSEMBLE

Deva Suite, for recorder trio DTrT [Chester Waits' Tune; Air; In Folksong Manner; Finale (Jig and Trio)] (Boosey and Hawkes, 1956)
Ded. 'To Carl Dolmetsch'
Threesome, for recorder quartet DDTrTen [Short Preamble; Two Wedded Tunes (Quodlibet); Chasing-Tunes (Canon)] (Piper, 1980)
Tunes from Down-Under, for recorder consort in four parts (DDTrTr) [Quodlibet and Canons; Botany Bay; Finale (Variants on Waltzing Matilda] (Bardic)
Ded. 'For Brian Wright & the recorder players of Moorfield Junior School'
MS at RNCM

GUITAR(S)

Neil's Reel (Variants on 'The Keel Row'), composed c.1988
Ded. 'For Neil Smith'
MS at RNCM (photocopy with MS annotations)
Rhythm Cycle: Four Studies in Irregular and Cross-Rhythms, for two guitars [Allegretto grazioso; Moderato lusingando; Poco solenne e con dignità; Allegro moderato giocoso], composed 1983 (Lewis Dyson)
Ded. 'for the Albany Duo'
MS at RNCM
Sonatina in A minor [Prelude; Variations on a Russian Theme] (Belwin Mills, 1958)
20 Simple Traditional Airs from England, Ireland, Scotland and Wales (Hinrichsen, 1964)

PIANO ACCORDION

Sonata [Preludio; Corale; Scherzetto; Danza], composed 1963 (MAP Editions)
Ded. 'To Pearl Fawcett'
Kalinka (Charnwood, 1971)
'Dedicated to Pearl Fawcett'
Song of Rest (Charnwood, 1972)

HARMONICA

Sonatina [Prelude; Siesta; Fanfare; Interlude; Postlude on a French Tune]
MS ('ed. JMF') at RNCM

HARP

Eleven Miniatures [First Little Jig; First Ostinato; Imitation; First Little Waltz; Second Little Jig; Cossack Lullaby; Third Little Jig; Second Ostinato; Fourth Little Jig; Second Little Waltz; Rippling] (Peters, 1976)
Folk Songs from Near and Far, for clarsach or harp (Adlais, 1982)
Ded. 'To Margaret Walker'
Sonatina, for clarsach or harp [Allegretto grazioso; Variations on a Russian Vesper Hymn] (Broekmans & Van Poppel, 1982)
Ded. 'to Mair Roberts-Jones'
Sonatina, for harp [Introduction – Moderato, poco flessibile; Melody from Fragment of Welsh Air] (Hinrichsen, 1958)
Ded. 'To Osian Ellis'

PERCUSSION

Motley Suite, for five percussion players [Woodpeckers; Caribbean Interlude; Scottish March (Quodlibet)]
    MS at RNCM
Sonata, for xylophone [Introduction; Intermezzo; Reel; Toccata] (Peters, 1967)
    Ded. 'for Eric Woolliscroft'
Sonata, for five unaccompanied timpani [Variations on a Three-Note Tune; Sonor Evening Landscape; Coda] (Lewis Dyson, 1985)
    Ded. 'To John Moate'
Sonatina, for percussion [Palindrome; Scherzo; Finale (Carol-Canons)] (Seesaw, 1976)
    Ded. 'To James Blades'

CHAMBER MUSIC

Alla Espagnola, for violin and cello*
Andante, for string quartet*
Chorale and Scherzo, for string quartet and piano [Movement 1 of 'Chanticleer']
    MS lost, but RNCM has photocopy score and MS parts in another hand
Chromatic Study, for string trio*
Contrapuntal Study, for string quartet*
Dirge, (?) for violin, cello and piano*
Diversions on a Nursery Tune, for string trio and guitar
    MS lost (microfilm at RNCM)
Divertimento for Oboe Quartet (oboe and string trio) [Toccatina; Pastorale; Intermezzo; Finale], composed 1966–7 (Mayhew, 1996)
    Ded. 'For Leon Goossens' and prefaced by the following verse: 'He pipes his pastoral way – / now seventy summers gone / down music's avenues / with avian retinues, / and every goose a swan.'
Duetto for Clarinet and Viola [Preludio; Transizione I; Canzone; Transizione II; Giga] (Seesaw, 1977)
    Ded. 'for Alison Waller & Nicholas Logie' (not on published edition)
    MS at RNCM
Epigraph, based on fragments from an Arensky ostinato, for violin, cello and piano
    Ded. 'For the Arensky Trio'
    MS at RNCM (score + violin and cello parts)
Fugue, for string trio*
Fun-Piece: see Icumin In
Household Symphony, for piano (4 hands), percussion, and various alternative instruments [Allegro moderato; Allegretto grazioso; Allegro moderato leggiero; Finale: Moderato piacevole] (Boosey, 1962)
Icumin In (previous title Fun-Piece), for four interchangeable instruments and piano [1 Piccolo/glock/violin/flute/recorder. 2 Recorder/clarinet/oboe/violin. 3 Recorder/viola/clarinet/horn. 4 Cello/bassoon]
    MS at RNCM (score + four instrumental parts)
Lyric Trio (Trio no. 2), for violin, cello and piano [Allegro marcato; Larghetto solenne/Allegro quasi allegretto; Allegro], composed 1948–9
    MS location unknown (photocopy with MS parts at RNCM)
Lyric Waltz, for recorder, cello and piano

Meditation and Canon, for violin, oboe/clarinet and piano
  Ded. 'To Reggie and Eileen Stead'
  MS at RNCM (score and parts in another hand)
Miniature Trio, for violin, cello and piano
  Finale broadcast 24 Feb 1936 (Midland Chamber Concerts); Norris Stanley, Harry
  Miller, Michael Mullinar
Minuet and Trio, for string quartet (OUP, 1940)
Modal Theme and Variations in Old English Style, for string quartet*
Pastoral, for violin, cello and piano (Cecilian Press [Cary])
Prelude in A minor, (?) for violin, cello and piano*
Prelude in D minor, (?) for violin, cello and piano*
Quartet, for piano and strings*
Quartet in E minor, for violin, viola, cello and piano [Allegro moderato; Air and
  Variations; Lento – Allegro gaiamente]
  FP 12 May 1945, Bolton; Martin Milner, Leila Hall, Norman Wright, Doris Staton
  MS lost or destroyed
Russian Dumka, for brass quintet
  FP 24 June 1983, St Mary's Church, Bolton; Holst Brass Ensemble
  MS at RNCM
Russian Dumka, for brass sextet
  MS at RNCM
Russian Dumka, for saxophone quartet
  MS at RNCM
Strata, for recorder and guitar [Andante con dignità; Allegretto grazioso]
String Quartet
  MS lost (no copies known to survive)
Themes (previous title A Linkage of Themes), for string quartet [Amabile; Divoto;
  Malinconio; Moderato piacevole; Con dignità (Air and Canon) – Homage to Vaughan
  Williams]
  MS at RNCM (full score, short score, parts)
Three for Six: Suite for brass sextet (2TrHn2TbTuba) [Scherzetto; Canzonet;
  Variations on a Nursery Tune] (Molenaar, 1972)
  FP 20 Jan 1971, Goethe Institute, Manchester; Northern Brass Ensemble
Trio, for flute, oboe and piano [Prelude; Elegiac Nocturne; Scherzo] (Augener, 1953;
  Piper, 1983)
  Ded. 'For the Zephyr Trio'
Trio, for oboe, bassoon and piano [Prelude; Scherzo; Pavan; Scottish Air with
  Variants] (Augener, 1956; Piper, 1984)
  Ded. 'For the Camden Trio'
Trio, for piano, violin, and cello [Molto moderato; Andante pastorale; Allegro moderato
  ma agitato], composed 1930 (OUP, 1933)
  Ded. 'To Alice M. Astbury'. FP (private) 16 March 1933, OUP concert, London;
  Louis Godowsky, Sheridan Russell, Hubert Foss. FP (public) 29 Oct 1933, Sunday
  Chamber Music Society, London; New London Trio (John Pauer, Jean Pougnet,
  Norina Semino)
Two Nautical Sketches, for descant recorder and guitar [Meditation on Tom Bowling;
  Reel on the Keel Row]

Ded. 'For John Turner and Neil Smith'
Variegations, for flute, oboe and piano [Varied Theme; Little Nocturne; Noel] (Chappell, 1962)
Ded. 'To the Cambrian Trio'

SOLO VOICE WITHOUT PIANO
Desdemona's Song: see below, SOLO VOICE WITH INSTRUMENTS
Iago's Songs [And Let me the Canakin Clink; King Stephen was a Worthy Peer]
    MS at RNCM

SOLO VOICE WITH PIANO
Auprès de ma blonde (tr. TBP)
    MS at RNCM (working sketch but apparently complete; words omitted)
Birds about the Morning Air (TBP) (Forsyth, 1989, in Selected Songs)
    For a later arrangement of the song see SOLO VOICE WITH INSTRUMENTS
Birdsong in the Morning (TBP) [arr. of Lyric Waltz]
    Ded. 'for K'
    MS at RNCM
Break of Day (John Donne) (Augener)
By the Dee at Night (TBP) (Cramer, 1964): see SOLO VOICE WITH INSTRUMENTS
    Ded. 'To Owen Wynne'
Candle Carol
    MS with John Turner (intended for a Christmas card)
Carol-Lullaby (TBP): see UNISON VOICES WITH PIANO
The Carrion Crow (trad.) (Cramer, 1952; Forsyth, 1989: new version, in Selected Songs)
    Ded. 'To Margaret Hyde'
Charming Gabriella, arr. and tr. TBP
    MS at RNCM
Cheshire Soul-Caking Song
    MS at RNCM
    For another version see ACCOMPANIED CHORUS
The Child Hears Rain at Night (TBP) (Forsyth, 1989, in Selected Songs)
Christmas Lullaby (TBP) (Cramer, 1934, rev. 1988; Forsyth, 1989, in Selected Songs)
    Broadcast 24 Feb 1936; Peter Howard, Michael Mullinar
City Child's Lament
    Broadcast 24 Feb 1936; Peter Howard, Michael Mullinar
    MS lost or destroyed
The Crescent Boat (John Grecon Brown) (Forsyth, 1989, in Selected Songs)
    MS at RNCM
Cuckoo and Chestnut Time (Robert Faulds) (Cramer, 1938; Forsyth, 1989, in Selected Songs)
Desdemona's Song (Shakespeare), unaccompanied, or with piano/harp/celtic harp (Cramer, 1957)
    Ded. 'To Mary Rowland'
Donkey Riding, coll. Thomas Wood (Cramer, 1966)
The Exile (TBP)
    Ded. 'To Kay Molinari'

For another setting of the same words see below, 'So Far from my Country'
A Fairy Song
    FP 23 March 1926, RMCM Students' Open Practice
    MS lost or destroyed
Faithful Johnny, adapted TBP (Forsyth, 1989, in Selected Songs)
    Ded. 'To Ena Mitchell'
Forgotten (AE)
    Broadcast 24 Feb 1936; Peter Howard, Michael Mullinar
    MS lost or destroyed
Four Canadian Folksongs, arr. and adapted by TBP [White Man, Let Me Go; The
    Stormy Scenes of Winter; Peter Amberley; no. 4 missing]
    Ded: 'for Robert Ivan Foster'
    MS: RNCM has MS of no. 2 and photocopy MSS of nos. 1 and 3
Four Little Songs (TBP) [Hilda Had a Garden; The Tortoise; Marketing; King
    Nebshazerod] (OUP, 1934; Brunton, 1984, in Recollections)
    See also UNISON VOICES WITH PIANO: Two Little Songs
Four Score Years and Ten (1992) (TBP)
    MS at RNCM
From Alderley (TBP) (Augener, 1953; Brunton, 1984, in Recollections)
    Ded. 'to Stephanie Baker'
Gawsworth: A Late-Year Afternoon (TBP)
    FP 4 April 1978, Bolton Central Library; Owen Wynne, Donald Holmes
    MS: RNCM has a lettered copy of the first page only; location of rest (and any
    copies) unknown
The Gentle Dove (Welsh), arr. and English words by TBP
    MS at RNCM
Heron (Phoebe Hesketh)
    MS at RNCM
Hunger (Mary Webb)
    Perf. 21 Nov 1931, Bolton Musical Artists' Association. Broadcast 24 Feb 1936;
    Peter Howard, Michael Mullinar
    MS lost or destroyed
In an Old Country Church (TBP) (Forsyth, 1989, in Selected Songs)
In Autumn (TBP) (Augener; Brunton, 1984, in Recollections; and composer, in
    booklet 'In Autumn')
    Broadcast 24 Feb 1936; Peter Howard, Michael Mullinar
    MS at RNCM (sketched version with clarsach)
In the Moonlight (Au clair de la lune, tr. TBP) (Cramer, 1942)
Into the Ark, for speaker and piano (Mostyn Music)
    See also SOLO AND ORCHESTRA
I've a Little Snuff (air J'ai du bon tabac, tr. TBP), arr. and piano acc. by TBP (Augener,
    1956; Brunton, 1984, in Recollections)
    Ded. (in Augener edition) 'To Peter and Grace Temple'
I've Got a Penny (TBP)
Jenny Kissed Me (Leigh Hunt), composed Feb 1996
    Ded. 'To Georgina Ann Colwell'
    MS at RNCM (several copies)

Limerick (TBP, from 'Limusics'), composed 1993
  Ded. 'A fiftieth birthday present for John Turner, setting a limerick on his name'
  MS at RNCM
Lingering Music, 1st setting (TBP) (Forsyth, 1989, in Selected Songs)
Lingering Music, 2nd setting, arr. from Night Music (TBP) (Forsyth, 1989, in Selected
  Songs)
The Lion (TBP) (Augener, 1940)
The Little Sorrow (Mary Webb)*†
  Broadcast 24 Feb 1936; Peter Howard, Michael Mullinar
  MS lost or destroyed
Lonely Spring (TBP) (Curwen)
The Miller of Dee (words and tune adapted from 18th-century song)
  MS at RNCM (with pencilled recorder part added)
Naiad (Dennis Jones) (Forsyth, 1989, in Selected Songs)
The New Hat (TBP)
  MS at RNCM
Nonsense Song: Spick and Span (TBP), composed 1995
  MS at RNCM (together with rough sketch score)
O Say Not (Charles Wolfe)*†
Pain
  Broadcast 24 Feb 1936; Peter Howard, Michael Mullinar
  MS lost or destroyed
The Policeman (TBP) (Cramer, 1934)
Polish Drinking Song (tr. and arr. by TBP)
  MS at RNCM
Prayer to thee Father of Heaven (John Skelton)*
Rue (With rue my heart is laden) (A.E. Housman), composed 1992
St Melangell and the Hare (TBP), for female narrator and piano (Mostyn Music)
  See also SOLO AND ORCHESTRA
The Sands of Dee (Charles Kingsley) (Forsyth, 1989, in Selected Songs)
  FP 3 Dec 1953, Crewe; Margaret Hyde, Nina Walker
  MS at RNCM
Sea Dirge
  FP 23 March 1926, RMCM Students' Open Practice
  MS lost or destroyed
Separation
  Broadcast 24 Feb 1936; Peter Howard, Michael Mullinar
  MS lost or destroyed
September Lovers (TBP) (Cramer, 1947; Forsyth, 1989, in Selected Songs)
  Ded. 'To Henry Cummings'
Shadow March (Robert Louis Stevenson) (Forsyth, 1989, in Selected Songs)
Shepherd Boy's Song (John Bunyan)
  Perf. 7 July 1933, Sandon Studios, Liverpool
  MS lost or destroyed
A Shropshire Lass, for mezzo-soprano and piano: see SOLO AND ORCHESTRA
  MS at RNCM (includes 2 MSS of the piano introduction)
The Silver Crown (Scottish song arr. and adapted by TBP)

MS at RNCM
Six Short Rhythm Studies for Singers [Three Letters (Phoebe Hesketh); Partnership (TBP);
Tell me where is Fancy Bred (Shakespeare); Autumn Swallows (TBP); Simple Simon
(trad. and TBP); Green, Brown and White (TBP)] (Hinrichsen, 1967)
Ded. respectively 'To Dora Gilson', 'To Elsie Thurston', 'To Maimie Woods', 'To
Winifred Busfield', 'To Hélène Pax', 'To Gwilym Jones'
Autumn Swallows also published by composer in booklet 'In Autumn'
Skeleton Bride (Phoebe Hesketh), for speaker and piano
FP 2 June 1961, RMCM; Sheila Barlow, John McCabe
MS at RNCM
Used for 'Sinister Dance' in Minors for piano duet
So Far from my Country (arr. TBP) (Forsyth, 1989, in Selected Songs)
Song of Compassion (TBP) (Forsyth, 1989, in Selected Songs)
See also UNISON VOICES WITH PIANO (Two Songs)
Sparrow (TBP) (subtitle: '(3) Scherzino (vocal sonatina)')
MS at RNCM
Storm Clouds (TBP)
Broadcast 24 Feb 1936; Peter Howard, Michael Mullinar
MS lost or destroyed
Swallow (TBP)
MS at RNCM
Three Nursery Songs [I Had a Little Nut Tree; Baa, Baa, Black Sheep; Hilda Had a
Garden]
Perf. 21 Nov 1931, Bolton Musical Artists' Association
Three Score Years and Thirty, composed 1993 (TBP)
Tibbie Fowler (TBP)
To Evening (TBP)*†
Two French Songs {Passing through Lorraine; In the Moonlight]
Perf. 21 Nov 1931, Bolton Musical Artists' Association
MS lost or destroyed
The Unfulfilled (Pushkin, tr. Alice Pitfield, English verse by TBP) (Forsyth, 1989, in
Selected Songs)
Vesper (TBP)*†
The Wagon of Life (Pushkin, tr. Alice Pitfield, English verse by TBP) (Cramer, 1944;
Forsyth, 1989, in Selected Songs)
Ded. 'To Alice, with love' (in Forsyth edition)
Walking at Night (Edward Shanks)*†
Willow Song (Shakespeare) (Francis, Day & Hunter, 1950; Forsyth, 1989, in Selected
Songs)
Ded. 'To Christine Grey'
Winter (Walter de la Mare)
Perf. 7 July 1933, Sandon Studios, Liverpool; Dorothy Reid, Norman Suckling
MS lost or destroyed
Winter Dusk (TBP) (Augener, Brunton, 1984, in Recollections)
MS: RNCM has MS dated Jan 1992 of 'Winter Dusk (II)' 'written on the skeleton of
Winter Dusk (I) publ by Augener 193–'
Winter Evening: Dunham Park (Forsyth, 1981)

Ded. 'To Honor Sheppard and Robert Elliott'. FP 30 April 1983, Eddisbury Hall, Macclesfield; Honor Sheppard, Stephen Reynolds
MS at RNCM
Winter Song (Katherine Mansfield), rev. 1978 (Five Line Publishing, 1987, in Première Issue no. 3; Forsyth, 1989, in Selected Songs)
See also SOLO VOICE WITH INSTRUMENTS
You Frail Sad Leaves (TBP) (Forsyth, 1989, in Selected Songs; and composer, in booklet 'In Autumn')

UNISON VOICES WITH PIANO
Adeste fideles. Descant to the carol (last verse)
MS at RNCM (working MS)
Autumn Evening Song (TBP) (published by composer, in booklet 'In Autumn')
Birdsong in the Morning (TBP) (Bardic, nd)
A Ceremonial Song (Epilogue from the Cantata 'House of Song') (TBP), for unison voices with 2 pianos (piano I optional) (Joseph Williams, 1944)
Cameo Carol (TBP), for voices and piano/organ
Ded. 'For Bolton School, Girls' Division'
Carol-Lullaby (Oecumuse, 1979)
The Christ Child (TBP), for unison voices with piano/organ (Augener, 1952)
Come All You Christian Gentlemen (Herefordshire Carol) (coll. Michael Mullinar) (Elkin, 1950)
The Country Road (Muriel Hilton) (Banks, 1947)
Festival Hymn (TBP) (Augener, 1954). Tune 'Wilmslow' (first published in programme for Wilmslow Christian Arts Festival, 1–18 May 1952)
Good Night Song (James Pass and Co.)
Hills of my Country (TBP) (Augener, 1938)
The Hobby-Horse (tr. TBP) (Curwen, 1956)
Ded. 'For the Dorothy Mellor Junior Choir'
Homeland Treasures (TBP) (Leonard, Gould and Bolttler, 1945)
In Excelsis Gloria, unison/3-part carol with piano, composed 1936 (Augener)
In Tuneful Union (TBP), unison song with optional descant (Leonard, Gould and Bolttler, 1952)
Ded. 'For The County Grammar School for Girls, Macclesfield'
I've Got a Penny (TBP) (OUP, 1963)
John Mouldy (de la Mare) (OUP, 1937)
Kalinka (tr. Alice Pitfield and TBP), unison voices with optional 2nd voice part and optional percussion (OUP, 1964)
Memorials (TBP) (Year Book Press, 1947)
Monstrous Monsters: Eight Unison Songs [The Puddlypaddler; The Spodliwonk; The Flitzibat; The Duophonion; The Scrumph; The Chodliwog; The Rotagilla; The Bellsicat]
MS at RNCM
New-Old Carol (TBP) (Cramer, 1939)
Parkdale Song (VS Song), composed 1991. Versions for voice and piano, voice and guitar, and 4-part chorus
MS at RNCM

Patriot's Hymn of Peace (TBP) (composer, nd, but 1937 or 1938 according to his recollection)
Patriot's Song of Peace (TBP), unison song with ad lib. descant (Curwen, 1945). Version of preceding item
Prince of Peace, carol for unison voices and piano, composed 1936
    MS at RNCM (hand-lettered booklet including the music and text)
The Robbers' Song and The Woodcutters' Song (from 'The Barnyard Singers') (Roberta Foster) (Hinrichsen, 1955)
The Runaway Snowman (Year Book Press)
So Far from my Country (arr. TBP), unison/solo song (OUP, 1957)
    Ded. 'To William Coombes'
Song of Concord (TBP) (Cramer, 1948). Alternative SATB version for second verse
    Ded. 'For Bamber Bridge Training College' (the dedication is pasted over in the MS, and does not appear in the published song)
    MS at RNCM (decorated and lettered copy)
Song of Sleep (TBP), for altos with trebles (hummed) ad lib. (Curwen, 1949)
The Song of the Christmas Waits (Herbert Palmer) (Augener, 1934)
Song of Unity (TBP) (Gwynn, 1954)
The Steam Roller (TBP), composed 1938
Three Cheshire Folksongs [The Spanish Lady; The Plains of Waterloo; William and Mary] (Curwen, 1954)
Three Nonsense Songs (TBP) [Miss Cod; Lilly Lipton; Cluck, Cluck] (Curwen, 1937)
Three Old French Songs (tr. TBP) [Near to my Fair One; Through Lorraine as I Went Walking; Hans, Hans de Schnöckelock] (Elkin, 1948; published individually)
Three Russian Folksongs (English verse by TBP tr. Alice Pitfield) [The Silver Birch; The Pedlar; Sleep my Child] (OUP, 1943)
    Also version with string orchestra
Two Little Songs (TBP) [Hilda Had a Garden; Marketing] (OUP, 1934)
    See also SOLO VOICE WITH PIANO (Four Little Songs)
Two Metrical Psalms [Psalm 23; Psalm 127] (paraphrase by Addison), unison voices and piano/organ (Hinrichsen, 1958)
Two Noels (arr. TBP) [Sing we all; Go forth] (OUP, 1962)
    Ded. 'To Allan Wicks'
Two Russian Children's Songs (English tr. by Alice Pitfield, arr. and English verse by TBP) [The Billy-Goat; Little Wood-Creatures] (OUP, 1942)
    Also version with string orchestra
Two Songs (TBP) [Morning and Evening; Winter Night] (Novello, 1964)
    Ded. 'For Bowdon Preparatory School'
    See SOLO VOICE WITH PIANO for separate solo publication of no. 2 as Song of Compassion
The Steamroller (TBP) (Cramer, 1938)

SOLO VOICE WITH INSTRUMENTS
Birds about the Morning Air, for soprano, descant recorder and piano
    See also SOLO VOICE WITH PIANO
Bones (de la Mare) for speaker and xylophone
    FP 2 June 1961, RMCM; Sheila Barlow, TBP

MS at RNCM
By the Dee, song cycle for medium voice/countertenor, strings/string quartet and piano
[The Sands of Dee; By the Dee at Night; The Miller of Dee; From Upland Springs]
The Carrion Crow, for soprano, flute/violin and piano
   MS at RNCM (violin part)
   See also SOLO VOICE WITH PIANO
Desdemona's Song (Shakespeare), for soprano and guitar (Forsyth, 1989, in Selected
   Songs)
   See also SOLO VOICE WITH PIANO
Donkey Riding, folk song for ensemble, for voice, 2-part instruments and piano
Doubles, for soprano, countertenor, recorder, xylophone, timpani and piano, composed
   1983
   Ded. 'To Alice for performance on her 82nd birthday, January 6th 1984'
   MS at RNCM (score and vocal part)
Faithful Johnny, for voice and guitar
   MS at RNCM
Faithful Johnny, for voice, recorder/violin and piano
   MS at RNCM (solo recorder and violin parts)
Folksong Suite, for medium voice, flute and piano [Faithful Johnny; So Far from my
   Country; The Billy Goat; I Live not where I Love; Carrion Crow]
   MS at RNCM (The Billy Goat, incorporating part of published voice and piano
   version)
The Forelock, for voice, violin/viola/recorder and piano
   MS at RNCM (violin and viola parts in D minor, with score in another hand in C
   minor for countertenor, recorder and piano)
Five Russian Folk Songs (tr. Alice Pitfield and TBP), for voice and guitar (optional 2nd
   guitar part) [The Bold Pedlar; The Forelock; The White Whirlwind; Sleep my Child;
   The Billy Goat] (OUP, 1959)
Four Russian Folksongs (TBP), for soprano, violin and piano [The Billy Goat; The
   Forelock; Cossack Cradle Song; Kalinka]
   MS at RNCM (score of Cossack Cradle song and violin part of The Billy Goat, almost
   identical with flute part: see above, Folksong Suite)
Happy Birthday, arr. with acc. for harp/clarsach by TBP
Hellelujah (TBP), for unison voices and guitar
   MS at RNCM (2 copies)
The Hobby Horse; Up the Lofty Mountain (Tyrolean Song), for voice and guitar
   MS at RNCM
John Gilpin's Ride, for (?) speaker, flute, guitar and percussion (?incomplete)
   MS at RNCM (incomplete working MS)
Kalinka, for soprano, flute and piano
   MS at RNCM
Lingering Music, for voice and guitar
   MS at RNCM (in another hand, possibly Alice Pitfield's)
   This is a different setting from the two published settings for voice and piano
Little Triptych (de la Mare): Three Miniatures for mezzo-soprano, viola and harpsichord/
   piano [The Horseman; Alone; A Fiddler]
   Ded. 'For the Primavera Trio'

MS at RNCM
See also below, Three Miniatures
The Miller of Dee, for voice, recorder and piano: see SOLO VOICE WITH PIANO
The Nightingale (TBP), for medium voice, violin and piano
    MS at RNCM (score and violin part)
Parkdale Song, for voice and guitar: see UNISON VOICES WITH PIANO
Porton Down, song for voice and guitar, written after seeing BBC feature on chemical
    and biological warfare
    MS at RNCM
Rain (de la Mare), for speaker, piano, and xylophone
    FP 2 June 1961, RMCM; Sheila Barlow, John McCabe, TBP
    MS at RNCM (marked in pencil 'Temporary copy only')
Rocking Song (Careful Hands), Nigerian song arr. TBP, for voice and Celtic harp
    MS at RNCM
Round: Apples and Carrots, for 4-part voices, with optional 2-part ostinato, piano and
    percussion
[Scottish Folksongs], for voice and clarsach (clarsach specified as accompaniment only
    in no. 5) [nos. 1 and 2 lost; 3 Coming Through the Rye; 4 Leezie Lindsay; 5
    Tullochgorum Reel]
    MS at RNCM (nos. 3. 4, and 5 only, with a further MS of no. 5 with clarsach or harp)
Serenade (TBP), for voice and guitar
    MS at RNCM (in another hand, probably Alice Pitfield's, with faint annotations by
    TBP)
The Short-Tempered Singer (TBP), soprano and descant recorder/piccolo (Forsyth, 1983,
    in A Birthday Album for Thomas Pitfield)
    FP 30 April 1983, Eddisbury Hall, Macclesfield; Honor Sheppard, John Turner
The Singer (from 'A Sketchbook of Men'), for voice, violin and piano
    MS at RNCM (solo violin part only)
So Far from my Country, for soprano, flute and piano
    MS at RNCM (MS flute part pasted over published voice and piano version)
Soulcaking Song, for soprano (with percussion), recorder/flute, cello/bassoon and
    harpsichord/piano
Sweet Suffolk Owl (Vautor), for soprano, tenor recorder/violin/viola/clarinet and piano
    (Lengnick, 1985)
    Ded. 'In memory of William Alwyn'
Three Drolleries (TBP) [Bats in the Belfry; The New Hat; Mary Jane], for soprano,
    clarinet and piano
    MS at RNCM (score and clarinet part)
    Also version for soprano, recorder and harpsichord
Three Miniatures (de la Mare) [The Horseman; Alone; The Fiddler], for soprano and
    violin (Forsyth, 1989, in Selected Songs)
    Ded. 'To Honor Sheppard'
    See also above, Little Triptych
Three Night Creatures [The Bat; The Owl; The Rat], for countertenor, cello and harpsi
    chord/piano
    FP 11 Nov 1969, Manchester City Art Gallery; Owen Wynne, Rosalind Gonley, Alan
    Cuckston

MS at RNCM
Threnody for Tracey Chadwell, for soprano, recorder/flute and piano, composed 1996
MS at RNCM (includes material from Birds about the Morning Air: see above)
Tibby Fowler, Scottish folk song arr. and words adapted by TBP, for voice, violin and piano
MS at RNCM (score and solo violin part)
Two by Two (trad.), canon for 2 voices and any instrument
MS at RNCM
Two Songs of Exile [So Far from my Country; no. 2 lost], for voice, guitar and keyboard
MS at RNCM (no. 1 only)
Vandal's Song (TBP), for voice and guitar
MS at RNCM
The Willow (TBP), for medium voice, treble recorder/flute/clarinet and piano/ harpsichord (Forsyth, 1989, in Selected Songs)
Ded. 'To Owen and Dorothy Wynne'
Winter Song (Katherine Mansfield), for voice, sopranino recorder/flute/oboe and piano (Forsyth, 1989, in Selected Songs)
MS at RNCM (recorder part only)

CHORUS A CAPPELLA
A Benediction, SATB
MS at RNCM
Antiphon to the Holy Spirit (Agnes M.F. Duclaux): Choric Hymn for SSAATTBB (Nov 1965).
MS at RNCM
This the first version, in A flat; for later version in A see ACCOMPANIED CHORUS (Prelude and Choric Hymn)
The Bold Pedlar (words tr. Alice Pitfield, arr. and English verse by TBP), SATB (OUP, 1947)
Candle Vesper, SATB (Augener, 1960)
The Carrion Crow (trad.), SATB (Cramer, 1952)
Ded. 'To the Wilmslow Guild Choral Group'
Cheshire May Day Song (trad.), SATB (OUP, 1954)
Child and Beast, SATB (Bardic, nd)
The Combat (TBP), SATB (Schofield & Sims, 1946, in The Wayfarer's Part Song Book, ed. John Horton)
Come all you Christian gentlemen (arr. TBP), SSA (Elkin, 1959)
Ded: 'To May Walley and the Bedford Girls Singers'
Divertissements (TBP) [La Cloche du village; Madame la Lune; L'Aiguille; Invitation au sommeil; Le Retour du printemps; Le Moulin à vent], SSA (Hinrichsen, 1953)
Elegy for a Little Boy
FP 29 Jan 1955, Bolton Musical Artists' Association, Central Library, Bolton, in a concert of vocal and instrumental works by TBP; Dormel Singers, Dorothy Mellor
MS possibly destroyed. In a printed list of works for women's voices, it is deleted by TBP, and marked in red 'REMOVE'. No copies known to survive.
Four Choral Miniatures (TBP) [The Singer; Wordless Song (tune heard in dream 22 June 1993); The Spider; Rain, Rain, Go Away], SATB and (nos. 1 and 4 only) piano (Bardic, nd)

Ded. 'to Altrincham Choral Society'
MS at RNCM
The Grasshopper and the Ant, SSA
MS at RNCM
The Haunted Wood (TBP), TTBB (OUP, 1938)
Here Lived a Quiet Lady, SSA (Ascherberg, 1957)
Ded. 'To The Grove Singers'
Hymn of Penitence (TBP), SATB (Oecumuse, 1989)
Previously part of A Short Community Service
Hymn of Trust (TBP), SATB (Oecumuse, 1989)
Previously part of A Short Community Service
The Idle Mill (TBP), TBB (Stainer and Bell, 1938)
In an Old Country Church (TBP), TTBB (Augener, 1952)
Ded. 'To Gordon Thorne'
Lament (Wordsworth), TTBB (Augener, 1931)
The Lord's Prayer, SATB choir and congregation (Oecumuse, 1989)
Marriage Song (Shakespeare), SSA/TBB/SSATBB (Curwen, 1963)
Ded. 'to Tony and Anna'
MS at RNCM
Meg Merrilies (Keats), SATB (Cramer, 1941)
New Year's Carol (Staffordshire), tune from H.W. Sinall (?), words adapted and music
arr. TBP, SATB
MS at RNCM
Night Music (TBP) [Horseman Night; Lingering Music; Midnight Wind; Inverse
Serenade; Sleep], choral suite for 4, 5 and 6-part voices (Augener, 1947; Bardic 1993)
Ded. 'For the Blackfriars Singers'. FP 27 June 1941, Wigmore Hall, London;
Blackfriars Singers, J.A. Coombs
For a solo version of Lingering Music see SOLO VOICE WITH INSTRUMENTS
The Night Watch (arr. TBP), part-song for mixed voices (Pass, 1957)
The Owl (TBP), SATB (Augener, 1937)
Parkdale Song, for 4-part chorus: see UNISON VOICES WITH PIANO
Pax Musica (TBP), double choir a cappella (Augener, 1953; Bardic, nd)
Ded. 'To Willis Grant and the Birmingham Bach Society Choir'
The Pilgrim (Threnody) (TBP), SSATBB (Curwen, 1963; Bardic, 1993)
Ded. 'For the Northern Consort's 10th Anniversary'
Rain Rain (TBP), composed Nov 1977, SSA/TTB/SSATBB
Commissioned by BBC Radio Manchester
Requiem-Nocturne (Emily Brontë), SMezA (Elkin, 1938)
Round for Peace (TBP), 4-part round (Berea College Press, Berea, KY, 1974, in 'Come
Let us Sing')
Sanctus Dominus (Revelation 4: 8), 6-part mixed voices
Ded. 'For Wallis Grant & the University of Bristol XXXII Choir'
MS at RNCM (2 MSS: one, marked '(3)', includes an optional organ part; this may be
one of the Motets and Choric Hymns: see ACCOMPANIED CHORUS)
Storm Clouds (TBP), SATB (Stainer and Bell, 1938)
Tramping Song (TBP), TTBB (Elkin, 1955; Braydeston, 1978)
Ded. 'To Herbert Spencer and the Nelson Excelsior Glee Union'

Two Angel Songs (TBP) [Angels' Song; Lullaby], SSA (Cramer, nd)
Two Short Litanies (Ruth Pitter) [For Evening (Little Vesper); Cure me with Quietness,
    Bless me with Peace] (Pitman Hart)
    Ded. 'To Ronald Frost and the Longford Singers'
Two Single Chants, SATB
    MS at RNCM
Twogethers: 'Universal' duets for instrumentalists or singers on folk and traditional tunes
    MS at RNCM (also a photocopy with optional bass parts and some MS parts)
A Young Virgin; Joyous Nightingale; Neighbour and Shepherd (no collective title), SSA
    MS at RNCM

ACCOMPANIED CHORUS
Anthem for an Arts Festival, SATB and organ
    MS at RNCM (two copies)
Ballad of a Minstrel, 2-part voices and piano (Banks, 1939)
The Carrion Crow, SSA and piano (Cramer, 1954)
Chanticleer, for chorus and instruments [Chorale and Scherzo; Canzone; Coxtrot and
    Fughetta]
    Ded. 'for Freddie Cox July 15th 1970'. FP 15 July 1970, RMCM; Maryrose
    Moorhouse, Katherine Gerrard, Leonard Williams, Patrick McGuigan, Walter Jorysz,
    Paulene Smith, Frederick Riddle, Paul Ward, Wilf Collinge, Clifton Helliwell, Kathleen
    McGrath, Leonard Foster, Sidney Coulston, TBP, Colin Price, Stephen Pilkington,
    John Wray
Cheshire May Day Song (words trad., music arr. TBP), SSA and piano (OUP, 1953)
Cheshire Soul-Caking Song (music arr. and words adapted by TBP), 2-part voices and
    piano (OUP, 1971)
Cheshire Souling Song, SSA (and S solo) and piano (Cramer, 1963)
    Ded. 'To Doris Parkinson and the choir of Wirral County Grammar School for Girls'
Chorestra: A Suite of eight dances for choir, piano duet, percussion and guitar [Summer
    Dance; Jaunty Dance; Lazy Afternoon Dance; Reel on the Keel Row; Dream Dance;
    Derbyshire Fandango; Winter Dance; Cheshire Morris Dance]
    Ded: 'For the boys of Chetham's Hospital School, Manchester. Conductor: Gerald
    Littlewood'
    MS at RNCM (sketch score only)
The Christ Child (TBP), SATB and piano/organ (Augener, 1953)
    Ded. 'For Robert Keys'
Christmas is Come (John Clare, ed. TBP), SA, piano and optional percussion (Bayley
    and Ferguson, 1967)
The Citizens of Chartres, carol for SATB, piano/organ, percussion and optional wind
    MS at RNCM
The Combat (TBP), 2-part voices and piano (OUP, 1954)
Deo Gratias: A Short Festival Cantata, for SATB choir, unison voices and organ [Refuge
    (Phoebe Hesketh); Festival Hymn (TBP); Praise (adapted TBP); Thanksgiving
    (Winkworth)] (Augener, 1960)
    Ded. 'For Bowdon Church Centenary'
The Divine Image (Blake), anthem for unison voices and organ (Oecumuse, 1989);
    previously part of A Short Community Service

Dunham Massey (TBP), round for 3 voices/instruments with piano/2 guitars
MS at RNCM

Eleven Minutes, for voices, percussion and other instruments [Old Jim John; King Nebshazerod; Clippetty Clop; Lonely Moon; Young Kitty Clark; A Queer Animal; A B at C; Rain at Night; Sleigh Ride; Mingled Jingles; Rain rain go away] (Chappell, 1963)
Ded. 'For John Gavall'

Evening Service for Men's Voices (Magnificat and Nunc Dimittis), TTBB (solo quartet/ choir) and organ (Hinrichsen, 1963; Oecumuse, 1989; Bardic, 1994)
Ded. 'For Manchester Cathedral'

Everyman's Prayer (TBP), SATB and organ/piano (Curwen, 1951); extracted from stage work 'Everyman'
Ded. 'To Denbigh and Muriel Hilton'

Festival Hymn (TBP), SA, men's voices and organ (Mayhew, 1994, in New Anthem Book, vol. 2)
MS at RNCM

A Flourish of Carols, for mixed choir, audience, children's choir and brass band [Unto Us a Boy is Born; Come All You Christian Gentlemen [see also UNISON VOICES WITH PIANO]; Three Kings of Orient; The Little Room; Catalan Carol; Silent Night; The Journey to Bethlehem; Ballad of the Little Jesus; Interlude; The Holly and the Ivy; Candles; Bell-Vesper; The Christ-Child; God Rest you Merry Gentlemen]
FP 20 Dec 1975, Victoria Hall, Bolton; Bolton Choral Union, Church Road Primary School Choir, Wingates Temperance Band, Michael Greenhalgh
Commissioned by the Bolton Choral Union

A Flourish of Carols: Five Carols for women's voices and piano accompaniment, arr. TBP [The Little Room; Catalan Carol; Ballad of the Little Jesus; Candles; Bell Vesper] (Piper, 1985)

Funfare, unison songs with instrumental obligato [The Euphonium; The Violin; The Clarinet; The Piano; The Trombone; The Xylophone; The Double-Bass; The Flute; The Guitar; The Trumpet]
MS at RNCM (photocopy only)

Fur and Feather: A Sequence of Tunes for equal treble voices, one piano four hands, and optional percussion (TBP) [The Fox; Ducks; The Hedgehog; The Seagull; Kitten in the Well; The Tortoise; Brown Hen; Creatures of the Night; The Stag; Ponies; Rabbits; The Camel; The Squirrel; The Highland Cow; Piglets (Polka)]
FP June 1970, Cransley School
MS at RNCM

Grieg Choral Suite (TBP), for mixed voices and piano [Watchman's Song; Cowkeeper's Song; Dirge: The Death of Ase; Solvejg's Song; Dusk in Autumn; Norwegian Melody] (Hinrichsen, 1958)

The Hills: Choral Variations on the 121st Psalm, for mixed voices with optional boys' voices and organ (or full orchestra with optional organ), composed 1960 (Hinrichsen, 1961)
Ded. 'In celebration of Macclesfield's 700th anniversary of the granting of a Borough Charter'. FP 12 Oct 1961, King's School, Macclesfield; Paul Ward
MS at RNCM

Homage to the Year's Beauty, for chorus and orchestra, composed 1937

MS lost or destroyed

House of Song: A Short Cantata for 2-part trebles, tenors and basses (ad lib.), 2 pianos, and percussion band (ad lib.) [Prologue; House of Dream (de la Mare); The House that Jack Built; By the House; Epilogue (published separately as 'A Ceremonial Song')] (Joseph Williams, 1944)

FP 17 June 1944, Tettenhall College; TBP

Hymn of Compassion, SATB and organ
MS at RNCM

I Live not where I Love (arr. TBP), SA and piano (Cramer, 1964)

If God build not the house (Phineas Fletcher), SSA and piano (or full/string orchestra with organ) (or 2 pianos) (Hinrichsen, 1957)
Ded. 'for Bolton School – Girls' Division'

Kalinka (tr. Alice Pitfield and TBP), TTBB and piano (OUP, 1969)
Ded. 'For Colin Jones and the Rhos Male Voice Choir'

Lazy Liza (Florence Harrison), 2-part voices and piano (Elkin, 1938)

The Lincolnshire Poacher (trad.), 2-part song with piano (Ascherberg, 1963)
Ded. 'To Mary Balders and the Grimsby Junior Philharmonic Choir'

The Little Watch (TBP), 4-part sopranos and piano (OUP, 1954)

The Lonesome Monster: A Cantata for Children, for unison voices, piano, recorders, violin and percussion
MS at RNCM

Marching Song (Robert Louis Stevenson), 2-part song with piano (Curwen, 1938)

Miniatures (TBP), for voices in 2 parts with piano and optional percussion [The Village Bell; The Needle; The Windmill] (Hinrichsen, 1963); arr. from Divertissements
Ded. 'For the Westmorland Schools Music Making'

Motets and Choric Hymns, for double choir and organ [1 Pax Musica (see below); 2 For an Arts Festival (TBP) (SATB and organ); (no. 3 missing); 4 Praise (Mary Webb) (SATB and Organ); 5 Meditation (organ solo) 6 The Word (Phoebe Hesketh); 7 Antiphon (Agnes Ducleaux)]
MS at RNCM (nos. 1 and 2, plus photocopy of no. 4 and part of Sanctus Dominus [possibly no. 3; see CHORUS A CAPPELLA])

My Grandma's Goat: Russian Nursery Song, for 3-part female voices and piano (Banks, 1953)

Now Thank we all our God, for unison voices, SSA choir (with optional violins) and organ/piano (Augener, 1957)
Ded. 'For Levenshulme High School for Girls'

Oh, Daughter Get Married (adapted TBP), 2-part voices and piano (Ascherberg, 1955)

On This Day (tr. TBP), SATB, audience and orchestra/organ/piano (Sam Fox, 1968)

Pax Musica (TBP), double SATB choir and organ (Bardic, 1993)

Pilgrim Song (John Bunyan), SATB and piano/organ (Augener, 1951)
Ded. 'For St. Paul's Church Choir, Macclesfield'

Planibestiary: A Zoological Sequence in Space* (TBP), for speakers, soloists, SAB choir, flute, oboe, bassoon, piano and percussion [Introduction; The Marsihog; The Cosmicock; The Venusian Lizard; The Minimeteormite; Link 1; The Mercurian Sphinx; The Lunarape; Link 2; The Uranian Winicorn] (Lengnick, 1972)
FP 8 Dec 1966, RMCM

Prayers from the Ark (tr. Godden), for 6 singers/SATB choir, speakers, organ and percussion

MS at RNCM

Prelude and Choric Hymn, SSAATTBB [Prelude: The Word (Phoebe Hesketh); Choric Hymn (Agnes M.F. Duclaux)]; a later version of Antiphon to the Holy Spirit: see CHORUS A CAPPELLA

Ded. 'For Cyril Dawes, and the Northwich district Festival Choir'

Rant (Founded on the Cheshire 'Souling Song'), SATB, piano and percussion (ad lib.) (Cramer, 1939); version for 4-part voices (male/female), piano and optional percussion (ed. Martin Shaw) (Cramer, 1952)

FP 27 May 1940, Wigmore Hall, London; Fleet Street Choir, T.B. Lawrence

Rhymes and Rhythms (TBP), pieces for youth choir, piano, percussion and various optional instruments [Abergavenny; Apples and Carrots; Jack's House; The Headless Woman; Melody Heard in a Dream; Modern City] (Hinrichsen, 1970)

The Rhyming Shopman (TBP): A Whimsical Cantata for chorus, baritone solo and orchestra (or strings and piano) [Introduction; Greeting; To his Love; Wedding Song; Lullaby; Dream; Customers' Chorus; Litany; Round; Epitaph], composed 1940 (Joseph Williams, 1944)

Ded. 'Inscribed to Hubert J. Foss'. FP 9 Nov 1942; BBC Chorus, Henry Cummings, BBC Orchestra, Clarence Raybould

MS at RNCM (MS vocal score: Trafford Libraries)

Rocking Song: Yoruba (Nigerian) melody from Josef Olubokau, arr. and English verse by TBP, SA and piano

MS at RNCM

School Songs, treble voices and guitar(s) with optional piano [The Bells of York (TBP); My Wife's Dead (Anon.); Faithful Johnny (adapted TBP); The Robber's Song (Roberta Foster) (from The Barnyard Singers); Little Nocturne (TBP); Up the Lofty Mountain (TBP)] (Mills, 1957)

A Sexton's Dozen: Twelve Epitaphs for bass voice, strings, piano and percussion (TBP) [Introduction; For Luke Warm; For Anne Tiquity; For Mark Time; For Will Nott & May Nott; For Percy Vere; For Jim Nastic; For Molly Coddle; For Polly Syllable; For Dan Druff; For the Rev. Eddie Fye; Epitaph for Anne Dante; Epitaph for Sam O'Var (marked in full score 'cancelled and superseded by Peter Out')], composed 1963

Ded. 'To Owen Brannigan' (not in published version)

There is a later version, composed 1968, for chorus, piano duet and percussion: Introduction; Anne Tiquity; Mark Time; Percy Vere; Jim Nastic; Molly Coddle; Dan Druff; Polly Syllable; Will Nott & May Nott; The Rev. Eddie Fye; Anne Dante; Peter Out (Galliard, 1970)

A Short Community Service, for choir, congregation and organ [Organ Prelude on 'Hymn of Trust'; Hymn of Trust; The Lord's Prayer; Anthem (The Divine Image – Blake); Hymn of Penitence; Organ Postlude on Hymn of Penitence] (Hinrichsen, 1964)

The Silver Birch (English verse by TBP tr. Alice Pitfield), Russian folk song arr. for mixed voice and piano/string orchestra (OUP, 1943)

A Sketchbook of Animals (TBP), cantata for 4- to 6- part mixed voices with piano and optional percussion, or strings, piano and percussion [The Aberdeen Terrier; The Calculating Cat; The Obsolete Horse; The Goldfish; The Chiffchaff; The Caged Lion; The Constant Cuckoo; The Hungry Hippopotamus; The Human Animal] (Hinrichsen, 1955)

A Sketchbook of Men (TBP), cantata for 3-part male voices with baritone solo, with piano and optional percussion, or strings, piano and percussion [Introduction; The Motor Mechanic; The Poet; The Policeman; The Composer; The Singer; The Old Man; The Company Director; The Preacher; The Farmer's Lad; The Politician; Conclusion] (Hinrichsen, 1953)
    Ded. 'To Arnold Haskell'
    MS at Trafford Libraries
A Sketchbook of Women (TBP), cantata for 3-part female voices with soprano solo, string orchestra and piano (or piano alone) [Introduction; The Singer; The Gossips; The Old Woman; The Schoolmistress; The Mother; Instrumental Interlude; The Seamstress; The Witch; The Dancer; The Housewives; Conclusion], composed 1951 (Hinrichsen, 1953; The Seamstress published separately)
    Ded. 'To Dorothy Mellor and the Dormel Singers'. FP 20 June 1952, BBC Home Service; Dormel Singers, Dorothy Mellor, Maurice Aitchison, BBC Northern Orchestra, John Hopkins
    MS at RNCM, which also has cello obbligato part to no. 10 (Sarabande)
The Spirit of the Lord: Introit for SATB and organ
    Ded. 'for Robin Coulthard and Bowdon Parish Church Choir'
    MS at RNCM (photocopy only)
Suite: Everyman, for chorus and orchestra
    FP 6 May 1951, Wilmslow; Wilmslow Guild Choral Group, Wilmslow and District Orchestra, Clarice Dunnington
Three Festive French Carols, SSA, piano and percussion [Sing Noel; Born is He; The Citizens of Chartres]
    MS location unknown (MS percussion part for xylophone and glockenspiel at RNCM)
Three Nonsense Brevities, for 2-part choir and piano [Silly Lilly; The Starling; Flippetty Flop] (Boosey and Hawkes, 1955)
Threnodies, SATB, brass and organ [On the Death of Vaughan Williams; Homage to John Ireland; On the Death of Walter de la Mare], composed Oct–Nov 1978; 'Commissioned for John Ireland 100th anniversary by Bowdon Festival, 1979'
    FP 15 July 1979, Bowdon; John Ireland Singers, Northern Brass Ensemble, Martin Merry
    MS: RNCM has working score for no. 1 and parts for two trumpets, tenor trombone and bass trombone, with photocopy full score
Triptych [Meditation, organ solo; The Word (Phoebe Hesketh), SSAATTBB; Choric Hymn, for 8-part mixed chorus, organ, glockenspiel and tubular bells] (Bardic, 1992)
    MS of Choric Hymn at RNCM
Two Folk Carols, SSA and piano [Ballad of the Little Jesus; Spanish Carol] (OUP, 1953); Spanish Carol republished as Catalan Carol (Piper, 1984)
    Ded. 'To Anne Crick and the Crewe Central Townswomens' Guild Choir'
Two Seasonal Songs, for 2-part choir and piano [The Cuckoo; Winter Song (see also SOLO VOICE WITH PIANO and SOLO VOICE WITH INSTRUMENTS)] (OUP, 1953)
Two Short Songs (TBP), SSA and piano [The Staring Moon; City Children] (Boosey and Hawkes, 1955)
    Ded. 'To Reginald Redman'
Whims and Frolics (TBP): Choral Suite, for school or (optional) mixed youth choir ac
    companied by orchestra, or piano duet and percussion [Fast Waltz; The Ill-Matched

Partners; Evening Song; Choral Reel] (Hinrichsen, 1965)
Ded. 'To Louise Lamigeon'
Why, neighbour, are you so uneasy? Dialogue between the Humble and the Worldly Shepherdesses (tr. TBP), for 2-part voices and piano (Novello, 1963)

COVERS FOR MUSIC BY OTHER COMPOSERS
This list is not complete. In later years TBP destroyed many of his file copies of the covers, and very few survived in his own collection.

William Alwyn: Naiades – Fantasy-Sonata, flute and harp (Lengnick)
Marion Anderson: Trail Ends, piano (Leonard, Gould and Bolttler)
Ernest Austin: Meadowland and Mountain, piano (Elkin)
Ernest Austin: Moods and Melodies, piano (Elkin)
J.S. Bach: Toccata and Fugue in D minor, arr. for two pianos by York Bowen (Elkin)
Cecil Baumer: Five Impressions, piano (Elkin)
Benjamin Britten: Simple Symphony (OUP)
John Brydson: Noah's Ark, piano (Lengnick)
F. Percival Driver: Tang o' the Heather, piano (Elkin)
Henry Duke: My Day Out, piano (Lengnick)
F.T. Durrant: A-Hiking we will go, piano (Augener)
Festival Series of Piano Duets (Curwen)
Eric Fogg: Ode to a Nightingale, baritone solo, string quartet, harp (Elkin)
John Väinö Forsman: Songs of Innocence, piano (Augener)
Robert Groves: Twelve Hymn-Tune Preludes, organ (Elkin)
H. Heale: Eight Christmas Carols (Augener)
Barbara Kirkby-Mason: Surf-Riding, piano (Curwen)
Richard Krentzlin: From my Album, piano (Lengnick)
Richard Krentzlin: Pictures from Childhood, piano (Lengnick)
Edward Macdowell: To a Wild Rose, piano (Elkin)
Eric Mareo: Stories without Words, piano (Augener)
E. Markham Lee: Little Pictures, piano (Elkin)
Mischa-Leon: Fairy Songs (Augener)
Walter Niemann: Christmas Bells: Seven Short Variations on an Old-English Tune (1795) (Peters)
Eva Pain: Five Finger Flights, piano (Lengnick)
Alfred Reynolds: Five Centuries of Love, song cycle (Elkin)
Charles Ross: Going Forward, piano (Elkin)
Charles Ross: Right Foot Forward: A First Book on Pedalling for Adult Students (Elkin)
Eric Smith: Three Studies in Contrast, piano (Elkin)
Felix Swinstead: Pot Luck, piano (Elkin); original artwork at RNCM
The Two Piano Series, ed. Ethel Bartlett and Rae Robertson (OUP)

PUBLISHED BOOKS
Art Teaching (Evans Bros, nd)
The Poetry of Trees (London, nd [1944])
Words Without Songs, with Introduction by Walter de la Mare (Altrincham: Sherratt and Co., 1951)

Limusicks (Limericks, Linocuts and Lettering) (London, nd); rearr. and republished as Limusics: 40 Limericks (Studio Music Company, 1985)

'The Sneyd Collection of Music', *Transactions of the Ancient Monuments Society*, ns, vol. 4 (1956); lecture delivered at University College of North Staffordshire, 23 Nov 1955

The Clarendon Folk Song Books, vols. 1 and 2 (London: OUP, 1953); includes many text translations by TBP

Musicianship for Guitarists (London: Mills, 1959)

The Orchestra, by Mervyn Bruxner, illustrated by TBP (London: OUP, 1960)

Musicianly Scale Practice (London: Boosey and Hawkes, 1962)

No Song, No Supper: An Autobiography (London: Thames, 1986)

Recording a Region: Notes & Pen & Wash Drawings (Trafford MBC, 1987)

My Words (50 poems) (London: Thames, 1987)

A Song after Supper: Volume 2 of an Autobiography (London: Thames, 1990)

A Cotton Town Boyhood (Altrincham: Kallkwik, 1995) [originally issued by Bolton School Girls' Division]

Johnnyrobins: Rhymes and Nonsense Verse (Manchester: Royal Northern College of Music, 1995)

Honeymoon: Incidents from a Sixty Year Holiday Diary (Altrincham: Kallkwik, 1998)

PRIVATELY PRINTED BOOKLETS (undated)

A Sexton's Dozen: Epitaphs by Thomas Pitfield

Cheshire Verses both Grave and Gay: Script and Decorations by the author

Delicatesse (Vegetarian): Design & Calligraphy by Thomas Pitfield, Recipes by Alice Pitfield

In Autumn: Songs, Verse, M.S & Drawings by Thomas Pitfield

Current Discography

Goossens Family Collection Chandos CHAN7132

   Includes Rondo Lirico for oboe and piano (Leon Goossens and David Lloyd)

English Recorder Music Olympia OCD667

   Includes Recorder Concerto, for recorder, string orchestra and percussion, and Three Nautical Sketches for recorder and string orchestra (John Turner and the Royal Ballet Sinfonia, conducted by Gavin Sutherland)

Jonathan Scott; Bridgewater Hall Organ ASC Records ASC CS CD42

   Includes Short Sonata for organ

The Music of Thomas Pitfield Royal Northern College of Music RNCMTP3

   Includes Violin Sonata no. 1, Three Miniatures for soprano and violin, Rondo alla Tarantella for recorder and piano, Prelude Minuet and Reel for piano, Three Nautical Sketches for recorder and piano, Novelette in F for piano, Studies on an English Dance Tune for piano, Polka for oboe and piano, Oboe Sonata, Selected Songs: Winter Song, Birds about the Morning Air, The Sands of Dee, So Far from my Country, Naiad, Shadow March, Cuckoo and Chestnut Time, The Child Hears Rain at Night (Tracey Chadwell, John McCabe, Dennis Simons, Richard Simpson, Janet Simpson, Keith Swallow, John Turner)

Contemporary British Violin Music ASC Records ASC CS CD4

Includes Violin Sonata no. 2 (Andrew Long and Stewart Death)
Contemporary British Piano Music Volume 2 ASC Records ASC CS CD3
Includes Prelude Minuet and Reel for piano (John McCabe)
Manchester Accents ASC Records ASC CS CD45
Includes Theme and Variations for string orchestra (Northern Chamber Orchestra, directed by Nicholas Ward)
British Light Overtures I ASV CD WHL 2133
Includes Concert Overture (Royal Ballet Sinfonia conducted by Gavin Sutherland)
British Light Music Discoveries 5 Sanctuary Classics White Line CD WHL 2144
Includes Overture on North Country Tunes (Royal Ballet Sinfonia, conducted by Gavin Sutherland)
Piano Concertos nos. 1 and 2 Naxos, British Piano Concertos series, forthcoming
Also includes Arietta and Finale for piano, Studies on an English Dance Tune for piano, Toccata for piano, and Sonata for xylophone (Peter Donohoe, Anthony Goldstone, RNCM Symphony Orchestra, conducted by Andrew Penny)

The Manchester Tuesday Mid-Day Concerts Society, 1923–1972

ANTONY SLUCE

In 1923, a group of chamber music enthusiasts formed a society to continue the series of Tuesday Mid-Day Concerts which had been started during the First World War. Needing a new management structure for the series, they appointed Edward Isaacs[1] Director of Concerts, and he devised the format that has kept the concerts going for the last eighty years. This history finishes in 1972, at the point when it became clear that the society would have to change its name, as the concerts could no longer be held exclusively on Tuesdays; 1972 was also the year in which the second Director of Concerts, Laurance Turner,[2] retired. The present account, based on the archives held by the Manchester Mid-Day Concerts Society, is intended to give a flavour of the available information, which could become the basis of a more detailed study.[3]

In 1915, the Committee for Music in Wartime (Northern Section) started a series of lunchtime concerts in Manchester, the first being held on 9 November that year. The purpose was to raise money to provide musical entertainment in military hospitals. With no govern-

---

[1] Born on 14 July 1881, he attended Manchester Grammar School and Manchester University. From 1894 until 1903 he was a student at the RMCM, where he was the Hallé scholar in 1900. He continued his musical studies from 1903 to 1905 in Germany and Austria. In 1907 he returned to live in Manchester where he carved out a career as pianist, piano teacher, lecturer and composer. As a pianist he appeared as a soloist in the Proms, toured, broadcast and played in the Tuesday Mid-Day Concerts on a number of occasions. He was widely respected as a teacher, and established performers came to him for lessons when they were extending their repertoire. Some of his compositions had their first performances at Tuesday Mid-Day Concerts. His piano concerto was first played with the Hallé in 1905 and revived in 1952, a year before he died. Isaacs lost his sight in 1925, and set about learning to play the piano by touch. He appears not to have allowed his disability to interrupt his life at all. He wrote a book *The Blind Piano Teacher*, published in 1948.

[2] Director of Concerts from 1953. Born in 1901, he joined the Hallé in 1920, leaving to join the BBC Symphony Orchestra on its foundation in 1930. He returned to Manchester to lead the BBC Northern Orchestra, but decided to stay with the Hallé in 1943 when the latter severed connections with the BBC orchestra. Turner then led the Hallé under Barbirolli until 1957. He also formed the Turner Quartet, which played at many Tuesday Mid-Day Concerts. As director, he continued the policies of Edward Isaacs, maintaining high standards.

[3] The Society holds: bound copies of the programmes from 1915 to date; minutes of the committee from 1915 to date; notes on auditions from c.1920 to date; newspaper cuttings from 1915 to date; index of pieces played at the concerts arranged by composer and date of performance, 1915–67. Also used in this article was a collection of newspaper cuttings by Lucy Pierce of her concerts 1910–30, held by the Society.

ment grants to call upon, the charity had to be self-financing. When they began, the concerts, which lasted forty minutes, were held at the Houldsworth Hall in Deansgate under the directorship of William Eller. The first twelve were called 'Tuesday Popular Concerts'; thereafter they were known as 'Tuesday Mid-Day Concerts'. Following on their success, a Friday noon series of concerts was started, with Edward Isaacs as director, to raise money for Music at the Front, another charity.

It soon became clear that the concerts, in addition to raising funds, were of benefit to the business community. According to the *Musical Times*, 'Harassed business men went back to their tasks on the 'change recreated in a real sense: they had "seen a great light", and the memory of it did not easily fade away.'[4] And the music critic of the *Manchester Guardian* wrote:

The noon concerts are a legitimate development of our musical life and their success is the success of the musical movement purely and simply. The movement needs a strong and definite musical policy, and the elimination of anything second rate … as soon as a demand for music at midday is established, an important landmark in the development of the musical life in Manchester will have been passed.[5]

The commentator went on to suggest that concerts aimed at children should be included, and put forward T.C. Horsfall's name as a possible facilitator of such a development.[6] Nothing appears to have come of this directly, but after the war the Manchester Education Committee was persuaded to take a number of tickets to be used by school parties (a practice that continued until the 1950s). In the 1920s, a number of school choirs performed in the concerts. Contact with the music colleges in Manchester was also very important: many of the established performers were teachers at the colleges, and the students provided some of the promising newcomers. The colleges took blocks of tickets, as the schools did, but this too died out in the 1950s.

---

[4] *Musical Times*, 57 (1916), p. 424.
[5] *Manchester Guardian*, 2 August 1916.
[6] Thomas C. Horsfall (1841–1932), active in the arts (especially in the field of education), and a pioneer of town planning. He established the Manchester Museum of Arts in Ancoats.

Tuesday Mid-Day Concerts

HOULDSWORTH HALL, MANCHESTER.

(In connection with the Committee for Music in War-time. Northern Section.)
Registered under the War Charities Act, 1916.

147th Concert - - TUESDAY, November 26th, 1918

From 1-20 to 2-0 p.m.

Quintet, for Piano and Strings, in E Major

BY

SYDNEY H. NICHOLSON

(Organist-elect of Westminster Abbey)

Miss Lucy Pierce, Dr. Brodsky, Mr. C. Rawdon Briggs
Mr. S. Speelman, Miss Kathleen Moorhouse

STEINWAY & SONS' GRAND PIANOFORTE

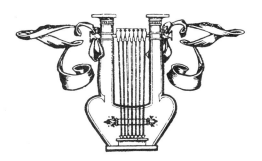

NEXT CONCERT, Tuesday, December 3rd.

Mrs. FLETCHER SHAW (Miss Nora Meredith) .... Singer
Miss ANNIE LORD ... ... Piano
At the Piano... .. .. Mrs. WILL MELLAND
At the Organ ... ... Mr. SYDNEY H. NICHOLSON

NO ENCORES.   **SMOKING ALLOWED.**

Director of the Tuesday Mid-day Concerts: William Eller, 1, Brazil St., Manchester.

Price 1d.   Entrance 6d. ; Tax 2d.

SEVIR, PRINTER, MANCHESTER   [P.T.O.

Sydney Nicholson,[7] then organist of Manchester Cathedral, was a prominent member of the committee. He was responsible for organizing up to eighty concerts a week in military hospitals in the area covered by the northern section of the committee. Several of his works were performed at the Tuesday Mid-Day Concerts, including a piano quintet in E major at the 147th concert, on 26 November 1918. As well as the money-raising and morale-boosting rationale for the concerts, some of the committee members – including William Eller, the Director of Concerts – regarded them as a way of providing employment for musicians in difficult times.

By the end of the war, the concerts were well established, and both Tuesday and Friday series continued. At the same time, the Brodsky Quartet was giving a series of concerts in the evenings: Manchester was indeed well off for chamber music! At this point, Tuesday Mid-Day Concerts were held in more than forty weeks of the year. However, audiences began to decline after the war, and by 1923 the committee found itself out of pocket. The decision was made to form a society which would charge annual subscriptions, to be channelled towards reducing the deficit. Thus the Manchester Tuesday Mid-Day Concerts Society was born, under the chairmanship of William Eller. It was lucky to secure the services of Edward Isaacs as Director of Concerts, and his personality shaped the society in a way that has enabled it to survive to the present day. As he began to lose his sight in 1925, Isaacs summarized in minute detail, in written form, the procedures for running the concert series.[8] This document gives examples of letters to be sent in connection with organizing auditions and contracts to be issued to performers, instructions on the printing of programmes and tickets, details of front-of-house duties in the hall on concert days, and so on: a real quality control strategy years before it became fashionable in industry.

The society planned to continue the series of over forty concerts a year with a mixture of celebrity artists and newcomers. The encourage-

[7] Sydney H. Nicholson (1875–1947) became organist of Manchester Cathedral in 1908, and of Westminster Abbey in 1919. In 1928 he founded the School of English Church Music (later the Royal School of Church Music). He was knighted in 1938.

[8] Edward Isaacs, 'See how they're run: the Manchester Tuesday Mid-Day Concerts and their management' (April 1937); unpublished document, held in the archive of the Manchester Mid-Day Concerts Society.

ment of the latter had been part of the policy of the concerts from the beginning, and in the early days the director had approached young artists who he thought might be suitable. This had led to occasional problems, so Isaacs instituted a system of auditions, held in London and Manchester. The archive of audition reports makes fascinating reading, even if only at the inquisitive level of 'Did the auditor get it right?' The society stuck to its policy of encouraging young performers for the next fifty years, despite the lack of enthusiasm displayed by some of the funding bodies to whom applications for grants were made.

The concerts struggled constantly to find a permanent home. Concert hall owners did not like their premises being rented for only a couple of hours at lunch time, which meant that more profitable whole-day rents had to be forgone. Over the years, the audience loyally followed the concerts from venue to venue. The suitable halls available in Manchester in the 1920s were the Houldsworth Hall in Deansgate, the Albert Hall in Peter Street, the Lesser Free Trade Hall, St Ann's Church, the Memorial Hall in Albert Square, and the Friends' Meeting House. None of them was ideal, but the society did the best it could.

The piano owned by the society was usually kept at the Houldsworth Hall and moved between locations as required. At the Albert Hall, with its steep flight of stairs, eight men were needed to move the instrument. The Lesser Free Trade Hall was an expensive alternative. St Ann's Church was not so comfortable for audiences. The Friends' Meeting House became a popular venue in the 1960s, but the audience was limited by the fire regulations to around three hundred.

In the 1920s and 30s the committee complained of low attendances. The society struggled to keep going, using the goodwill of performers and season ticket subscribers. In the late 1940s, however, average audiences appear to have been over six hundred, rising to seven hundred in 1947. Some concerts attracted audiences of over a thousand, and during this period the society was able to build up a cash reserve. Audience numbers fell off during the 1950s and 60s, down to an average of about three hundred – a size suitable for the Friends' Meeting House, where all concerts were held during the 1960s. There appears to be no discernible reason for the fluctuation in the popularity of the concerts, as the types of artist and the music performed had not changed significantly in the period considered. The boom in the late 1940s may have been due to the social changes in the immediate post-war period.

During the period under consideration, although the number of concerts each year was reduced, the balance of types of performer remained remarkably constant (see Table 1).

TABLE 1: Numbers of concerts and types of performers, 1917–1972

Year	Orchestra [a]	Chamber group [b]	Instrumental solo/duo	Choir [c]	Vocal solo	Inst'l/vocal group [d]	Total number of concerts	Average audience [e]
1917	3	13	7	9	7	12	51	n/a
1923	0	11	12	3	4	17	47	239
1933	1	3	12	2	0	11	29	n/a
1943	1	6	12	0	1	9	29	623
1953	0	4	12	0	0	10	26	440
1963	0	1	10	2	4	8	25	n/a
1972	1	13	1	1	7	1	24	n/a

Notes to Table 1

[a] Orchestras were chamber orchestras – usually from colleges or schools, but in 1943 the Boyd Neel Orchestra played.
[b] Chamber groups are wind or string groups larger than trios.
[c] Choirs include chamber choirs and choral groups performing extracts from operas.
[d] 'Instrumental/vocal' covers concerts where a mixture of sung and instrumental works was performed. These were usually the young artists.
[e] Audience figures are not available for all years.

Throughout the period considered, the instrumental groups tended to play from the standard repertoire with occasional first performances. A typical forty-minute programme consisted of a major work, with a shorter piece to fill the time if necessary. In 1923 for example the Brodsky Quartet gave three concerts, each devoted to a late Beethoven quartet. These were in marked contrast to others consisting of ten or twelve solo vocal items of a light-hearted nature. Programmes played by solo and duo instrumentalists altered over the years as musical tastes changed. In the early days, violinists would most often play a selection of Kreisler lollipops, pieces arranged by contemporary violinists, or movements from larger works. Later on they tended to play one or two pieces from the standard repertoire. A similar shift can be seen in programmes offered by other types of instrumentalists and by singers.

The list of artists who appeared early in their careers in the Tuesday Mid-Day Concerts and went on to make a name for themselves internationally is a long one. Edward Isaacs actively encouraged a number of performers, pianists like himself, among whom may be mentioned Myra Hess, Eileen Joyce, Moura Lympany, Cyril Smith and Phyllis Sellick. Thanks to the mix of celebrity artists and newcomers, the Tuesday Mid-Day Concerts played an important role in the musical life of Manchester and the wider world. This is borne out by the press coverage and letters from individual artists to be found in the archive.

The expenses of the society were: artists' fees, hall hire and administration (the last including publicity and programmes). Because the concert series originated as a money-raising charity, many established artists had given recitals for no fee. When the Tuesday Mid-Day Concerts Society was formed, some of the artists continued to perform gratis, or for reduced fees. The Brodsky Quartet were an example, and in recognition of this the committee used to give a donation to a college charity. For newcomers there was a different arrangement whereby they shared the surplus, if any, generated by their particular concert. As there was often more than one artist this was not a very advantageous arrangement, but the status of the series ensured that there was no shortage of newcomers willing to perform on these terms. One incentive for the artist was that there was always a review in the *Manchester Guardian* or the *Daily Telegraph*. There were no similar ways in which the society could economize on the cost of hire of halls. The Houldsworth Hall was eventually abandoned when it became too expensive as the audience numbers fell in the 1950s and 60s. Administration costs were subsidized by the administrators themselves: if the society had had to pay the true cost, it could not have survived.

The society's income came from ticket sales, subscriptions, grants and business sponsorship. The ticket prices and subscriptions were kept low, a fact that led to refusals of grants from some funding bodies! The committee always sought support from the business community in Manchester, and this varied over the years from firms allowing staff to carry out front-of-house duties at concerts to publishing free advertisements for the concerts. The committee also sold advertising space in the programmes. In 1954–5 advertising revenue together with the proceeds of programme sales equalled the grant from the Arts Council.

From its inception in 1923 the society enjoyed an association with the BBC. In the 1920s, the arrangement was that the society would draw up a list of artists it wanted to promote, from which the BBC would select a small number. For each concert broadcast a fee was paid to the society, which arranged for the artists' fee to include broadcasting rights. The society strove to maintain its freedom over choice of artists. During the Second World War, broadcasting of the concerts seems to have been suspended, resuming in 1953. The BBC abided by the original arrangement until the 1960s, when it decided it wanted to broadcast on Thursdays instead of Tuesdays. After much argument, the society gave way. By this time, only twenty-four concerts were being promoted each year: twelve on Tuesdays and twelve on Thursdays. By 1970, all the concerts were on Thursday and the society's name had become an anachronism.

From the foregoing, it can be seen that there is a great archive of information about the Tuesday Mid-Day Concerts Society and musical life in Manchester covering nearly sixty years of the last century. Besides those already mentioned, a number of other individuals prominent in Manchester music were involved with the society: Philip Godlee, for example, followed Alderman Will Melland as chairman in 1946. A more comprehensive list of artists who have appeared and the music played could usefully be produced, to form the basis for a study of changes in musical taste over the century.

The society survives to this date as the Manchester Mid-Day Concerts Society, still promoting twenty-four concerts a year (nowadays in the main hall of the Bridgewater Hall), and the gathering of archive material continues.

Antony Sluce was Chairman of the Manchester Mid-Day Concerts Society from November 1998 to November 2003.

The Long Road to Zion: Thirty Years of the Manchester Camerata

ROBERT BEALE

THE MANCHESTER CAMERATA embarked on its first full concert season in 1972–3, and so has now marked thirty years' existence. Historians of the music of the latter part of the twentieth century may well see something more significant in its survival than a mere numerical milestone. Few English freelance-based chamber orchestras of any significance have thrived outside London. Even those that appear to be sheltered under the wing of a larger organization can fall victim to the assassin's knife, as the late, lamented Bournemouth Sinfonietta's case shows.

The Camerata, though, is still alive, and made modest history when it became the first orchestra of its kind to benefit from the Arts Council's Lottery-funded 'stabilization' scheme in 2002: a step which proclaimed that 1. here was an organization too important to lose (the terms of such an award being that the client should be teetering on the edge of insolvency and 2. that the scheme should save it for the foreseeable future).

This fact argues that Manchester Camerata, thirty years ago an idealistic, risk-heavy project, is today a national institution. A glance at the literature of orchestral policy of the past decade shows signs of its growing significance. The Ritterman Enquiry consultation document of 1994 – the most comprehensive survey at the time of 'orchestral provision' in England,[1] and one of the first to recognize chamber orchestras as a sector in their own right – pointed to research from the immediate past in which, it is apparent, Manchester and its orchestral situation had played a central part.[2] It also presented statistical evi-

[1] *BBC/Arts Council Review of National Orchestral Provision: Consultation Document*, October 1994. This document's factual analysis, it seems to me, has been fundamental to subsequent Arts Council of England policy developments, despite the fact that the Consultation Report which followed (Janet Ritterman, *BBC/Arts Council National Review of Orchestral Provision: Report of the Consultation*, April 1995) contained a plethora of competing views and was widely criticized. The Arts Council's own *Strategy for the Support and Development of Orchestras and their Audiences*, July 1995, endorsed, among other things, the Northern Orchestral Consortium, formed in 1994, in which the Camerata played a major part, and declared a policy of investment in chamber orchestras.
[2] *BBC/Arts Council Review of National Orchestral Provision: Consultation Document*, October 1994, p. 8, referred to *Orchestral Concerts Research* (Harris Research Centre/ACE, December 1993), whose focus group of concert attenders was based entirely on a Manchester Camerata audience; *Customer Care in the Arts* (Millward Brown/ACE, June 1994), a survey based entirely on Manchester concert venues; and *Orchestral Concerts*

dence for the chamber orchestra sector gathered from six representative organizations, four of them London chamber orchestras, and the
others the Birmingham Contemporary Music Group and the Manchester Camerata.[3] Such things do not happen by accident, and the
Camerata's status as a leader and representative of its sector here was
due very much to one man: John Whibley (general manager 1975–96).
But the Camerata began as the vision of a few. The city had long had
a freelance pool of players (the Hallé, BBC Northern and Liverpool
Philharmonic orchestras all depended on it until the Second World War),
and any self-respecting choral society in need of an orchestra could
rely on them to provide a scratch band for its performances (the Manchester Mozart Orchestra, formed in 1963, was still playing for about
thirty of these a year in 1981 – and, from then, was under the management of Camerata Productions Ltd).[4] Pre-Camerata chamber orchestra
concerts were organised in the city by Paul Ward, a Hallé cellist (and
father of Nicholas Ward, now leader of the Northern Chamber Orchestra and City of London Sinfonia), and conductors included Charles
Groves and Norman Del Mar.[5]

The foundation of BBC Radio Manchester, one of the first local
radio stations, was however the catalyst for the creation of a concert-
giving chamber orchestra with higher ambitions. The decision to form
a chamber group under its auspices was taken in July 1971, and the
new Manchester Camerata gave its first concert in April 1972.[6]

'The orchestra, consisting basically of 23 players, was created to
provide public chamber orchestral concerts in Manchester, which had
so sadly lacked them', wrote Raphael Gonley, music producer with
Radio Manchester, in February 1973 to Dr Arthur Wolff, who became

---

Quantitative Research (Research Surveys of Great Britain/ACE, June 1994), research
into barriers to attendance at classical concerts, based on information from the Hallé,
Manchester Camerata, Northern Sinfonia and London Symphony Orchestra.
[3] *BBC/Arts Council Review of National Orchestral Provision: Consultation Document*,
October 1994, pp. 33 and 91.
[4] In 'Musical Britain: Manchester' (*Classical Music*, 29 August 1987) John Whibley is
quoted to the effect that the Camerata had its "origin" in the Manchester Mozart Orchestra.
[5] This brief account is based on recollections of John Whibley (personal communication).
[6] The dates are taken from a document summarizing the orchestra's history, prepared for
members of its newly formed Policy Committee in September 1979, when the BBC
ceased to be the orchestra's promoter (Camerata archives).

the first secretary of the orchestra's Association of Friends.[7] The Camerata was Gonley's 'baby'. By agreement with the Musicians' Union, Radio Manchester undertook to employ freelance musicians for a series of five concerts 'and thereby help to stimulate the profession outside the regular full-time orchestras'. It was the only local radio station in the country to make such a long-term commitment to an artistic venture.[8]

Frank Cliff was appointed conductor, and Fay Campey leader, and the first season's concerts were held in the Great Hall of the main building of UMIST in Manchester, promoted in tandem with Radio Manchester's recital series at the Friends' Meeting House, Mount Street. Christian Blackshaw was the piano soloist at the first series concert, on 30 September 1972, and Yossi Zivoni the violin soloist at the last, on 14 April 1973.

However, by that time two things had become apparent. One was that there was an immediate interest in the availability of the Camerata for outside engagements; the other that its own concerts in Manchester would lose money – about £400-£450 per concert in that first season.[9]

By January 1974, Manchester Camerata Ltd (a charity) had been created, a grant received from the North West Arts Association to make possible concerts 'throughout the North West', an advisory council set up,[10] and an Association of Friends begun.[11] Gonley was now aiming for an eight-month season, and to perform an average of two concerts per week, providing players with two weeks' work each month.[12]

He approached the newly formed Greater Manchester Council, and, not for the last time, the possibility of a merger with the Hallé was broached.[13] But by the end of 1974, the Camerata's identity had been preserved and the GMC had become its main provider, to the tune of £15,000 in a full year (to Radio Manchester's £3,500).[14] An ambitious

---

[7] The Hallé Concerts Society had considered the formation of a chamber orchestra from as early as 1965.
[8] Letter, 6 February 1973 (Camerata archives).
[9] Letter, Gonley to Wolff, 6 February 1973.
[10] Its first members were Dr Arthur Wolff, Dr Joyce Bourne, Anthony Burton of NWAA, Gerald Larner of *The Guardian* and John Reed, with John Manduell of the Royal Northern College of Music as chairman, later succeeded by John Reed.
[11] Advisory Council minutes, 24 January 1974 (Camerata archives).
[12] Advisory Council minutes, 7 March 1974 (Camerata archives).
[13] Advisory Council minutes, 13 June 1974 (Camerata archives).
[14] Advisory Council minutes, 26 November 1975 (Camerata archives).

series of concerts – originally to be three in every borough in the new Metropolitan County[15] – was planned for 1975–6.

At this point John Whibley, a former Hallé Orchestra cellist, was appointed part-time manager of the Camerata (Raphael Gonley, now on the staff of North West Arts, relinquished his post as director the following year).[16] Manchester Camerata Ltd from this point had a directorate of three,[17] and Szymon Goldberg, after a guest appearance, was appointed principal conductor in 1977.

For 1976–7, the Camerata season first took a shape recognizably similar to that of today: eight concerts in Manchester and fourteen outside, under GMC borough council auspices. Venues included Peel Hall, Salford; the Princess Rooms, Urmston; the Elizabethan Suite, Bury; the Victoria Hall, Bolton; the Grange Arts Centre, Oldham; Wythenshawe Forum; the Turnpike Gallery, Leigh; Romiley Forum and Stockport Town Hall. There were also two London area appearances by the orchestra (the Fairfield Hall, Croydon, and Rudolf Steiner Hall, London, on 24 and 25 September 1977).[18]

There was also another suggestion of merger with the Hallé – from the music panel of North West Arts, which noted that both the Camerata and the Northern Chamber Orchestra (also freelance-based, Manchester-orientated and regionally operative) were under-patronized, and, quoting the Peacock Report[19] of 1970 as authority, suggested the formation of a full-time chamber orchestra for the north-west, under Hallé administration.[20]

But the idea was not pursued, and under Whibley's guidance the Camerata found new venues and pioneered new concert styles of its own. In 1977–8 it began performing at the Royal Exchange Theatre in Manchester, a connection which continued for ten seasons, and established a presence at Nantwich in Cheshire, which (with a break from 1981 to 1985) continued for many years. In 1979 it became the resident orchestra for the Buxton Festival's opera productions, a relationship which continued until 1993, and in 1979–80 a chamber

[15] John Whibley (personal communication).
[16] Gonley later became manager of the London Sinfonietta.
[17] John Reed, Keith Naismith and Rhys Davies.
[18] Part of a Liszt festival organised by Chris de Souza. Szymon Goldberg conducted and Louis Kentner played *Malediction*.
[19] *Report on Orchestral Resources in Great Britain* (Arts Council of Great Britain, 1970).
[20] Advisory Council briefing paper, September 1977 (Camerata archives).

group was formed, directed by Manoug Parikian, which performed for five seasons at St Peter's House, the chaplaincy centre in Manchester University.[21]

By the end of 1979, a number of important changes had been made. New relationships had been established with Manong Parikian, appointed music director in January 1980, and Nicholas Braithwaite, principal guest conductor later that year. BBC Radio Manchester no longer promoted the RNCM concerts, although for a brief period they were still broadcast; instead, Manchester Camerata itself promoted these and an increasing number of outside concerts, in the north-west and beyond. Manchester Camerata Ltd continued as a registered charity, while John Whibley Management[23] employed two staff (an assistant manager and a publicity officer) and provided the orchestra of Northern Ballet Theatre (at this time Manchester-based, the arrangement continuing until 1983), as well as orchestral resources for local choral societies.

The North West Arts Board made a block grant (£6,000 in 1979–80), but the GMC's help now came in the form of guarantee rather than a grant. The Camerata's former Advisory Council became a 16-member Policy Committee, whose members included David Ellis of the BBC and Michael Kennedy of *The Daily Telegraph*.[24]

But increased activity brought increased risks, and by early 1980 it became apparent that Manchester Camerata Ltd's overdraft facility of £5,000 was in danger of being exceeded,[25] and that there would be a deficit of about that amount on the 1979–80 season alone, to add to the existing, though smaller, accumulated deficit. An audacious plan to hold a 'musical marathon', to dispose of all debts at one go and raise new funds for investment, was devised, with the agreement of the Musicians' Union and a target of £30,000. The orchestra and other musicians would perform for 36 hours on 22–23 May for no pay, and various celebrity figures would be involved.[26]

---

[21] The Goldberg Ensemble, a string ensemble formed in 1982 and named after Szymon Goldberg, was also managed by John Whibley until 1987; it continues today as an independent ensemble, directed by Malcolm Layfield (Camerata leader 1985–9).

[23] Camerata Productions Ltd (directors John Whibley and Keith Naismith) was created from John Whibley Management, to operate from April 1981, responsible for Manchester Camerata and (pro tem) the Northern Ballet Orchestra, with Whibley and two others as employees: Policy Committee, 18 November 1980 (Camerata archives).

[24] Policy Committee, 11 September 1979 (Camerata archives).

[25] Manchester Camerata Ltd directors' meeting, 19 February 1980 (Camerata archives).

[26] Policy Committee, 26 February 1980 (Camerata archives).

In the event, over 200 professional musicians took part, from the Hallé, BBC Philharmonic, Northern Chamber Orchestra and Camerata, with 22 conductors and 50 soloists, from 10 am on 22 May to 10 pm on 23 May: £9,000 net was raised, but the Marathon Concert was accounted 'outstandingly successful as a public relations and advertising exercise'.[27] It also proved a lifeline financially, allowing for more new ideas to be developed.

A Camerata tour to Norway took place, also in May 1980. Whibley had begun discussions with the Hallé general manager, Clive Smart, on the possibility of a Camerata appearance at the Free Trade Hall in February 1981, when the Hallé Orchestra would be on tour in Hong Kong. A performance with the Hallé Choir was also arranged: Bach's Mass in B minor was given at the RNCM in March 1982.[28]

New regional performance opportunities were investigated in Bolton, Oldham and Rochdale (it was a stroke of bad luck that, before the first Bolton concert could be given, the chosen venue, the Town Hall, was badly damaged by fire). North West Arts, however, was to reduce its grant,[29] and – inexplicably as part of a single policy – push for more contemporary music concerts for Manchester:[30] a performance on 25 April 1981 was given with its support and a 'money back if you don't enjoy it' offer to the audience. In the event, attendance figures were described as 'disastrous' (although no one asked for their money back).[31]

The Camerata also received an invitation from the pianist Moura Lympany, in 1981, to take part in a summer music festival at Rasiguères, in the foothills of the French Pyrenees, on an unusual basis: there would be no fees, but all the musicians would have free board and lodging and enter into every part of the festivities, and their friends could come as holidaymakers.[32] It proved extraordinarily successful[33] and continued as an annual frolic until 1992 (also leading to the Camerata's being the

[27] Policy Committee, 26 March 1981 (Camerata archives).
[28] Policy Committee, 25 November 1981 (Camerata archives).
[29] Manchester Camerata Ltd directors' meeting, 21 September 1981 (Camerata archives).
[30] Policy Committee, 18 November 1980 (Camerata archives).
[31] Policy Committee, 25 November 1981 (Camerata archives).
[32] As John Whibley tells it, the sequence of events was as follows: Moura Lympany visited the Camerata in Manchester to play a concerto, and at the party afterwards was talking about her new house in Rasiguères. 'She said she was going to have a festival and "You must all come". Then she phoned up a bit later, said she'd spoken to the mayor and so on, it was all going ahead and "See you there!"'
[33] Manchester Camerata Ltd directors' meeting, 21 September 1981 (Camerata archives).

first British orchestra to visit the Azores, in 1986 – and again in 1988 and 1990).

Manchester Camerata also decided to join the Association of British Orchestras[34] – a step which, in the light of subsequent history, was highly significant.

And so the orchestra reached its tenth anniversary, with GMC help now of £12,000 per annum[35] and a North West Arts grant of £7,000,[36] but still finding it difficult to make ends meet. An accumulated deficit of nearly £7,000 by 1982[37] (when a tour to Hong Kong took place) was to rise inexorably over the following three years.

In 1983 the baroque specialist conductor Nicholas Kraemer began an association with the Camerata which has continued to this day, and after the departure of Manoug Parikian in 1984, Nicholas Braithwaite was appointed principal conductor; at the same time Sir Charles Groves was appointed president of the orchestra, a position he held until his death in 1992.[38] (A name change to simply 'Camerata', without the 'Manchester', was tried at the same time, but did not last long.)[39]

In 1983, Camerata Productions Ltd became temporarily responsible for the activities of the Northern Chamber Orchestra,[40] which was facing financial problems, and as a result a concert series in Crewe and Warrington became available for 1984–5. A major new landmark also appeared: self-promoted Camerata concerts in the Free Trade Hall. 1 January 1984 saw the first of what has become a tradition of annual Viennese programmes to welcome the new year.[41]

The hall was booked again for an ambitious concert in the autumn. Given on 27 October 1984, it featured the former prime minister, Edward

---

[34] Manchester Camerata Ltd directors' meeting, 16 December 16 (Camerata archives).
[35] Manchester Camerata Ltd directors' meeting, 14 September 1983 (Camerata archives).
[36] Manchester Camerata Ltd directors' meeting, 12 January 1982 (Camerata archives).
[37] Policy Committee, 19 November 1982 (Camerata archives).
[38] Similar to the Hallé Concerts Society's procedure in 1934, when Beecham was made president (a non-constitutional position), in succession to Elgar, and became in effect principal guest conductor.
[39] Manchester Camerata Ltd directors' meeting, 17 January 1984 (Camerata archives).
[40] Policy Committee, 24 May 1983 (Camerata archives).
[41] The event took the Camerata's mailing list from 700 to 5000 at a stroke: 'Who calls the financial tune?', *Manchester Evening News*, 27 July 1989.

Heath, as conductor[42] and Moura Lympany as soloist,[43] and was intended to be the launch-pad for a new appeal: concerts in venues in
Greater Manchester were also arranged, with the harmonica-player Larry
Adler as soloist. Unfortunately none was very successful, and the accumulated deficit grew from £12,000 (1984) to £16,000 in 1985.[44]

At the same time it became apparent that the forthcoming demise of
the GMC would seriously disturb the orchestra's grant income (as it
would, to a far larger extent, that of the Hallé in the long term). Already
players were being paid late,[45] and the North West Arts grant, though
now £17,000, was to be frozen for 1985–6.[46] Fund-raising events such
as a Viennese concert in the Free Trade Hall (5 May 1985) in which the
players donated their services, and an auction of musical memorabilia,
were held, raising £3,400 altogether[47] – but the dying GMC's 'deficit
grant' of £16,000[48] finally saved the day.[49] (An Easter performance of
Handel's *Messiah* was given in the Free Trade Hall in 1986, as a mark
of thanksgiving, and was repeated each year until 1994.)[50]

The Camerata continued to struggle for existence throughout the
remainder of the 1980s, but a pattern evolved which gradually led to
stability. There were visits to Portugal in 1986 and Macao in 1988.
John Whibley was able to report, in summer 1987, that 30% of the
content of Camerata programmes at the RNCM was twentieth-century
music, and that the Camerata played 30 self-promoted concerts and
about 45 engagements every year.[51] In 1989 players were provided
with about a hundred days' work.[52]

---

[42] The *Manchester Evening News* review found a distinguished historical parallel:
'Gladstone felled trees. Edward Heath conducted … a solid and worthy account of movements from the Water Music.'
[43] The same review hailed 'this extraordinary lady' for 'a performance of superb style,
beauty and unfailing enjoyment'.
[44] Manchester Camerata Ltd directors' meeting, 3 October 1985 (Camerata archives).
[45] Manchester Camerata Ltd directors' meeting, 25 January 1985 (Camerata archives).
[46] Manchester Camerata Ltd directors' meeting, 8 March 1985 (Camerata archives).
[47] Manchester Camerata Ltd directors' meeting, 14 May and 18 June 1985 (Camerata
archives).
[48] Policy Committee, 17 December 1985 (Camerata archives).
[49] As, indeed, a similar and much larger grant did for the Hallé at the same time.
[50] Policy Committee, 17 December 1985 (Camerata archives).
[51] 'Musical Britain: Manchester', *Classical Music*, 29 August 1987.
[52] 'Manchester Rovers', *Classical Music*, 20 May 1989.

Most significantly, it was discovered that Free Trade Hall performances could be made to pay. The annual Viennese concert was ex-
panded with a New Year's Eve programme as well as that on New
Year's Day (from 1985–6),[53] and a popular programme of around six
concerts was promoted from that season also.

Figures for the three seasons from 1989–90 to 1991–92 show annual turnover increasing from £341,000 to about £460,000, with small
surpluses in two of the three seasons. Grant income was around 15% of
the total, earned income grew from 71% to nearly 80%, and corporate
income and sponsorship made a significant contribution (it was to be
7% of all income in 1992–3).[54]

Malcolm Layfield became leader of the orchestra in 1985 (he was
succeeded by Richard Howarth in 1989), and the clarinettist Janet Hilton
became a Camerata principal around the same time.[55] She formed the
Camerata Wind Soloists, to be known as a highly distinguished group
in the late 1980s and early 90s.[56] Carlo Rizzi, after conducting the
Camerata in Donizetti's *Torquato Tasso* at the Buxton Festival in 1988,[57]
began a close relationship with the orchestra which continued until
1992.

In 1990–1, Manchester Camerata was able to put on eight concerts
at the Free Trade Hall, six at the RNCM, eight at Crewe and Nantwich,
four in a new series which began that season at Colne, and the first in
what was to become an annual visit for an open-air fireworks concert
at Cholmondeley Hall, Malpas, in Cheshire, as well as taking part in a
multitude of engagements including performances at Beaumaris (the
festival), Leeds, Skegness, Dewsbury, Blackpool, Sheffield, Grimsby
and Harrogate.

Tragically, Sir Charles Groves suffered a stroke while in rehearsal

---

[53] Perhaps the high spot of all these was that of 1993, when Rosalind Plowright, Dennis
O'Neill and Willard White brought the curtain up on Manchester's year as City of Drama
1994, although the first Bridgewater Hall New Year, with Susan Bullock, Andrew Shore,
Bonaventura Bottone and Willard White, was another magnificent occasion.

[54] John Whibley, personal communication.

[55] She remained with the Camerata until 1998, when she was appointed head of woodwind at the Royal College of Music in London.

[56] Her performances of Mozart's Clarinet Concerto and Clarinet Quintet were among the
most magical I have heard. The following was the impression of the Quintet's slow movement in 1993: 'Just now and then in music-making, there is one of those moments when
people forget to cough, stop rustling their programmes and hardly dare breathe lest they
break the spell. It happened on Saturday.'

with the orchestra on 21 February 1992.[58] The following September, Nicholas Kraemer was appointed principal conductor and (in 1993) musical director. He introduced an inventively themed approach to programming, 'Distant Echoes', which linked major twentieth-century works with classics from the past, and set up an education programme in four centres (Crewe, Colne, Chester and Widnes) on the same theme.

John Whibley had joined the board of the Association of British Orchestras in 1991, to represent the chamber orchestras sector. It was a commitment on his part that was to bear fruit in years to come.

The Camerata also proved itself adroit in attracting sponsorship from commercial firms – so much so that it won a special Arts Council of Great Britain grant of £22,500 for 1993–4 – a 'first' for a chamber orchestra. By this time, with other grants of £22,000 (from the North West Arts Board), £12,000 from Crewe and Nantwich together with Cheshire County Council, and £15,000 from AGMA (the Association of Greater Manchester Authorities, successor to the GMC in arts funding in the region), it was able to count on over £73,000 (i.e. about 11%) of unearned income in the year, with turnover of around £644,000.[59]

The staff of Camerata Productions Ltd now consisted of five full-time and five part-time. Audience figures were rising (for which marketing manager Jeremy Hamilton and staff member Patsy Lawler were particularly praised), and visits were arranged to Halle in Germany and Barossa in Australia.[60] The organization won a 'Flying Start' award from Granada TV for its good business practice.[61]

John Whibley remembers 1992–6 as the "halcyon days". The Free Trade Hall series contained between nine and twelve concerts per season; the RNCM between six and ten; Nantwich, Crewe and Colne yielded another eight; and there was the usual variety of engagements in and outside the north-west.

It was not all plain sailing financially. The Arts Council of Great Britain cut back North West Arts' resources for 1994–5, and a 7% cut to clients was proposed.[62] The results for 1993–4 were not as good as

---

[57] His first appearance in this country, which moved the *Times* critic to say: 'He made the Manchester Camerata sound better than I have ever heard them.'
[58] He was preparing a performance of the Schumann Cello Concerto with Steven Isserlis as soloist. He died some months later.
[59] Manchester Camerata Ltd board minutes, 17 March 1993 (Camerata archives).
[60] Manchester Camerata Ltd board minutes, 27 July 1993 (Camerata archives).
[61] Manchester Camerata Ltd board minutes, 17 January 1994 (Camerata archives).
[62] Manchester Camerata Ltd board minutes, 17 January 1994 (Camerata archives).

had been expected (a major disaster had been the Cholmondeley fireworks concert, where, with an operatic programme in May, a loss of £25,000 was sustained). By the end of 1994, Jeremy Hamilton, whose post had been paid for by the ACGB 'Incentive Funding', had left.[63]

The 1994–5 season resulted in an overall loss of £35,000, and a loan of £50,000, interest-free over three years, was negotiated with the Musicians' Union. The North West Arts Board's approach seemed curiously irrelevant: it conducted an appraisal which commended the Camerata's financial controls, at the same time as the Camerata board heard that a large overspend on marketing in 1994–5 had 'just come to light' and that covenant, trust and sponsorship income were all less than expected; and, in the light of this financial plight, it called for better conductors and soloists and more new works to be programmed.[64]

But there were encouraging signs for the future. In its new policy document of 1995[65] the Arts Council committed itself for the first time to the support of freelance-based chamber orchestras; the prospect of the new Bridgewater Hall as Manchester's principal concert venue from 1996 onwards was raising many expectations; the Camerata had formed a link with the BBC Philharmonic to promote Saturday concerts in the new hall;[66] and Sachio Fujioka had been appointed principal conductor (Nicholas Kraemer becoming principal guest conductor).

Finances were eased by the successful reclaiming of VAT on three years' income from Cholmondeley firework concerts – yielding a total of £40,000[67] – and a grant of £20,000 from the Arts Council of England towards development in the Bridgewater Hall.[68]

John Whibley, however, brought his era to an end by accepting the post of Artistic and Planning Director for the Hallé, briefly remaining a director of Manchester Camerata Ltd[69] but finally severing his connection in June 1997. Chris Knowles, oboist and former chairman of the

[63] Manchester Camerata Ltd board minutes, 18 July and 17 October 1994 (Camerata archives).
[64] Manchester Camerata Ltd board minutes, 20 March 1995 (Camerata archives).
[65] *Strategy for the Support and Development of Orchestras and their Audiences*, Arts Council, July 1995.
[66] Manchester Camerata Ltd board minutes, 12 September 1995 (Camerata archives).
[67] Manchester Camerata Ltd board minutes, 23 October 1995 and 11 March 1996 (Camerata archives).
[68] Manchester Camerata Ltd board minutes, 5 February 1996 (Camerata archives).
[69] Manchester Camerata Ltd board minutes, 5 February 1996 (Camerata archives).

orchestra committee, became a board member and then general manager in Whibley's place.[70] He was to leave just over a year later to work
for the Raymond Gubbay organization.[71] Gavin Reid, former principal
trumpet, became education officer.[72]

In spring 1996, shortly before the opening of the Bridgewater Hall,
Manchester Camerata took its closest step yet towards joint operation
with the Hallé. The two orchestras' corporate development departments
were merged, and the Camerata office moved into the Bridgewater Hall.[73]

But this was as close as the two partners ever came to consumma-
tion. The Camerata secured a tour of Japan for 1998, pioneered a concert series in the Queen Elizabeth Hall, Oldham, and took part in the
Chester Festival.[74] Lucy Potter, formerly administrator of the Orchestra of St Martin-in-the-Fields, was appointed general manager, and the
board decided that the Camerata 'had to remain a separate organization'.[75]

Thus the present status of Manchester Camerata became established.
Disengagement from the Hallé became the new agenda;[76] and a vision
statement was drafted (by Gavin Reid, now chairman of the players'
committee and a board member) which said that: 'The enduring thing
about the Manchester Camerata is its flexibility. It is a wonderfully
creative resource capable of fulfilling many roles within the music
industry.'[77]

The Musicians' Union froze its outstanding loan;[78] a bid for education funding under the Arts4Everyone scheme won £54,000;[79] and Lucy
Potter devised a three-year plan and a proposal for 'stabilization' de-

[70] Manchester Camerata Ltd board minutes, 7 May 1996 (Camerata archives).
[71] Manchester Camerata Ltd board minutes, 10 March 1997 (Camerata archives): the resignation took effect on 31 May.
[72] Manchester Camerata Ltd board minutes, 9 September 1996 (Camerata archives).
[73] Manchester Camerata Ltd board minutes, 3 April, 15 July and 9 September 1996 (Camerata archives). The move drew criticism from the BBC's head of music, Trevor Green, who cancelled a planned press launch of the joint BBC Philharmonic/Manchester Camerata 1996–7 season and complained of being gazumped: 'Manchester Orchestras Locked in Merger Battle', *Classical Music*, 11 May 1996.
[74] Manchester Camerata Ltd board minutes, 10 March 1997 (Camerata archives).
[75] Manchester Camerata Ltd board minutes, 2 June and 14 July 1997 (Camerata archives).
[76] Manchester Camerata Ltd board minutes, 3 November 1997 (Camerata archives).
[77] Manchester Camerata Ltd board minutes, 14 July 1997 (Camerata archives).
[78] Manchester Camerata Ltd board minutes, 24 March 1998 (Camerata archives).
[79] Piloted by Gavin Reid: Manchester Camerata Ltd board minutes, 23 September 1998 (Camerata archives).

signed to bring the orchestra's ambitions for self-promoted events back within realistic limits.[80] When she left in 2002, to be succeeded by Gavin Reid, the process was well under way.

Stabilization paid off the accumulated deficit of £120,000 (and the Musicians' Union wrote off total debt of £70,000), and provided extra funds for balancing the books in 2002 and 2003, plus the salary of a full-time development and marketing officer. It also meant a scaling down of activity. The self-promotion of the Cholmondeley fireworks concert was abandoned after a poor year in 2000, coupled with an unsuccessful attempt at repeating the formula at Castle Howard in Yorkshire (it poured with rain and the Camerata lost a substantial amount: the Cholmondeley concert continues, with the Camerata providing the music, but the Camerata no longer promotes it).[81] Bridgewater Hall concerts came down from ten per season to five in 1999–2000, and now number four plus the New Year festival. Royal Northern College of Music concerts were reduced to five per season, then four (but there are six in the present season). Regular self-promotions in the Manchester region continue: four in Crewe and four in Colne.

But the appointment of Douglas Boyd as the Camerata's principal conductor from 2000, after a near-instant, unanimous vote of confidence from the orchestra itself, has resulted in a new atmosphere of optimism. The 2002–3 programme, marking thirty years of Camerata concert seasons, has been a chance to celebrate – and in some style.[82] North West Arts and AGMA have both increased their revenue grants substantially.

One of Lucy Potter's first dispatches to the Camerata board, in 1997, began with these words: '1. A map of how to get to Zion.' It was a reference to the location of the new offices at the Zion Arts Centre (formerly the Zion Institute) in Hulme, Manchester. But as a statement of intent it remains appropriate. The road to salvation may be a long and winding one, but Manchester Camerata, after thirty years, goes marching on.

---

[80] Manchester Camerata Ltd board minutes, 2 November 1998 and 25 January 1999 (Camerata archives).
[81] 'Stable mates', *Classical Music*, 17 August 2002.
[82] Concerts with Douglas Boyd have included a masterly *Eroica* symphony, and with Nicholas Kraemer a memorable Bach B minor Mass.

Chairmen of Manchester Camerata Ltd
Raphael Gonley (Director 1972–7)
John Reed (1977–84)
Rhys Davies (1984–92)
Simon Sperryn (1992–3)
Alan Watson (1993–6)
Mike Grindrod (1996–2004)

Principal conductors of Manchester Camerata
Frank Cliff (1972–7)
Szymon Goldberg (1977–80)
Manoug Parikian (music director 1980–4)
Nicholas Braithwaite (1984–90)
Nicholas Kraemer (1992–5; musical director 1993–5)
Sachio Fujioka (1996–2000)
Douglas Boyd (2000–)

Leaders of Manchester Camerata
Fay Campey (1972–84)
Malcolm Layfield (1985–9)
Richard Howarth (1989–)

General managers of Manchester Camerata
John Whibley (1975–96)
Chris Knowles (1996–7)
Lucy Potter (1997–2002)
Gavin Reid (2002–)

Appendix: Discography of the Manchester Camerata

Serenades from Old Vienna (1986)
Camerata Wind Soloists, directed by Janet Hilton
Valerie Taylor, Christopher Knowles (oboes), Janet Hilton, Ruth Ellis (clarinets), Julie Price, Susan Scott (bassoons), Elizabeth Davis, Christopher Morley (horns)
    Krommer: Octet-Partita in F op. 57
    Schubert: Minuet and Finale D72
    Beethoven: Rondino in E flat G146 (WoO 25)
    Beethoven: Octet in E flat op. 103
Tape cassette: Musette (Camerata Productions Ltd) MSTC 1003

Serenade for Susan
Laurence Perkins (bassoon), Manchester Camerata, conducted by Sir Charles Groves
The orchestra appears on the following tracks:
    Walking Tune (Swedish trad. folk melody, arr. Perkins)
    Fauré: Petite pièce (orch. Perkins)
    Michel Legrand: The Summer Knows (arr. Perkins)
    Three Hebridean Melodies (Scottish trad., arr. Perkins)
    I just fall in love again (Dorff–Herbstritt–Sklenov–Lloyd, arr. Perkins)
Released by IMP/Pickwick in 1991

Camerata Celebration
Manchester Camerata, conducted by Carlo Rizzi
    Mozart: overture Le Nozze di Figaro K492
    Vivaldi: Concerto in C for two trumpets RV537 (soloists Gavin Reid, Anthony Briggs)
    Senaillé: Allegro spiritoso (arr. Perkins) (soloist Laurence Perkins)
    Weber: Concertino for clarinet and orchestra op. 26 (soloist: Janet Hilton)
    Stravinsky: Suite for small orchestra no. 2
    Bartók: Divertimento for strings, Sz113
    Haydn: Symphony no. 83 ('La Poule'), first movement
Released by Manchester Camerata in 1992

Music by Takashi Yoshimatsu (b. 1953)
Kyoto Tabe (piano), Manchester Camerata, conducted by Sachio Fujioka
    Piano Concerto 'Memo Flora' op. 67
    And Birds are Still ... op. 72
    While an Angel falls into a Doze ... op. 73 (with Kyoto Tabe, piano)
    Dream Colored Mobile II op. 58a
    White Landscapes op. 47a
Chandos CHAN9652 (recorded 10–11 May 1998, New Broadcasting House, Manchester)

Bassoon Concertos
Laurence Perkins (bassoon), Manchester Camerata, conducted by Douglas Boyd
    Mozart: Concerto in B flat κ191
    Michael Haydn: Concertino in B flat, Perger 52/5
    Karl Stamitz: Concerto in F major
    Weber: Andante e Rondo ungarese op.35
    Weber: Concerto in F major op.75
Hyperion CDA67288 (released January 2002)

Old City New Image
Chamber music of John McCabe and David Ellis, played by the Camerata Ensemble
    McCabe: String Trio (1965)
    McCabe: String Quartet no. 2 (1972)
    Ellis: Trio for Violin, Viola and Cello (1954)
    Ellis: String Quartet no. 1 (1980)
Campion Cameo 2027 (released 2003)

(with thanks to Lawrence Perkins)

ROBERT BEALE is music critic of the *Manchester Evening News* and author of *The Hallé: A British Orchestra in the 20th Century* (Manchester, 2000).

Book Review

MARTIN THACKER

ANDREW LAMB, *Leslie Stuart: Composer of Florodora* (cover title: *Leslie Stuart: The Man who Composed Florodora*). New York and London: Routledge, 2002. 295 pp. ISBN 0 415 93747 7
LESLIE STUART, *My Bohemian Life*, edited and annotated by Andrew Lamb. Croydon: Fullers Wood Press, 2003. 135 pp. ISBN 0 9524149 3 7

... an audience found itself gazing in astonishment ... on an elderly, silver-haired, sad looking man, sitting all alone at a grand piano. His strong mouth was closed in a firm line, his eyes gazed far away as if oblivious of his surroundings ... then, quite softly, he began to play ...

WITH THE EXCEPTION of the silver hair, this description of Leslie Stuart is exactly confirmed by the picture on the cover of *My Bohemian Life*, and by another showing him at the piano in *Leslie Stuart: Composer of Florodora*. Stuart smiled in none of his photographs, but in his earlier days he looked thoroughly sure of himself. The later look of sadness and worry adds a layer of interest to his story, for, although he never recovered financially from his bankruptcy of 1913, the non-photographic evidence would suggest that he was not someone to let such trifles worry him. This was the man who spent money like water, who castigated his children when they showed a momentary tendency to thrift; the man whose confidence in his own marketability never waned. Andrew Lamb also quotes evidence that Stuart was an alcoholic and a womanizer. Yet there he sits, a churchwarden-like figure: neat, prim, and mysteriously sad.

A British composer of light music for the stage, with a background in church music; of Irish parentage; sometimes accused of wasting his talent; a victim of musical piracy; a habitual all-night composer; fond of society; a gambler and heavy smoker, who witnessed a falling-off in his popularity during the last years of his life. Surely this is a description of Sullivan? The latter's mantle has been said to have fallen on Edward German, but German was far less like him as a person. As Andrew Lamb points out, Stuart's first great success, *Florodora*, was produced in London in November 1899, just eighteen days before Sullivan's last completed operetta, *The Rose of Persia*. Add to that Stuart's influence on Jerome Kern (another speciality of Lamb's), and you can claim for him, in the words of Rodney Milnes quoted on page 266, the status of 'a palpable missing link in the development of the popular musical'.

Born Thomas Augustine Barrett, son of a cabinet maker and stage carpenter, Stuart differed from his predecessor in that he married and fathered several children, in that he was a Roman Catholic, active in Irish Nationalist politics, in that he often wrote the words of his own songs, and most particularly in the exceptional degree of showmanship in his character. He grew up in a theatrical atmosphere and appeared as a child extra in Liverpool, when some of the leading theatrical person-alities of the day were performing on the same stage. As a child he put on a home-made show (with pyrotechnic display) to other children, and played the piano in a public house. As a young man he was lucky to escape unharmed from an (unjustly) irate audience in Radcliffe, and as a concert impresario in Manchester he had to depend for financial survival on his wits and instinct, being almost (but not quite) the first manager in England to engage Paderewski. Showmanship was not en-tirely absent, either, from his tenure as organist and choirmaster at Salford Roman Catholic Cathedral and at the Church of the Holy Name, Man-chester; and the once-famous 'double sextet' in *Florodora* was as much a triumph of showmanship as of musicianship.

This trait, coupled with Stuart's present-day obscurity, has made Lamb's task of laying the foundations of a biography a hard one. For Stuart was keener on impression than on total accuracy: he preferred to believe that he had become a cathedral organist at 14, instead of the hardly less remarkable 16, and so muddied the waters about his precise year of birth; he felt it necessary to continue to give the impression of being rich while in the process of sliding spectacularly into debt. On the other hand, he assisted his biographer enormously by producing a series of memoirs, published as a serial by the magazine *Empire News* shortly before his death. These are elegantly written and engaging, suf-fering only occasionally from the species of heavy irony which was a feature of the humorous writing of the day, and they provide quotations which help to make the narrative more vivid. Naturally, Lamb could not incorporate the whole of these memoirs into his main book, and so he has edited them and published them separately, under the title *My Bohemian Life*, as a labour of love. His services to Stuart, as to the history of the musical theatre in general, are exemplary.

In spite of Stuart's vagueness over some details, and his wrong-headed attempt to discredit Germany over her treatment of her native composers (chapter 5) he is generally a reliable raconteur, and Lamb proves this with copious footnotes, which add enormous value and authority to the finished product. He also corrects numerous misspellings and other slips, rearranges the material from its original lucky-dip form to make a roughly chronological narrative, and adds material from earlier autobiographical fragments by Stuart.

We occasionally receive an impression – necessarily in the memoirs, but even in the biography – that we are being told Stuart's story the way Stuart the showman wants it told. For many of the vivid details cannot be verified by even the most industrious research. He says, for example, that he was offered a small fortune by F.W. Woolworth to compose an early form of corporate anthem for the eponymous retail chain. No doubt he was, but unfortunately we will only ever have his word for it. There are no diary entries, coded or otherwise; no files of correspondence; no detailed financial accounts (except the sad ones documenting his progress through the bankruptcy court): just Lamb's strenuous efforts to get as close to the truth as possible, using newspaper reports, street directories, census returns – anything to establish a reliable factual bedrock. He has also been able to make contact with Stuart's surviving descendants – he was just in time to catch the last person alive who knew him personally – and these reminiscences add immeasurably to the authority of the biography.

Naturally, the biography and the memoirs are full of information not only about Stuart, but about his world: the turn-of-the-century musical stage, dominated in London by producer George Edwardes, and in New York by the Shubert brothers. There is copious detail about the business of creating, financing and casting an early musical, and much too about the problems of music piracy in the early twentieth century. Stuart suffered the vexation of seeing illegal editions of his songs hawked openly on the streets, and was moved on one occasion to physical violence, for which he was duly fined at Marlborough Street Police Court. Then there are the large number of still-famous people whom Stuart knew and could give sidelights on: Rudolph Valentino is a particularly interesting example.

Lamb does a great deal to make us thirsty for a taste of Stuart's music, helped by vivid quotations from contemporary newspaper re-

ports of the shows: the closest we can come to experiencing these remarkable productions. And he includes quotations from other eminent
writers in support of Stuart: not only Walter Macqueen-Pope (author of
the one at the head of this review) but Neville Cardus, Eric Sams and
Rodney Milnes. All are mesmerized by 'Tell me, pretty maiden', the
'double sextet' from *Florodora*; Milnes (p. 266) refers to its asym-
metrical phrase-lengths, supporting Stuart's own claim (*My Bohemian
Life*, p. 58) that in writing his own texts he was enabled to free his
songs from the normal constraints of prosody. Cardus (p. 91) likens its
opening to the beginning of a Brahms symphony (not, surely, one of
the four that the rest of us know), but they both give away the truth that
at least some of the attraction of the piece is the visual element – 'all
eyes, teeth and winsomeness', says Milnes. And when Cardus mentions it in the same breath as the quintet from *Die Meistersinger* he is in
company with President Harry S. Truman, who compared it (p. 133) to
the sextet in *Lucia di Lammermoor*. I must enter a mild protest here, for
by continually referring – even in the revised *New Grove Dictionary of
Music and Musicians* – to 'the double sextet from *Florodora*', Lamb
and others give the impression that some deep vein of classical training
in Stuart had led him to include an outstanding feat of part-writing in a
musical comedy. Classical training he certainly had, but the so-called
double sextet is musically just a duet performed team-handed: scarcely even
that really, more like two interspersed solos that occasionally overlap.

Lamb is not blind to the fact that many of Stuart's compositions
betray a strong family likeness, referring frequently to 'trade-mark dotted rhythms'. This can be verified by reference to some of his most
famous productions: the introduction to 'Lily of Laguna', for example,
is clearly a shorter forerunner of that to 'Tell me, pretty maiden,' dotted
rhythms and all. Why the latter appear so often is a mystery: if they
were not to be found in *Florodora* one would think that they were a
feature of the dance style of Eugene Stratton, the black-face performer
for whom 'Lily of Laguna' and other Stuart music-hall numbers were
written. Each of these includes a dance, usually with the dotted rhythm;
in describing this style we might also cite interpolated triplets and a
baroque tendency for a single line to simulate two-part counterpoint,
which in Stuart's case produces a pleasantly yodelling effect. This can
be said without fear of relegation to the same pseuds' corner which
Cardus risked in comparing Stuart to Brahms and Wagner. Those com-

posers he does not resemble: but the dotted rhythms could be believed to have derived from some of the eighteenth-century music – Bach's *Praeludium* BWV552 (St Anne) for example, or John Stanley's *Trumpet Voluntary* from op.6, no.5 – that Stuart might have known in his organ-playing days. Or are they whistling tunes rather than yodelling ones; do they perhaps memorialize Stuart's admiration for Alice Shaw, the American *siffleuse* who invariably saved his bacon when ticket sales for his Manchester concerts were looking unhealthy?

Lamb's own astonishing collection of theatrical memorabilia is one of the stars of this particular show. He doesn't have to visit libraries (or not many), looking for rare pictures of Stuart shows, of Stuart himself, or even an autograph manuscript of 'Soldiers of the Queen'. On the contrary, others would have to visit him. His enthusiasm for what might be called the semi-facsimile – a reproduction by typography, not pho-tography, of a concert or theatre programme, showing (presumably) the layout of the original, within a border – is much in evidence through-out his account of the succession of Stuart first nights. I feel (others may differ) that this looks like a computer screen gone wrong when it spreads onto two, and occasionally three, pages. Surely borders are supposed to *contain* their contents? As could be seen in Lamb's article on Stuart in last year's *Manchester Sounds*, the effect is considerably improved by leaving out the border: there is less of an impression of disruption. But better still would be a simple table, as found in Kurt Gänzl's *The British Musical Theatre*, and in other publications.

Whether all the information contained in these semi-facsimiles is actually necessary is also open to question. Most is to be found in ref-erence sources, such as Gänzl's book. And many a worthy biography of a composer has been written without detailing, down to the smallest part, the first-night casts on both sides of the Atlantic.

One further quibble about an otherwise excellent book, this time over something outside Lamb's control: his publishers' disregard for what until now has been the normal use of the running title: name of the book on the left-hand page of an opening, chapter title or number (or both) on the right. Routledge in their wisdom replace this with: author's name (ascending vertically) low down on the left, book title (descending vertically) high up on the right – the latter in a fancy font, to boot. A fat lot of use when you want to know where you are in this fascinating story of Stuart's life and music!

CD Reviews

MICHAEL KENNEDY, GEOFF THOMASON, SAM KING, ROBERT
BEALE, LYNNE WALKER AND DAVID FANNING

Elgar
Symphony no. 1 in A flat, *In the South, In Moonlight*
(Christine Rice, mezzo-soprano)
Hallé Orchestra, conducted by Mark Elder
HLL7500

Elgar
Variations on an Original Theme (Enigma), Serenade in E minor for
strings, *Cockaigne (In London Town)*, *Chanson de Matin*
Hallé Orchestra, conducted by Mark Elder
HLL7501

Nielsen
Symphony no. 5, Flute Concerto (Andrew Nicholson, flute),
Entrance March from *Aladdin*
Hallé Orchestra, conducted by Mark Elder
HLL7502

THE HALLÉ has followed the example of the London Symphony Orchestra, the Royal Liverpool Philharmonic, English National Opera
and some other musical organizations in setting up its own record label. It has done so in association with Sanctuary Classics, and this
should ensure wide distribution – a necessity if the venture is to suc-
ceed. The first three discs, with some works recorded in the Bridgewater
Hall and some in Studio 7 of New Broadcasting House, were issued in
the spring at £9.99 each (dearer than the LSO Live label), all produced
by the widely experienced Andrew Keener. Two of them are devoted
to music by Elgar, thereby issuing a declaration of intent by Mark Elder
to continue the orchestra's honourable Elgar tradition which stretches
back to Frederic Cowen in 1898 but even more significantly to Hans
Richter's championship of the *Enigma Variations* in 1899 and of *The
Dream of Gerontius* in 1900. The composer himself regularly conducted his own works in Manchester, the last time in January 1933
(*Gerontius*). Sir Hamilton Harty made famous recordings of the *Enigma
Variations* and the Cello Concerto, and when Elgar was too ill to con-

duct a Hallé concert in February 1934 his place was taken by the young John Barbirolli who, more than any of his predecessors as Hallé conductor, was later to identify the orchestra and himself with Elgar's music. Their recordings still sell steadily, but Elder is undeterred by this daunting shadow and he is right not to be, for he brings his own interpretative powers to bear on these great works.

Considerable thought has gone into the constitution of the discs. For example, as an appendix to the performance of the *Enigma Variations* we can hear the original somewhat abrupt ending, 96 bars shorter, which Elgar discarded for the third performance and which was not heard again until Frederick Ashton's ballet in 1968. It was also played at a BBC Philharmonic concert in Manchester conducted by Yan Pascal Tortelier in 1999, but this is its first appearance on disc. Then, after the performance of *In the South*, the mezzo-soprano Christine Rice, with Elder at the piano, sings *In Moonlight*, the song with words by Shelley which Elgar derived from the *canto popolare* viola solo in the orchestral work. This is something of a rarity, and although the words and music are sometimes an uneasy fit, it has considerable charm.

The First Symphony is, of course, dedicated to Richter and was first performed at a Hallé concert, so it has a special place in Mancunian lore. The playing on this disc shows the orchestra of today in splendid form, with rich string tone and mellow brass. I find Elder's interpretation a little inhibited in emotional expression, although some will welcome that approach. Yet having said that, I should add that he takes slightly longer over both the second movement and the Adagio than Barbirolli in both of his recordings. The performance of the *Enigma Variations*, recorded live, is magnificent, each of Elgar's 'friends pictured within' being vividly characterized, notably Troyte and Dorabella, and there is sumptuous cello sound in B.G.N., while the *pianissimo* start of Nimrod is magical, leading to a truly powerful climax. *In the South*, *Cockaigne* and the Serenade are given excellent performances and that of *Chanson de Matin* has the authentic Elgarian poetry.

The sound-quality encourages high hopes for this venture and is nowhere more exciting and faithful than in the cracking performance of Carl Nielsen's Fifth Symphony, one of the staggering masterpieces inspired by the First World War. Many audiences in Britain came to know this work through performances by Barbirolli's Hallé, and Mark Elder is clearly a champion of it too. The episode when the side-drum overwhelms the rest of the orchestra is of course the most famous part of this work, but there is much more to it than that, and Elder's dramatic driving force and cohesive grasp of structure can be felt in every bar.

The Flute Concerto, superbly played by Andrew Nicholson, is no *Syrinx*-like afternoon daydream but a quirky virtuosic exploration of all the moods of which the instrument is capable, and some others besides. On this disc, too, there is an unusual appetizer. Nielsen's large score of incidental music for *Aladdin* at Copenhagen in 1919 (recorded some years ago) had an Entrance march at Aladdin's wedding which was replaced at the two performances by the 'Oriental Festive March'. This Hallé performance is in all probability the discarded piece's world première. It lasts only two minutes, but it is good to have it. All three discs can be inserted in the CD drive of a computer to reveal a website dedicated to the disc.

                                                                    Michael Kennedy

Rawsthorne
Piano Concertos nos. 1 and 2 (Peter Donohoe, piano),
Variations on a Theme by Constant Lambert
Ulster Orchestra, conducted by Takuo Yuasa
Naxos 8.555959 (British Piano Concertos series)

THE EARLIEST WORKS to come from the pen of the Lancastrian composer Alan Rawsthorne might suggest a promising career as a writer. Instead he opted first for dentistry at Liverpool University, abandoned that in favour of architecture, and finally entered the Royal Manchester College of Music, where his teachers included the pianist Frank Merrick and from where he graduated in 1929. The early interest in composition which had been nurtured in Manchester bore fruit in the ensuing decade in a number of successful works and a growing reputation both at home and abroad, as well as bringing Rawsthorne into contact with a number of fellow artists in music and her sister arts.

The First Piano Concerto of 1939 stands as the culmination of that eventful decade. Rawsthorne wrote it initially for an orchestra of strings and percussion but rescored it three years later for full orchestra, in which form it has been recorded with its later companion by fellow Lancastrian Peter Donohoe and the Ulster Orchestra as part of the Naxos

British Piano Concertos series. Neither concerto can really claim to have established itself as a repertoire work (although the late John Ogdon was a champion of the Second), so Naxos have done us a good service by reminding us of the riches we are neglecting. If anything it is the earlier concerto that needs and gets the more powerful advocacy here. It is a fascinating work, with two bravura movements framing a central Chaconne in which both Donohoe and his orchestra beautifully point the fascinating colours of Rawsthorne's score, not least the delicate percussion writing which remains from the original version. Takuo Yuasa (helped by the Naxos engineers) is also careful throughout not to let the richer textures of the 1942 version swamp the solo line.

The Second Concerto, a 1951 Festival of Britain commission, is a bigger work in four movements, with the extra movement a volatile scherzo in which Rawsthorne's natural wit cannot resist a backward glance to the obvious Brahmsian precedent. A more 'public' piece, it requires a superabundance of brilliance and certainly gets it from pianist and orchestra alike. Anyone to whom this is unfamiliar territory should dip first into the finale, where the Ulster Orchestra and Donohoe run rings round each other to see who can most realize the unbuttoned humour of a movement which every so often appears to burst into *El salón México*. If the piano wins, then the orchestra gets its own back in a polished performance of the *Variations on a Theme of Constant Lambert* – a homage in more than one sense, given that Lambert's widow became Rawsthorne's second wife.

Geoff Thomason

John R. Williamson
Music for Piano, vol. 2. Murray McLachlan (piano)
Dunelm Records DRD0176. Available from 2 Park Close, Glossop, Derbyshire SK13 7RQ; e-mail info@dunelm-records.co.uk

Horizons
New music for oboe and harp, by Philip Grange, Jinny Shaw, Howard Skempton, Lynne Plowman and Judith Bingham
Jinny Shaw (oboe), Lucy Wakeford (harp)
ASC Records, ASC CS CD51 <www.ascrecords.com>

Concertos for Orchestra
by Edward Gregson, Alun Hoddinott and John McCabe
Royal Liverpool Philharmonic Orchestra, conducted by Douglas
Bostock.
Classico CLASSCD384. Available through D I Music; e-mail
dimus@aol.com

THE THREE DISCS reviewed here demonstrate the great variety of contemporary music-making created, inspired and supported by Manchester's alumni and institutions.

Volume 9 of Classico's *British Symphonic Collection* brings the series up to date with no fewer than three world première recordings of
concertos for orchestra by senior figures in British composition. All
three works originated in the 1980s, though Edward Gregson's *Contrasts: A Concerto for Orchestra* was revised extensively in preparation for this recording.

Both the excellent booklet and the round-table discussion between
the three composers and the writer Lewis Foreman, included as a bo-
nus track on the CD, mention prestigious antecedents in this genre; not
just the familiar and popular work by Bartók, but also ground-breaking
examples by Hindemith and Kodály. Since these examples, the genre
has become a favourite vehicle for those composers who wish to maintain a spiritual or technical link, however distant, with the symphonic
mainstream of the later nineteenth and early twentieth centuries, but
who are also excited by the kaleidoscopic colour resources of the modern symphony orchestra, including its extended percussion section. The
concept of virtuoso display enshrined in the Romantic concerto is trans-
ferred away from the individual towards the ensemble, but also towards the composers themselves, as the genre offers the opportunity to
manipulate these resources in order to produce arresting new combinations of timbre. This all three composers certainly do with panache
and, as Gregson states in the discussion, the RLPO and Douglas Bostock
clearly relish the opportunity to demonstrate their prowess; more importantly, they play with commitment to the communicative purpose
of the music.

There is enough common ground between the works to make the
disc seem an eminently coherent piece of programming, yet the simi-
larity of date and genre allows for fascinating comparisons of approach

and voice. Both Gregson and Alun Hoddinott stay within generic conventions by adopting the fast–slow–fast movement sequence handed down from the Baroque period and also make use of the tried and trusted device of cyclic recall of themes towards the ends of their works. However, John McCabe favours a multi-movement design akin to Schumann's strings of characteristic miniatures linked together. Broadly speaking, these formal characteristics have stylistic parallels; Gregson, whose watchword is accessibility, is closest in rhetoric to the symphonic mainstream, while the sense of continuity in McCabe's work is more elliptical, abrupt even, as the enigmatic ending demonstrates.

Gregson's music is at its most characteristic when exploiting bold and exhilarating orchestral primary colours, particularly those of wind and percussion. The first movement is launched by an angular and urgent theme for horns and soon develops an almost Beethovenian propulsion through the insistent repetition of a dotted rhythm. A rampant percussion section takes control at the height of this opening paragraph. Sonata-style contrast is provided by a more smoothly contoured and regularly phrased melody on solo woodwinds. This description might make the music seem rather formulaic, but an interesting innovation on Gregson's part is the inclusion of aleatoric mutterings on muted brass, which undercut the refined lyricism of this 'second subject' and eventually swamp it.

Hoddinott's tonal palette is less obviously flamboyant than Gregson's but full of subtlety. The exquisite opening of the work, whose repeated-note figure was apparently inspired by the rhythmic cooing of doves in the composer's garden, is a case in point: against a background of sustained high strings, perky woodwinds intone the theme with delicate punctuation from pizzicato lower strings, harp, tambourine and flexatone. Hoddinott is a persuasive advocate for the right of the percussion section to be regarded as an equal of the other orchestral departments. His work is scored for no fewer than 23 percussion instruments, and yet they are handled with a refinement reminiscent of Debussy. Perhaps the most ear-catching moment comes near the very end, where tuned percussion and sleighbells create an effervescent froth which is brutally slashed at by tutti octaves from the rest of the orchestra.

This disc can be wholeheartedly recommended to anyone with an interest in twentieth-century orchestral music, creating as it does an impression of sustained brilliance of invention and execution alike.

The contemporary chamber music specialists Okeanos have produced an exceptionally well thought-out programme of music for oboe and harp. Two important themes run through the disc; one is that of classical Greek antiquity, perhaps inspired by the idea of the lyre and reed pipe (Philip Grange's _Diptych_, based on the myth of Daedalus and Icarus, Jinny Shaw's _The House of Asterion_, based on Borges's version of the Minotaur legend, and Judith Bingham's _The Island of Patmos_, which weaves together visions of Artemis and Apollo with those of the Book of Revelation); the other theme is contemplation, whether of natural phenomena or of artworks (Grange's _The Knell of Parting Day_, Lynne Plowman's _The Mermaids' Lagoon_ and _Floating, turning, spinning_, Howard Skempton's _Three Preludes_ and _Horizons_). As well as duets, the programme includes solo works for each performer and also affords the oboist Jinny Shaw the opportunity to vary the tonal palette by using the cor anglais (in Grange's _Daedalus's Lament_) and the gorgeous oboe d'amore (in _Floating, turning, spinning_). One might expect this particular combination of instruments to produce exclusively delicate textures, but in fact there is a great deal of steely brilliance in the sound, particularly in the first part of Grange's _Diptych_ and in the fourth of Skempton's _Horizons_. These two composers represent opposite poles of utterance. Grange builds long paragraphs of mounting intensity, during which the listener is drawn in by the expressive tension inherent in individual intervals or even in individual notes – the tolling bell effect of _The Knell_ being the clearest example. Skempton, on the other hand, creates gem-like miniatures of a more static quality. Of the other composers, Judith Bingham's piece stands somewhat apart stylistically in its more Brittenesque exploitation of tonality, while in her own work Jinny Shaw demonstrates a fascinating array of contemporary performance techniques.

The compositional voice and method of John R. Williamson is a distinctive one, sympathetically realized by Murray McLachlan in this second disc devoted to his solo piano music. Many of the works featured rely on the composer's use of palindromic structures. One of the compositional problems in this is to create melodic lines which make as much sense played 'backwards' or 'upside-down' as the 'right' way. Williamson solves this cannily through frequent recourse to the pentatonic scale, which is free of the directional pulls inherent in a major or minor scale. Beneath these often oriental-sounding melodies, the harmony is richly chromatic, reminding one of some of the riper passages in Ravel's music. These pieces are as well crafted as one would expect of a one-time pupil of Lennox Berkeley, demonstrating a fluent command of keyboard textures in an early twentieth-century idiom.

Sam King

Hat Box
Music for recorder and guitar by Alan Bullard, John Duarte, David Ellis, John Golland, Peter Hope, Štìpán Rak, Ernest Tomlinson *et al.*
John Turner (recorder), Neil Smith (guitar)
Campion Records CAMEO 2020

Old City: New Image
Chamber music by John McCabe and David Ellis
Camerata Ensemble
Campion Records CAMEO 2027

Celtic Magic
Chamber music and songs by Peter Crossley-Holland, John Manduell, Edmund Rubbra, Julius Harrison, John Ireland, David Cox, Benjamin Britten
Lesley-Jane Rogers (soprano), John Turner (recorder), Richard Simpson (oboe), Keith Swallow (piano), Richard Howarth (violin), Tom Dunn (viola)
Campion Records CAMEO 2026

All three discs available from D I Music; e-mail dimus@aol.com

STOCKPORT IS the undoubted focus of the recital by John Turner (recorder) and Neil Smith (guitar). Its title is taken from the suite of eight pieces which come first of the 31 tracks, and indicates the Stopfordian connections embodied in them. Stockport has long been famous for its hat-making industry (the expression 'mad as a hatter' comes from one of the unfortunate effects of the chemicals used in the process), and both members of the Turner–Smith duo are resident in the town. Not only that: the recordings were partly made in Chadkirk Chapel, Romiley, and the producer, David Ellis, is a Bramhall inhabitant.

The non-verbalized theme, which pervades the collection, is dancing. Alan Bullard's *Hat Box* – written specially for the recording – is
a deliciously parodistic suite, comprising Quadrille, Valse, Mexican
Hat Dance, Shuffle, Jig, Stomp, Waltz and Galop. David Ellis's *Fred's
Blue Ginger Staircase Music* recalls the routines of Fred Astaire and
Ginger Rogers (it was written to celebrate the renovation of the me-
dieval Staircase House in Stockport). John Golland's *New World
Dances* (written for Smith and Turner) consist of a Ragtime, Blues
and Bossa Nova. John Duarte's *Un Petit Jazz* (and its 'encore', *Un
Petit Bis*) – likewise written for Smith and Turner – explores rhythms
of three, four, alternate five and six, and twelve beats. Peter Hope's
Bramall Hall Dances (Stockport-born composer, Stockport locale)
are a fascinating combination of old and new styles in a Round Dance,
Pavane, Ostinato (actually a kind of rumba), Waltz and Galop – again
written for Turner and Smith.

In addition the duo provide two glimpses of seventeenth-century
Dutch music for recorder and guitar (*Variations on Dowland's
Comagin*, by Jacob van Eyck, and Three Pieces from *'t Uitnement
Kabinet* by Pieter de Vois and others), and two more recent melodic
gems: a lovely neo-baroque *Arioso* by Štipán Rak (b. 1945), and
Chadkirk Idyll, composed in 2002 especially for this recording by
Ernest Tomlinson, which is also a tribute to Stockport, where
Tomlinson spent part of his wartime RAF training.

This is a remarkably varied and constantly delightful collection,
which captures some of the best of the duo's live performance.

The focus for "Old City: New Image" is Liverpool – proud bearer
of the 'City of Culture' title for 2008 – and the Liverpool Institute for
Boys in particular, two of whose old boys remind us that The Beatles
were not the only creative talent to come out of that place.

David Ellis and John McCabe both continued their education at
the Royal Manchester College of Music: Ellis (b. 1933) is the elder
and provides the earliest piece of the set: Trio for Violin, Viola and
Cello, written in 1954, when Ellis was a member of the 'Manchester
School' of student composers and indeed 'fixer' of their earliest London concerts. His other piece is much more recent: String Quartet no.
1, of 1980. John McCabe (b. 1939) wrote his String Trio in 1965, on
the occasion of Alan Rawsthorne's sixtieth birthday, and his String

Quartet no. 2 in 1972, for the Macclesfield Festival of that year.

Two trios, then, and two quartets, played by (unnamed) members of the Camerata Ensemble. The McCabe pieces are free in structure, spare in texture and challenging to the ear, while Ellis, though never simplistic, writes in (modified) classical forms and with direct emotional appeal.

Peter Crossley-Holland (1916–2001) was a Londoner and educated at Oxford, but his teacher at the Royal College of Music was John Ireland and he lived in Wilmslow during and after the Second World War. Ireland (a son of Bowdon, as we must never forget) is represented in this collection by the Christmas evergreen 'The Holy Boy', in its violin and piano arrangement, warmly played by Richard Howarth and Keith Swallow. Crossley-Holland's own 'The Nightingales', to a Robert Bridges poem, was written in Wilmslow in 1945 and opens the collection, making an interesting companion to the late work for recorder and piano, *Ode To Mananan*, written in 1999 and first performed by these artists at Port Erin in 2000. It is notable how little his elegiac, and almost sentimental, style had changed in fifty-four years.

Crossley-Holland loved the avian characteristics of the recorder, and they are heard in two songs, 'The Philosopher Bird' (the poem, by his son Kevin, is the only text included in the liner notes), and 'Fairy Workers' – each entertaining, whimsical and slightly tongue-in-cheek. Other little charmers are another pair of songs, 'The Weather the Cuckoo Likes' and 'The Piper'; his early, sweet 'Lullaby', here for violin and piano; his wartime Trio for recorder, oboe and viola; and 'Twilight it is' (Masefield's poem) for soprano and piano – a lovely valediction.

The disc is based on a concert given at the Bridgewater Hall in August 2002, and into the bargain the listener is offered a tribute to 'C-H', by John Manduell, for violin and viola (using the German nomenclature as its basis), Rubbra's Sonata in C for oboe and piano, Julius Harrison's *Midsummer Night's Dream* settings, 'Philomel' and 'I know a Bank' (for soprano and piano), Britten's *Six Metamorphoses after Ovid* (for solo oboe), and a beautiful vocalise by David Cox (his last work) called 'The Magical Island', for soprano, recorder and piano. Indeed, there is much magic here.

Robert Beale

John Casken
Darting the Skiff, Maharal Dreaming, Cello Concerto, *Vaganza*
Northern Sinfonia, conducted by John Casken and Heinrich Schiff
NMC Ancora NMCD086

THE GREAT STRENGTH of this new CD featuring four works by John
Casken, Professor of Music at the University of Manchester, lies in the
character not only of the music but also of the performances. Casken
and the Northern Sinfonia go back a long way to the fruitful years
when, as its Composer in Association, he produced a number of sure-
footed and substantial works, three of which appear on this recording.
  Maharal Dreaming (1989) is a short orchestral fantasy, a sort of
prequel to Casken's first opera, *Golem*. The dream envisages the man
of clay (Golem) stirring to life with an impersonal, nightmarish quality.
The dragging of his steps, the sinister menace of his movements, the
feverish activity of his actions – all these are vividly imagined in a
score which, in this recording, fairly burns at its central climax. *Vaganza*
(premiered by Aquarius in 1985) is 'a serious entertainment' in six
movements. Its theatrical dimension is contained in several engaging
'scenes' that segue swiftly into one another, though never at the expense here of an assured ensemble. The atmosphere is enhanced in this
performance by a general feeling for the unpredictable and coloured by
sinuously shaped woodwind parts, pellucid percussion and an oddly
sinister chamber organ.
  In the exuberant *Darting the Skiff* (1993) the Northern Sinfonia keeps
on course in the scudding instrumental lines and the vigorously charged
currents that propel this magical work along. It is one of my favourites
pieces by Casken. The curiously evocative title is from a line by Gerard
Manley Hopkins: 'You'll dare the Alp – you'll dart the skiff?', and,
though the music is indisputably abstract, it has pictorial associations
with boats and reflected light on Lake Como, where Casken began
composing it. The Northern Sinfonia never falters in what amounts to
a balancing exercise between lively rhythmic articulation and broad
melodic sweep.
  More than any other work on this CD the Cello Concerto displays
Casken's distinctive manner of generating new material out of vari-
ously shaped and sized melodic themes, in a way that is both unsettling
and intriguing. The 'landscape' of this composition, as Casken puts it,

is defined by five lines of poetry which he wrote alongside the music and which the cello 'sings'. Heinrich Schiff's account of the taxing solo part is notable for the way in which he allows its character – at times haunting, at times urgently communicative – to unfold. His shaping of the dreamily decorative lines is sensitive, his control of the more dynamic discourse impressive. With its wealth of instrumental inventiveness and its tonal and textural variety the Concerto makes a surprisingly symphonic impression. It is confident, mature and rich in detail. At its premiere in Lichfield Cathedral in 1991 Schiff himself directed the Northern Sinfonia (as on this recording), adding an edge to the occasion by dropping his bow. He successfully retrieved it and continued, with aplomb. Casken conducts the three other works here, his unmannered approach clearly bringing out the best in the Northern Sinfonia.

All credit to the excellent NMC label for reinstating these fine recordings (previously released on Collins Classics) as part of its Ancora series.

Lynne Walker

Edward Gregson
Blazon, Clarinet Concerto (Michael Collins, clarinet), Violin Concerto (Olivier Charlier, Violin), *Stepping Out*
BBC Philharmonic, conducted by Martyn Brabbins
Chandos CHAN 10105

EDWARD GREGSON, Principal of the Royal Northern College of Music, is also a prolific composer. A new CD from Chandos, featuring two of his seven concertos – following on from a mini-festival devoted to his music, presented at the RNCM and supported by the BBC Philharmonic – demonstrates something of the extrovert plasticity and dazzling ease of his artistry. A miniature concerto for orchestra, propelled by a restless rhythmic drive, *Blazon* (1992) is Waltonian in its spirited athleticism, throwing up echoes of Britten in felicitous woodwind flutters and, at one point, a particularly attractive long-spun oboe melody. It is impossible to dismiss the bold visual images for which this music – with its striding tunes, heraldic brass fanfares and busy percussion – would provide the perfect big screen partner. There is even a great stretch to accompany the 'main title' and rolling credits.

From a post-modernist cultural perspective Gregson doesn't break any new ground in his engagement with tonality. Indeed the leisurely opening of the second part of the Clarinet Concerto (1994, revised 2002), so curiously like part of an interlude from Britten's *Peter Grimes*, inspires such lush playing from the BBC Philharmonic strings, pointing up the music's elegiac quality, that it could easily become the new Barber *Adagio*. With Michael Collins as soloist the Clarinet Concerto unfolds with complete conviction on this airing. But I wish that all the Waltonesque flurries, the undulating aggression, the unleashed sugary musical vision and a shrill touch worthy of Malcolm Arnold's *Tam O' Shanter* concealed more complex layers beneath the colourful surface.

The Violin Concerto was a brave millennium commission by the Hallé from Gregson. The turn-of-the-century timing gave Gregson a genuine excuse to indulge in retrospective glances: 'I found it impossible to resist the temptation to look back and give some respectful nods in certain musical directions.' Lines by Wilde and Verlaine inspired the first and second movements, while another poetic voice, the Irish bodhrán (a traditional hand-held drum), carries the third movement to its ebullient conclusion. Olivier Charlier's glowing account of the solo violin part, generous in tone in the legato lines and nimble in the execution of the tumbling cascades in the finale, firmly avoids overt gushing in the wistful nostalgia of the central slow movement – another exercise in dark-timbred moodiness.

The BBC Philharmonic, under Martyn Brabbins, is bright and breezy in its treatment of these works, and the CD as a whole provides an entertaining glimpse into the output of a genial and technically assured musical voice, apparently untouched by so many of the seismic musical developments of the major part of the twentieth century.

Lynne Walker

Robin Walker
Instrumental Works
Riverrun Records RVRCD66. Available from Riverrun Records, PO Box 30, Potton, Bedfordshire SG19 2XN <www.rvrcd.co.uk>

RESIDENT FOR the past fifteen years in Delph, near Oldham, Robin Walker was for seven years before that a lecturer at Manchester University. No one who has had contact with his music can doubt its integrity and distinctiveness. His style, though it has recently mellowed from its early hard-edged modernism, has always been marked by seemingly incompatible archetypes and affinities – asceticism and ecstasy, shyness and inner strength, landscapes of the Yorkshire moors and the Orient, music of both Anglican and Catholic traditions, echoes of Stravinsky, Boulez, Birtwistle, Tippett and the Kinks. Yet this panoply is no more than necessary means for expressing the complex drives of the inner man; and rich though the pool of influences may be, in his strongest work Walker passes every note through a refining fire before allowing it onto the page.

Placed first on the disc, *Dance/Still* (1982) reflects the 'rhythmic liberation' he experienced following a visit to India to hear the music of the Buddhist temples. Knowing that, it is certainly possible to hear an ethnic tinge in the pervasive drumbeats, and the revolving near-repetitions have something of the trance-like beauty of another India-inspired piece, John Cage's String Quartet. Yet it is the astringent harmonies – delicately scored for seven players, and nicely balanced on this recording by the RNCM's New Ensemble conducted by Clark Rundell – that first catch the ear. Walker's juxtaposition of motion and stasis is superbly controlled, and had *Dance/Still* been titled 'Homage to Stravinsky' (it was composed around the time of Stravinsky's death) it would surely have been hailed as a fitting tribute.

The solo organ piece *Dances with Chant and Chorales* (1986) handles similar polarities with comparable deftness and is played with immense flair by Jonathan Scott, who conjures weird and wonderful colours from the University of Huddersfield organ. Messiaen is somewhere in the background here, but as so often with Walker's music, a touch of self-denial too that gives the piece a unique flavour. Of the three short works from 1994, *Mr Gilbert dines at the Modern Hindu Hotel* for recorder and piano (here John Turner and Peter Lawson) is a whimsically titled yet toughly composed tribute to the composer Anthony Gilbert; *Invention* is another solo organ piece of strongly profiled contrasts, paying homage to Marcel Dupré; and *I Thirst* is a movement for string quartet (the players here drawn from the Camerata Ensemble) based on one of the Seven Last Words of Christ from the Cross, startling in its initial euphony which is destined to be first parched, then restored in ethereal harmonics.

Halifax, a zany study for player-piano with teasing excursions into 'Oranges and Lemons', fulfils its aim to explore the relationship between objective purity and expression. But the longest and most impressive work on the disc is another tribute to Walker's Yorkshire roots; *At the Grave of William Baines* pays homage to the Yorkshire composer who died in his early twenties. Walker's evocation of his 'wild spirituality' (characteristic phrase!) encompasses the ecstasy of Skryabin and the pounding energy of Rzewski and makes a fine vehicle for the versatility and virtuosity of Peter Lawson. The disc concludes with another recorder and piano piece, *His Master's Voice*, a more modest yet still beautifully focused tribute, this time to Walker's erstwhile composition teacher, David Lumsdaine.

Performances on this disc are uniformly strong, and the recording quality, though variable according to venue and on the whole rather dry, is quite acceptable. Presentation would have been the better for longer gaps between tracks, and neither the jewel-case nor the booklet gives timings for the eight individual pieces. Apart from the intrinsic rewards of the music, it would be marvellous if this CD led to recordings of Walker's most ambitious scores, such as his breathtaking symphonic poem, *The Stone Maker*.

David Fanning

First Performances in Greater Manchester and Neighbouring Towns, 2002

Compiled by GEOFFREY KIMPTON

Each entry is a world première unless otherwise stated

Aagaard-Nilsen, Torstein
Pentagram, for wind orchestra
22 March
Royal Northern College of Music, Theatre
RNCM Wind Orchestra, conducted by Clark Rundell

Antal, Mikhail
White Note Partita, for chamber orchestra
27 March
Royal Northern College of Music, Concert Hall
Sale Chamber Orchestra, conducted by Jonathan Brett

Ball, Michael
Cambrian Suite, for brass band
18 January
Royal Northern College of Music, Concert Hall
Black Dyke Band, conducted by Nicholas Childs

Basford, Daniel
Esoteric Ether, for contrabassoon solo
26 June
Royal Northern College of Music, Studio Theatre

Basford, Daniel
Pathetic Clowns, for E flat clarinet and celesta duet
26 June
Royal Northern College of Music, Studio Theatre

Bayliss, Colin
Piano Sonata no. 3 (B121)
31 August
Chetham's School, Whiteley Hall
Murray McLachlan

Beck, David
Hinterludes, for bassoon and piano
8 October
St James' Church, Gatley
Graham Salvage and Janet Simpson

Beck, David
Lord Nelson, for recorder, oboe, bassoon and piano
8 October
St James' Church, Gatley
John Turner, Richard Simpson, Graham Salvage and Janet Simpson

Beck, David
Sound Bites, for descant recorder and piano
8 October
St James' Church, Gatley
John Turner and Janet Simpson

Bedford, David
Bash Peace, for percussion ensemble (première earlier in tour)
(commissioned by Ensemble Bash with funds from the Arts Council)
20 November
Royal Northern College of Music, Concert Hall
Ensemble Bash

Bertrand, Christophe
La Chute du Rouge, for violin, viola, cello, double bass (+ bass guitar),
clarinet, flute, trumpet, guitar (+ electric guitar), piano and percussion
13 September
Zion Arts Centre, Hulme
Ensemble 11, directed by Gavin Wayte

Bitensky, Larry
'Awake, you Sleepers', for trumpet and wind orchestra
(Fromm Music Foundation commission)
2 July
Royal Northern College of Music, Concert Hall
John Hagstrom, RNCM Wind Orchestra, conducted by Timothy Reynish

Bullard, Alan
Sonata for Three, for recorder, bassoon and harpsichord
10 September
St Ann's Church
John Turner, Graham Salvage and Pamela Nash

Callahan, Moiya
Four-Way Sextet, for flute, clarinet, violin, cello, percussion and piano
13 September
Zion Arts Centre, Hulme
Ensemble 11, directed by Gavin Wayte

Camilleri, Charles
Valletta Images, for piano
(City of History and Elegance, Saturday Night at the Auberge, Churches
and Bells, Merchant Street)
31 August
Chetham's School, Whiteley Hall
Murray McLachlan

Carroll, Fergal
Winter Dances, for wind ensemble
23 March
Royal Northern College of Music, Theatre
All North Cheshire Concert Band, conducted by Mark Heron

Cetiz, Mahir
In Trace of the Memories Lost in the Infinity of Time, for ensemble
18 October
Royal Northern College of Music, Concert Hall
RNCM New Ensemble, directed by Clark Rundell

Clarke, Simon
Introduction and Allegro, for instrumental ensemble
26 February
Royal Northern College of Music, Concert Hall
New Ensemble, directed by Max Xinyu- Liu

Clay, Paul
Network/Ruin, for trombone and tape
(first performance of this version)
26 June
Royal Northern College of Music, Studio Theatre

Copeland, Stewart
Breather, for percussion ensemble (première earlier in tour)
(commissioned by Ensemble Bash with funds from the PRS)
20 November
Royal Northern College of Music, Concert Hall
Ensemble Bash

Crossley-Holland, Peter
Lullaby, for violin and piano (first performance of this version)
27 August
Bridgewater Hall, Stalls Foyer
Richard Howarth and Keith Swallow

Crossley-Holland, Peter
Trio for recorder, oboe and viola (1940/?2001)
(Prelude, Dance, Country Song, Three Duets (Jig), Musette)
27 August
Bridgewater Hall, Stalls Foyer
John Turner, Richard Simpson and Tom Dunn

Dawson, Ben
Cube, for piano, tuba and percussion
25 June
Royal Northern College of Music, Lord Rhodes Room
New Art Ensemble

Dean, Brett
Huntington's Eulogy, for cello and piano
17 January
Bridgewater Hall
Alban Gerhardt and Steven Osborne

Debussy, Claude, orchestrated by Colin Matthews
Prelude, 'Canope'
24 October
Bridgewater Hall
Hallé Orchestra, conducted by Jean-Bernard Pommier

Dodgson, Stephen
Warbeck Dances, for recorder and harpsichord (revised version)
10 September
St Ann's Church
John Turner and Pamela Nash

Dodgson, Stephen
Warbeck Trio, for recorder, bassoon and harpsichord
10 September
St Ann's Church
John Turner, Graham Salvage and Pamela Nash

Dowrick, Mick
Reflected Images, for three saxophones, three trumpets, three
trombones, bass and piano
20 June
Royal Northern College of Music, Concert Hall
Ensemble 11, directed by André de Ridder

Duddell, Joe
Generation, for string ensemble
16 February
Royal Northern College of Music, Concert Hall
Goldberg Ensemble, directed by Malcolm Layfield

Ellerby, Martin
Euphonium Concerto (première of wind version)
23 March
Royal Northern College of Music, Concert Hall
David Childs, Central Band of the Royal Air Force

Ellis, David
Vetrate di Ricercata, for organ
29 October
St Ann's Church
Ronald Frost

Ferguson, Sean
Corranach, for flute, cello and piano
14 March
Royal Northern College of Music, Studio Theatre
Trio Phoenix

Fitkin, Graham
Shard, for percussion ensemble (première earlier in tour)
(commissioned by Ensemble Bash with funds from the PRS)
20 November
Royal Northern College of Music, Concert Hall
Ensemble Bash

Fox, Christopher
Shadow Cast, for string ensemble
17 February
Royal Northern College of Music, Concert Hall
Goldberg Ensemble, directed by Malcolm Layfield

Garland, Tim
Concerto for saxophone and wind orchestra
22 March
Royal Northern College of Music, Theatre
Tim Garland, RNCM Wind Orchestra conducted by Clark Rundell

Gilbert, Anthony
Sonata no. 3, for piano
10 May
Royal Northern College of Music, Concert Hall
Peter Lawson

Górecki, Henryk
Ad Matrem, for soprano, chorus and orchestra (UK première)
14 December
University of Manchester, Whitworth Hall
Rebekah Coffey, University of Manchester Chorus and Symphony
Orchestra, conducted by John Casken

Grange, Philip
Diptych: Sky-maze; Daedalus' Lament, for oboe/cor anglais and harp
7 March
University of Manchester, Department of Music
Jinny Shaw and Lucy Wakeford

Gregson, Edward
Fanfare for DK (Dame Kathleen Ollerenshaw)
6 December
Royal Northern College of Music, Concert Hall
RNCM Symphony Orchestra, conducted by Elgar Howarth

Hayes, Nick
dance play, for percussion ensemble (première earlier in tour)
(commissioned by Ensemble Bash with funds from the PRS)
20 November
Royal Northern College of Music, Concert Hall
Ensemble Bash

Heaton, Wilfred
Variations, for brass band
10 February (RNCM Festival of Brass)
Royal Northern College of Music, Concert Hall
Fairey Band, conducted by Sian Edwards

Hesketh, Kenneth
Alchymist's Journal, for brass band
18 January
Royal Northern College of Music, Concert Hall
Black Dyke Band, conducted by Nicholas Childs

Hesketh, Kenneth
Festive Overture, for concert band
23 March
Royal Northern College of Music, Concert Hall
Central Band of the Royal Air Force

Hill, Jackson
Philomel, for soprano, recorder, cello and harpsichord
11 May
Bridgewater Hall, Barbirolli Room
Elizabeth Atherton, John Turner, Jonathan Price and Janet Simpson

Hong, Sungji
Impetuoso, for clarinet and string quartet
13 September
Zion Arts Centre, Hulme
Ensemble 11, directed by Gavin Wayte

Hope, Peter
Four Sketches, for oboe, bassoon and piano
28 April
Chetham's School of Music, Whiteley Hall
Jennifer Galloway, Graham Salvage and Janet Simpson

Hope, Peter
Two Songs, to poems by Robert Herrick,
for counter-tenor, recorder, cello and harpsichord
4 October
University of Manchester, Department of Music
James Bowman, John Turner, Jonathan Price and Pamela Nash

Hopson, Graeme
Quintet, for flute, clarinet, cello, percussion (1 player) and piano
13 September
Zion Arts Centre, Hulme
Ensemble 11, directed by Gavin Wayte

Ingoldsby, Tom
Dances and Dirges: chamber concerto for two pianos and eleven
instruments
28 November
University of Manchester, Department of Music
Christian White and Angie Wilson, University New Music Ensemble,
conducted by Gavin Wayte

Ireland, Robin
Pairings 2, for two violas (Fantasia-Scherzo-Adagietto–Canon–
Ostinato)
18 April
University of Manchester, Department of Music
Robin Ireland and Louise Williams

Jackson, Hannah
Plus ça change —, for piano, trombone and percussion
25 June
Royal Northern College of Music, Lord Rhodes Room
New Art Ensemble

Johnson, Chris
Norwegian Folk Tale no. 1, 'The Cock and the Fox', for three
saxophones, three trumpets, three trombones, bass and piano
20 June
Royal Northern College of Music, Concert Hall
Ensemble 11, directed by André de Ridder

Johnson, Liz
de l'herbe qui s'éveille, for string ensemble
17 February
Royal Northern College of Music, Concert Hall
Goldberg Ensemble, directed by Malcolm Layfield

Joseph, Julian
The Road of Kharma, for saxophone and piano
3 October
Royal Northern College of Music, Concert Hall
Federico Mondelci and Kathryn Stott

Kamen, Michael
Angels dancing on the head of a pin, for percussion and orchestra
17 July
Bridgewater Hall
Evelyn Glennie, Hallé Orchestra, conducted by Kristjan Järvi

Keeling, Andrew
Ave verum corpus, for choir
17 March
Bolton Parish Church
Choir of Bolton Parish Church, directed by Stephen Carleston

Kenmuir, Callum
Preludes 1–12, for piano
31 August
Chetham's School of Music, Whiteley Hall
Murray McLachlan

Kim, Mina
Tantalization, for flute, clarinet, trumpet, guitar (+ electric guitar),
piano, percussion, violin, viola, cello, double bass (+ bass guitar)
13 September
Zion Arts Centre, Hulme
Ensemble 11, directed by Gavin Wayte

Kokoras, Panayiotis
Friction, for flute, clarinet, trumpet, guitar (+ electric guitar), piano,
percussion, violin, viola, cello, double bass (+ bass guitar)
13 September
Zion Arts Centre, Hulme
Ensemble 11, directed by Gavin Wayte

Lehto, Jukka-Pekka
Rhapsody, for bassoon and wind ensemble
23 March
Royal Northern College of Music, Theatre
North Cheshire Concert Band, conducted by Mark Heron

McGarr, Peter
Britain Seen from the North, for string ensemble
16 February
Royal Northern College of Music, Concert Hall
Goldberg Ensemble, directed by Malcolm Layfield

Mackey, Steve
Physical Property, for electric guitar and string quartet (UK première)
30 November
Royal Northern College of Music, Theatre
Steve Mackey and Psappha, conducted by Nicholas Kok

McNeff, Stephen
Overture for concert band
22 March
Royal Northern College of Music, Concert Hall
RNCM Wind Orchestra, directed by Clark Rundell

MacPherson, Gordon
Joshua Sketch, for five trumpets
4 July
Royal Northern College of Music, Lord Rhodes Room
Scottish Consort of Trumpets

Malone, Kevin
Bassoon Concerto (UK première)
23 November
University of Manchester, Whitworth Hall
Benjamin Hudson, University of Manchester Symphony Orchestra,
conducted by Clark Rundell

Manduell, Sir John
'C-H' – Recitative and Aria in Memoriam PC-H, for violin and viola
27 August
Bridgewater Hall, Stalls Foyer
Richard Howarth and Tom Dunn

Manning, Sasha Johnson
Psalm 91, for choir
22 June
St George's Church, Stockport
St George's Singers, conducted by Stephen Williams

Maric, Dave
Exile, for two pianos, percussion and live electronics
30 October
Bridgewater Hall
Katia and Marielle Labèque, Colin Currie and Dave Maric

Maric, Dave
Lifetimes, for 12 strings and percussion (commissioned by Rococo Strings)
18 June
Bridgewater Hall
Rococo Strings, Adrian Spillett

Masmanian, Daniel
Moody Food, for cello solo
26 June
Royal Northern College of Music, Studio Theatre

Masmanian, Daniel
Three Miniatures, for piano
26 June
Royal Northern College of Music, Studio Theatre

Matthews, Colin
Aftertones (Edmund Blunden), for mezzo-soprano, choir and orchestra
2 May
Bridgewater Hall
Leah Marian Jones, Hallé Choir, Hallé Orchestra, conducted by Lu Jia

Matthews, Colin
Vivo, for orchestra
7 November
Bridgewater Hall
Hallé Orchestra, conducted by Mark Elder

Mawhinney, Simon
Shimna: concerto for marimba and strings, from spnm workshop
15 February
Royal Northern College of Music, Studio Theatre
Julian Warburton, Goldberg Ensemble, directed by Malcolm Layfield

Meechan, Peter
Concerto for alto saxophone and orchestra
23 April
Royal Manchester College of Music, Concert Hall

Millard, Russell
Still Not Finding, for flute, clarinet, trumpet, guitar (+ electric guitar), percussion, piano, violin, viola, cello, double bass (+ bass guitar)
13 September
Zion Arts Centre, Hulme
Ensemble 11, directed by Gavin Wayte

Montague, Stephen
Rim Fire, for percussion ensemble (première earlier in tour)
(commissioned by Ensemble Bash with funds from the PRS)
Royal Northern College of Music, Concert Hall
Ensemble Bash

Notareschi, Loretta
Now, More Than Ever, for flute, clarinet, trumpet, guitar (+ electric
guitar), percussion, piano, violin, viola, cello, double bass (+ bass guitar)
13 September
Zion Arts Centre, Hulme
Ensemble 11, directed by Gavin Wayte

Parrott, Ian
Duo, for recorder and cello
5 October
Stockport Grammar School
John Turner and Jonathan Price

Parrott, Ian
'Fantasising on a Welsh Tune', for recorder, oboe, bassoon and
harpsichord
8 October
St James' Church, Gatley
John Turner, Richard Simpson, Graham Salvage and Janet Simpson

Parrott, Ian
Percyisms, for soprano, mixed chorus, recorder, cello and harpsichord
11 May
Bridgewater Hall, Barbirolli Room
Elizabeth Atherton, John Powell Singers, conducted by John Powell,
John Turner, Jonathan Price and Janet Simpson

Peci, Aleksander
Polycentrum, for strings (UK première)
15 February
Royal Northern College of Music, Studio Theatre
Goldberg Ensemble, directed by Malcolm Layfield

Pike, Jeremy
Aphelion, for violin and piano
30 January
Chetham's School, Baronial Hall
Jennifer Pike and Max Ritchie

Pike, Jeremy
Ballade, for piano
31 August
Chetham's School, Whiteley Hall
Murray McLachlan

Pitkin, Jonathan
Soundlessly Down, for brass band
5 November
Royal Northern College of Music, Concert Hall
RNCM Brass Band, conducted by John Miller

Poole, Geoffrey
Lucifer, a concerto for piano and twenty-one loud instruments
17 November
Royal Northern College of Music, Concert Hall
Philip Mead, RNCM Brass Ensemble, conducted by James Gourlay

Preger, Norma
David, a children's oratorio, for choir and accompanist
20 October
Norden Methodist Church, Rochdale
Norden Methodist Church Choir, directed by Barbara Richardson,
Norma Preger (accompanist)

Preger, Norma
Suite 'Noah', for piano
9 August
Cross Street Unitarian Chapel
Norma Preger

Psathas, John
View from Olympus, a double concerto for percussion, piano and
orchestra
26 July
Bridgewater Hall
Evelyn Glennie, Philip Smith, Hallé Orchestra, conducted by Mark
Elder

Riain, Ailis Ni
Dogs in Waiting, for double bass solo
26 June
Royal Northern College of Music, Studio Theatre
Matt Baker

Riain, Ailis Ni
Rogue Boar, Shot Dead, for drum kit, piano and trombone
25 June
Royal Northern College of Music, Lord Rhodes Room
New Art Ensemble

Riain, Ailis Ni
The Dead Live (2002), for five instrumental duos (bassopicco, boesoon, cellorn, pianarp, bassussion)
19 March
Royal Northern College of Music, Concert Hall
New Ensemble, conducted by James MacMillan

Roth, Alec
Venus Dancing, for recorder and piano
4 October
University of Manchester, Department of Music
John Turner and Peter Lawson

Rütti, Carl
Metamorphosis, for euphonium and wind orchestra
24 April
Royal Northern College of Music, Concert Hall
David Childs, RNCM Wind Orchestra, conducted by Clark Rundell

Sanders, John
The Age of Herbert and Vaughan (Edmund Blunden), for soprano, recorder, harpsichord and cello continuo
11 May
Bridgewater Hall, Barbirolli Room
Elizabeth Atherton, John Turner, Janet Simpson and Jonathan Price

Simaku, Thoma
Pas de deux, for children and string players
16 February
Royal Northern College of Music, Concert Hall
Children from local schools with Goldberg Ensemble principals

Simaku, Thoma
Soliloquy 3, for viola solo
16 February
Royal Northern College of Music, Concert Hall
Joel Hunter, principal viola, Goldberg Ensemble

Skempton, Howard
Horizons, for oboe and harp
7 March
University of Manchester, Department of Music
Jinny Shaw and Lucy Wakeford

Skempton, Howard
Sarabande, for strings
15 February
Royal Northern College of Music, Studio Theatre
Goldberg Ensemble, directed by Malcolm Layfield

Skempton, Howard
Slip-Stream, for percussion ensemble (première earlier in tour)
(commissioned by Ensemble Bash with funds from the PRS)
20 November
Royal Northern College of Music, Concert Hall
Ensemble Bash

Smith, Dave
Fractures, for wind orchestra
24 March
Royal Northern College of Music
Chetham's School Wind Orchestra, conducted by John Dickinson

Solomons, David
Scallywag's Kickwalk, for piano
25 October
Cross Street Unitarian Chapel
John Barton

Spratt, Alasdair
Paper Has More Patience (concerto for percussion and orchestra)
23 April
Royal Northern College of Music, Concert Hall

Stamatakis-Brown, Andrew
Two Septic Sketches, for trumpet solo
26 June
Royal Northern College of Music, Studio Theatre

Stamp, Jack
Four Maryland Songs, for mezzo-soprano and wind ensemble (UK première)
23 March
Royal Northern College of Music, Theatre
Susan Johnston, North Cheshire Concert Band, conducted by Mark Heron

Stevenson, Ronald
To Autumn (William Blake), for soprano and recorder
11 May
Bridgewater Hall, Barbirolli Room
Elizabeth Atherton and John Turner

Stevenson, Ronald
A Chinese Folksong Suite, for piano
31 August
Chetham's School, Whiteley Hall
Murray McLachlan

Stevenson, Ronald
Canonic Caprice on 'The Bat', for piano
31 August
Chetham's School, Whiteley Hall
Murray McLachlan

Sweeney, Eric
Saxophone Concerto
17 February
Royal Northern College of Music, Concert Hall
Sarah Field, Goldberg Ensemble, directed by Malcolm Layfield

Tucapsky, Antonin
Mala odpoledni hudba
18 May
Royal Northern College of Music
Cefiro Clarinet Quartet

Van Der Walt, Simon
Ha!, for string ensemble
15 February
Royal Northern College of Music, Studio Theatre
Goldberg Ensemble, directed by Malcolm Layfield

Vine, Ian
Ten White Leaves, for flute, oboe, two clarinets, horn, trombone,
percussion, piano, viola, cello and double bass
20 June
Royal Northern College of Music, Concert Hall
Ensemble 11, directed by Andre de Ridder

Watkins, Huw
Suite no. 1, for wind quintet, string quintet, harp and celesta
9 March
Royal Northern College of Music, Concert Hall
Manchester Camerata, conducted by Douglas Boyd

Wayte, Gavin
Strange Attraction, for solo flute and ensemble
21 March
University of Manchester, Department of Music
Amina Hussain, University New Music Ensemble, directed by Gavin
Wayte

Whitelaw, Timothy
Concerto for cello and orchestra
23 April
Royal Northern College of Music, Concert Hall

Wilby, Philip
Atlantic, for brass band
18 January
Royal Northern College of Music, Concert Hall
Black Dyke Band, conducted by Nicholas Childs

Wilby, Philip
Concerto 1945, for cornet and band
5 July
Royal Northern College of Music, Concert Hall
Roger Webster, Black Dyke Band, conducted by Nicholas Childs

Williamson, John
Seven Interval Studies 2001, for piano
31 August
Chetham's School, Whiteley Hall
Murray McLachlan

Wills, Simon
Sweet Song Variations, for trombone choir
17 November
Royal Northern College of Music, Concert Hall
RNCM/Chetham's Trombone Ensemble, directed by Chris Houlding

Willson, Flora
A Late Lark (W.E. Henley), for counter-tenor, recorder, cello and harpsichord
5 October
Stockport Grammar School
James Bowman, John Turner, Jonathan Price and Pamela Nash

Wilson, Dana
Leader Lieder, for trumpet and wind orchestra (ITG Commission)
2 July
Royal Northern College of Music, Concert Hall
James Thompson, RNCM Wind Orchestra, conducted by James Gourlay

Wolters, Michael
Monsterwalzer, for string ensemble
15 February
Royal Northern College of Music, Studio Theatre
Goldberg Ensemble, directed by Malcolm Layfield

Woolrich, John
Darker Still, for flute and piano (Royal Philharmonic Society/BBC commission)
22 February
Royal Northern College of Music, Concert Hall
Emily Beynon and Andrew West

Subscribers

Harry and Dorothy Acton-Wilson
Eric Adshead
Sir James Anderton
Margaret Arnison
Susan Astles
Dr Robert Aston
BBC Manchester
H. Valerie Bailey
Michael and Miriam Ball
William Ball
Philip Barnes
Roderick Barrand
Colin Bayliss
Robert Beale
David Beck
Dr Colin Beeson
Richard Beith
John M. Belcher
John Bethell MBE
Ronald Birks
Birmingham Central Library
Keith Bisatt
William Blezard†
Jean and John Blundell
J. P. Boydell
Elizabeth Bridge
The Bridgewater Hall
Gerald A. Brinnen
Britten-Pears Library
Rosemary Broadbent
Dr Terry Broadbent
John T. Brophy
Christine Brown
Christine Susan Buchan
Alan Bullard
Joan Burns MBE
Professor Donald Burrows
Bury Grammar School (Boys)
    Learning Resource Centre

Arthur Butterworth MBE
M. and B. Campbell Smith
Roger Carpenter
Douglas R. Carrington
Hazel and Michael Carter
William T. Cavanagh
Andrew Challinger
Margaret Challinger
Malcolm Chapman
Christina Chester
Chetham's School of Music
Bettie Cohen
Mr and Mrs John Colloff
Paul Conway
Barry A. R. Cooper
Cornell University
Christopher Cotton
Philip Cowlin
Philip Crookall
Dr Nicole Crossley-Holland
Sarah Crouch
George Davies, Solicitors
Glyn Davies
Harvey Davies
Lizzie Davis
Peter Davison
Jeffrey Dean and Penelope Gouk
Basil Deane
Dr James W. Dickenson
John A. Dickes
Dr T. Donald
Sir Edward Downes
Sally Drage
Paul Driver
John Duarte
Gail Dudson and Martin Roscoe
Julia Earnshaw
John East
John Eckersley

Patricia Elcombe
Martin Ellerby
John Ellis
Patricia and David Ellis
Mary Evans
Professor William Everett
Richard Fallas
David Fallows
Polly Fallows
David Fanning
Jean Fielden
Rosemary and Roger Firman
Roger Firth
James Flett
Dr Peter Flinn
Florida Pitfield Archive
Valerie Floyd
Lewis Foreman
Helen Foster
Paul Fowles
Mavis Fox
Ronald Frost
James Garratt
Maggie Gibb
Rachel Gick
Dorothy M. Gill
Hans and Sandra Glauser
Bill and Judith Godfrey
Richard and Alison Godlee
Anthony Goldstone
Raphael and Rosalind Gonley
Adam Gorb
James Gourlay
Professor Philip Grange
Michael Graubart
Terence Greaves
David Green
Professor Edward Gregson
Lady Groves†

Sir Ernest Hall
Tim Hall
Tony Halstead
Don Hargreaves
Sir Martin and Lady Harris
Michael Harris
Robert Hastings
Peter Henry
Nick Henshall
M. Elisabeth Hessey
Dr Peter Hick
Pat Higginson
Trevor Hill
Derek Hodgkiss
Clive and Hilda Holland
Peter Hope
Neil Horner
Michael Horwood
Stephen Hough
Alan R. Howarth
Bernard Howcroft
Jean Howes
Dr Crawford Howie
The Rt Revd Peter Hullah
The Hulme Grammar School
for Girls
Garry Humphreys
Patricia D. Hurst
Gillian Hush, MBE
Margaret Hutt
Vernon G. Hyde
Ishbel Isaacs
Geoffrey Jackson
Professor Douglas Jarman
Alexandra Jobling
John Rylands University Library
of Manchester
David Jones
David Ll. Jones

Eira Lynn Jones
Fae J. Jones
Philip Jones†
David Jordan
Anne Jubb
Ian Kemp and Sian Edwards
Serena and Janice Kay
Glenda Keam
Michael and Joyce Kennedy
David Kent
Geoffrey and Margarita Kimpton
Doreen and Harry Knipe
Andrew Lamb
Valerie Langfield
Beryl Langley
Louise Latham
Peter Lawson
John Leach
Raymond Leppard
Anwen Lewis
Colin Lomas
Alistair Lomax
James Loughran
Sherry Lowe
Andrew and Rachel Lucas
Peter Lyons
John McCabe CBE
Brendan McCormack
Patrick McGuigan
Ian Mackay
Philip Mackenzie
Murray McLachlan
Manchester Camerata
Manchester Cathedral
Manchester City Council:
    Henry Watson Music Library
Manchester Music Service
Sir John Manduell CBE and
    Lady Manduell

Derrick Margerson
John Beardwood Marsden
David† and Daphne Marshall
George A. Marshall
Andrew Mayes
Ron Merchant
Jennifer E. A. Merren
John and Mary Moate
Ruth Moon
John Myerscough
Dr Roy Newsome
New York Public Library
Northwestern Library,
    Evanston, Illinois
Ronan O'Hora
Mary I. Ohlson
Oldham Metropolitan Borough
    Council: Local Studies and Archives
Professor and Mrs P. Ormerod
Joyce Lindley Parker
Professor Ian Parrott
Jane and Bas Perrins
Brian Pidgeon
Valerie Pocklington
David Powell
John Powell and Martin Lessons
Michael and Judith Redhead
Maurice E. Ridge
Sheila W. Ridgway
J. Edward Rigg
Christopher Robins
Steven Robinson
Stuart A. Robinson
Antony Roper
Roger Rostron
Dr Alec Roth
Mark Rowlinson
Royal College of Music

Royal Northern College
                of Music Library
Peter Royle
Clark Rundell
Chinchinha Sainter
Sale Chamber Orchestra
Salford University
Graham and Yi Xin Salvage
Leslie Sayers
Jonathan Scott
Richard A. Scott
Stuart Scott
David Seddon
Charles Sellers
Honor Sheppard (Elliott)
Grahame Shrubsole
Mrs Elizabeth Siddall
Ronald Singleton
Antony Sluce
Anna Smart
Alan and Mary Smith
Helen I. L. Smith
Michael A. Smith
Neil Smith
Peter B. Smith
Roy Heaton Smith
John Snow
Peter Spaull
J. Martin Stafford
Dr Ronald Stevenson, FRMCM
Robin Stewart
Stockport Grammar School
Stockport Metropolitan Borough
                Council – Libraries
David Sumbler
Peter Syrus
Tameside Metropolitan Borough
        Council – Local Studies and
                Archives

Alex Temple
Martin Thacker
Sheila Thacker
Jonathan Thackeray
Kay Thomas
Callum L. Thomson
Brian N. Thorpe
Stephen and Kathleen Threlfall
Pamela Thurlow
Ernest Tomlinson
Colin Touchin
Jackson Towers
Trafford Metropolitan District
                Council – Libraries
Trinity College of Music Library
John and Margaret Turner
Roger Turner
John Tyrrell
Christopher Underwood
R. David Usher
Richard Valéry
Dr R. O. Vasey
Peter B. Waddington
Graham Wade
Peter Wainwright
Raymond J. Walker
Robin Walker
Professor Michael Waller
David S. Walton
Robin Walton
Tony Ward
Irving Wardle
William Waterhouse
David H. Watt
Joan Watt
Percy and Anne Welton
Christina K. B. Westwell
John and Helen Whibley
Kevin Whittingham

Alison M. Wilkinson
Stephen Wilkinson
Enid M. Williams
Gladys Williams and Dennis Dodge
Roger Williams
John Ramsden Williamson
Peter Willis
John and Janet Wilson
Ronald H. Wilson
Dr Susan Wollenberg
Myra Worsley
Christopher Yates
Keith Yearsley
Dr Percy M. Young
T. M. and A. C. Young
Young Musicians' Festival

Names in italics are founder
subscribers.

North West Composers'
NWCA
Association
Affiliated to the British Academy of
Composers and Songwriters

In addition to its principal aim – to raise and maintain the profile of new music – the Association promotes the talents of North West-based performers through its concerts and recordings. These CDs can be ordered from the NWCA, or from local music shops and distributors.

Further information is available from the NWCA Secretary: 0161 766 5950, or visit us on-line at www.nwca.org.uk.

The Wagon of Life – to mark the centenary of the birth of **Thomas Pitfield**, a new CD of songs performed by MARK ROWLINSON (baritone) and PETER LAWSON (piano) will shortly be made available, including music by Stuart Scott, Geoffrey Kimpton, Stephen Wilkinson, Joanna Treasure, John R. Williamson, Sasha Johnson Manning, Kevin George Brown, David Golightly, Philip Wood and David Forshaw.

Currently avilable recordings on CD:

Contemporary British Piano Music (Vol. 1) – JONATHAN MIDDLETON ASC CS CD 1
Music by Golightly, Jeremy Pike, Scott, Colin Bayliss, Treasure, Margaret Wegener.

Contemporary British Piano Music (Vol. 2) – JOHN McCABE   ASC CS CD 3
Music by Alan Rawsthorne, Pitfield, Forshaw, Williamson, Christopher Beardsley, Golightly.

British Clarinet Music – ROGER HEATON & STEPHEN PRUSLIN   ASC CS CD 2
Music by Kevin Malone, Pike, Forshaw, Stephen Plews, Kimpton, Golightly, John Reeman.

British Violin Music – ANDREW LONG & STEWART DEATH   ASC CS CD 4
Music by Walton, Geoffrey Kimpton, Stephen Plews, Pitfield, Stuart Scott, Jeremy Pike.

An Image of Truth – WILLIAM BYRD SINGERS, KEITH SWALLOW, JOHN TURNER, PETER LAWSON, ALISON WELLS, COULL QUARTET   ASC CS CD 6
Music of David Ellis.

Manchester Accents – NCO directedby NICHOLAS WARD   ASC CS CD 45
Music by Pitfield, Anthony Gilbert, James Langley, McCabe, Manduell, Terence Greaves.

Symphony No. 1 – PRAGUE PHILHARMONIC / GAVIN SUTHERLAND   Modrana Music
Music by David Golightly.

Fast Forward – LINDSAYS, CAMERATA, COULL and NOSSEK   ASC CS CD 11
Quartets for the new millennium by Kevin Malone, David Ellis, John Casken, Robin Walker, Geoffrey Poole and Anthony Gilbert.

Old City – New Image – CAMERATA ENSEMBLE   Cameo Classics 2027
Music by John McCabe and David Ellis (String Quartets and Trios).

Thirteen Ways of Looking at a Blackbird – JOHN TURNER / CAMERATA
Olympia OCD 710
Music by Leonard Bernstein, Robert Simpson, Richard Arnell, Matyas Seiber & NWCA members Beth Wiseman, Philip Wood, David Forshaw and David Ellis.

The Music of Thomas Pitfield –TRACEY CHADWELL, JOHN MCCABE, DENNIS SIMONS,
RICHARD & JANET SIMPSON, KEITH SWALLOW   RNCM TP 3

John and Peter's Whistling Book – JOHN TURNER & PETER LAWSON
Forsyth FS 001 / 2
Includes music by Geoffrey Poole, David Ellis and Kevin Malone.

Colin Bayliss – DAVID MARTIN (piano)   NCC 2001
Sonatas and other pieces for solo piano.

Colin Bayliss – RONALD FROST (organ)   NCC 2002
The complete music for organ recorded in St Ann's Church, Manchester.

Songs of Solomons – STEPHEN TAYLOR & JONATHAN LEONARD   NCC 2003
Music of David W. Solomons.

Twelve Housman Songs – NIGEL SHAW & JOHN WILLIAMSON   DRD 0133
The music of John R. Williamson with the composer as accompanist.

Music for Piano (2 volumes) – MURRAY MCLACHLAN   DRD 0134
The music of John R. Williamson   & 0176

Music to my Listening – GEORGINA COLWELL, STEPHEN VARCOE   Musica Ariosa
The songs of Margaret Wegener with Nigel Foster (piano)

Golden Jubilee Songs – SUSAN YARNELL & STEPHEN FOULKES   ENVO36CD
with Steven Kings (piano). Presented by the English Poetry and Song Society and the British Music Society. Finalists in the Jubilee Song Competition included NWCA Members Margaret Wegener, Geoffrey Kimpton and John R. Williamson. Also music by Elgar, Bax, Bliss, Walford Davies and Malcolm Williamson.

Music from Six Contintents – MORAVIAN PHILHARMONIC ORCHESTRA   VMM 3050
Including music by Sonja Grossner.

Metropolois – RNCM WIND ORCHESTRA   SER CD 2400
Timothy Reynish and Clark Rundell conduct – including music by Geoffrey Poole.

Earth and Moon & Move – TUBALATE [2CDs]   ASC CS CD 21 & TCD 4
This popular group plays music by Colin Bayliss, Stuart Scott and David Solomons.

The composers are grateful to the Manchester Musical Heritage Trust, the Thomas Pitfield Trust and the Ida Carroll Trust for their generous support of specific NWCA projects.